PRAISE FOR *PEACE TALKS*

"As a fellow pastor and one engaged in John 17 unity in my own city, I am delighted to recommend this book. It is a must read for anyone who would self-identify as a follower of Jesus or merely as one of His fans. With the increasing polarization and incivility in our society, especially in the area of politics, the author correctly points out the contribution that followers/fans of Jesus have made to the problem. He states the problem in this manner as an introduction to one of the chapters in the book: 'Any time we place our identity in anything secondary, tragedy results. When we try to ask of something more than it's equipped to provide, a letdown is inevitable.' The author then follows this quote with a powerfully transparent retelling of his own personal experience in the Donkey Elephant wars and how God directed his way to freedom and to the current ministry in which he is engaged. It is a privilege for me to be on this Kingdom journey with the author and all those in Tucson. May His tribe increase!"

—CLINT HALL
Director of Church Relations, The Sending Project,
Kansas City Metro

"Dave's understanding of how polarized the political system is gives us a handle to deal with the negative effects of this system gone wild. It also invites us to be a part of the solution rather than a part of the problem! God dwells in the praises of His people but maybe evil dwells in the Donkey Elephant wars where evil is traded for evil. Unholy political alliances may be where the believer's loyalty needs to shift from party loyalty to Kingdom loyalties by thinking through issues rather than being caught in emotional reactivity. Dave has done a great job of defining the problem, showing a Biblical worldview, and pointing to solutions for a sick system in need of love, unity, and healing. This is a much-needed book at the appropriate time in our history, with a call to the church to be salt and light in a world in need of light. Thank you, Dave."

Pastor, counselor, community developer, a

D1044369

"In *Peace Talks: The Good News of Jesus in a Donkey Elephant War*, my friend David Drum has written a timely book to help followers of Jesus navigate the troubling times we find ourselves in. The Good News is still good news for all of us, and for our country and the world, but we need grace and humility to recognize how affected we often are by our own cultural and political biases. Be encouraged! God is still working through His people all around the world. This book will sharpen your mind and challenge you and those you lead to be as impactful as possible in these vital times."

—Kevin Palau
President, Luis Palau Association
Portland, OR

"It is without equivocation that I recommend *Peace Talks: The Good News of Jesus in a Donkey Elephant War* to every believer or whoever wants a fresh, humorous but sobering perspective on faith and politics. Who would dare address such a potentially explosive topic? Dave Drum! Dave is well known throughout the Tucson community, state, and other Christian venues for his Kingdom work of connecting and bringing together people, ministries, pastors and churches to this end: unity in the Body of Christ (See Dave's book *Jesus' Surprising Strategy*). Being in the midst of such a time where hypersensitive politics is threatening to further divide our nation and the Body of Christ, such a person and such a book as *Peace Talks* is needed. Jesus declared 'If I be lifted up, I'll draw all men unto me!' That's the good news of Jesus that needs to be heard in this Donkey Elephant war."

—Warren Anderson
Apostle, Living Water Ministries
Tucson, AZ

"I began reading the manuscript of David Drum's timely and helpful book as President Trump declared a national emergency in response to the coronavirus. As I was concluding the final chapters of David's call to harmony, the White House and Democrats reached a deal on an economic relief bill. Amazing how an international crisis can make leaders face reality—work together or live with catastrophic consequences! David Drum's timely book unveils an even deadlier spiritual virus many followers of Jesus have been infected with—political idolatry. As a seasoned leader of gospel-shaped harmony, Drum helps us understand the source of our threat and how to work together to defeat it. He provides, in a very readable and memorable way, how to live as a citizen of the Kingdom of Heaven in the middle of a Donkey Elephant political war. Hardly a week goes by that I am not asked by other followers of Jesus how to live for Christ in our current politically-divided context. David's book provides sound and tested gospel-shaped answers to that vital question. His book is a must read and I plan on pointing many to its wise counsel."

—STEVE KING
Senior Pastor Emeritus, Cherrydale Baptist Church
Arlington, VA

"Politics so often divide, but Christ is the great unifier! There has never been a greater time for the message that comes from *Peace Talks: The Good News of Jesus in a Donkey Elephant War.* The content will challenge you to take Jesus out of the political box you may have put Him in and inspire you to see the issues of our day through the lens of the One perfect leader!"

—ELISA MEDINA
Executive Director, Hands of Hope
Tucson, AZ

PEACE
TALKS

The Good News of Jesus
in a Donkey Elephant War

DAVID DRUM

J17 MINISTRIES

David Drum has had the privilege of working full time for nine years to see Jesus' prayer in John 17 answered in his hometown of Tucson, AZ. He served as the Church Domain Director for 4Tucson for over seven years, and on October 20, 2018, founded J17 Ministries, devoted to uniting the Body of Christ FOR a divided world. He served as the solo/lead pastor of Community of Hope Lutheran Church from 1990-2011. He is also the author of *Jesus' Surprising Strategy: A Mandate and a Means for City Transformation* (published in both English and Spanish), and *If It Was Easy, Jesus Wouldn't Have Prayed For It: How Jesus' Strategic Prayer For Unity Can Revolutionize Your City, Congregation, and Home*. A Tucson, AZ native with a B.S. in Mechanical Engineering from the University of Arizona and an M.Div. from Trinity Lutheran Seminary, David and his wife Valerie have four children and one grandchild.

Published by J17 Ministries, Inc.
©2020 by David Drum
Printed in the United States of America

Cover design, typesetting, and illustrations by Cameron Hood
Author photo by Trevor Crosby

ISBN: 978-1-7348148-0-4

Contents

*To the Pastor Partnership of Tucson,
a group of African American and Anglo
Pastors meeting monthly to talk politics and
race and coming out stronger as a result.*

*This book would not have been possible
without all you've taught me.*

PROLOGUE

"Why is our own participation in scapegoating so difficult to perceive and the participation of others so easy?"
—RENE GIRARD[1]

Coronavirus seized our attention like nothing else in my lifetime. Almost no one had ever heard the word last Christmas, and within three months it was the only thing anyone talked about. That's partly because COVID-19 eliminated the competition, completely shutting down the sports and entertainment industries, and shuttering massive portions of the business and retail worlds as well. You couldn't even go shopping to drown your sorrows—either because you'd lost your job and had no money, or because you couldn't find a store open. And if you were looking for toilet paper, hopefully you brought along the tissues— the empty shelves and long lines might have moved you to tears.

---

1   Rene Girard, *Violent Origins: Walter Burkert, Rene Girard, and Jonathan Z. Smith on Ritual Killing and Cultural Formation*, ed. Robert Hamerton-Kelly (Stanford, CA: Stanford University Press, 1987), 79.

COVID-19 was first documented in Wuhan, Hubei Province, China in December 2019. The first confirmed U.S. case of the coronavirus was reported January 21, 2020—a Washington state man who had recently returned from China. The World Health Organization officially declared COVID-19 a global pandemic on March 11, 2020, and on March 13, 2020, President Trump declared a national emergency. Almost instantaneously much of the country and a significant percentage of the world was sheltering at home. The U.S. economy staggered immediately as millions were suddenly unemployed.

In the days immediately following the global and national declarations, a surge of bipartisanship swept through Washington. The first stimulus bills passed by over 90%. Rep. Ilhan Omar, one of President Trump's most outspoken critics, praised the President for the "incredible" job he was doing in fighting the pandemic.[2] President Trump praised both houses of Congress, and both parties, for their willingness to work hard and set aside differences in order to pass legislation that would aid a fearful and financially unstable citizenry.[3] During the congressional debates concerning the $2.2T stimulus bill, President Trump even gave Democrats the benefit of the doubt, one of the key solutions I'll be developing later on, a posture almost universally lacking in the Donkey Elephant war. On March 27, 2020, President Trump signed the largest bill in U.S. history after both houses of Congress had passed it by consensus on a voice vote.

Is the global pandemic COVID-19, commonly referred to as the coronavirus, an exception to the Donkey Elephant war? Or better yet, is the partisan war over, replaced by a war against an unseen enemy?

---

2   Gregg Re, "Ilhan Omar Praises Trump's 'Incredible' Response to Coronavirus Pandemic," *Fox News*, March 19, 2020, https://www.foxnews.com/politics/ilhan-omar-praises-trumps-incredible-response-to-coronavirus-pandemic.

3   Michael Bonner, "Coronavirus: President Donald Trump Praises Congress' Efforts to Pass Stimulus Bill, Says Easter Reopening May Be Flexible," *MassLive*, March 24, 2020, https://www.masslive.com/coronavirus/2020/03/coronavirus-president-donald-trump-praises-congress-efforts-to-pass-stimulus-bill-says-easter-reopening-may-be-flexible.html.

The enemy of my enemy is my friend

As much as I would love to believe that a global pandemic's silver lining would be that it brought about the end of the Donkey Elephant war, I don't really think that's what's happening. I suspect that playing nice is a temporary phenomenon. I cited a couple of shockingly positive statements above from people who are notoriously not-positive toward the other side, but I could just as easily have cited the countless jabs and counterpunches thrown as both the Donkeys and Elephants tried to position themselves as the winners. If coronavirus functions like the bucking chute in a rodeo, penning in our Donkeys and Elephants and preventing them from hurting each other too badly, you can already see the animal pushing against the restraint, just waiting to bust out and wreak some havoc.

I believe what's happening is merely that there's a new threat, a new enemy, that's large enough and dangerous enough to function like a magnet, drawing the competitive fighting energy toward itself and away from the other political party. How many times have we heard "enemy" language used in battling the coronavirus? "This is a war, and we will win," has been a battle cry universally voiced, not only by both political parties in our own country, but by leaders of nations all over the globe. As long as the casualty count is high, both in people suffering and dying as well as in the economy hemorrhaging, it could be that the partisan war will remain in the wings instead of center stage. We can certainly pray that's the case.

From a historical perspective, the "common enemy" phenomenon helps explain why partisanship is worse now than in previous decades. When would you say our country was the most united, the best equipped to do hard things over long periods of time at great sacrifice? I would argue that World War II was that time. The Axis powers, the Third Reich, and Adolf Hitler specifically were such a clearly identified enemy that people almost universally jumped at the opportunity to sacrifice for the cause. We haven't had a national enemy so clearly identified and labeled since then. The Cold War against the Soviet Union was probably the closest second, but our culture wars were raging internally at the same time, and I had to do a Google search just to remind myself of who the Soviet leaders were during the Cold War. September 11 united us for a brief season, but once the "what next" question surfaced, unity flew out the window. Hitler, though, is universally recognized as the bottom of the barrel of humanity. Nobody since then has been as magnetically negative. Without a common enemy to rally against, it becomes easier to take shots at one another.

In order to practice what I preach in the development of this book, I've learned what I could from a very wide variety of voices. Here's an example as it relates to the temporary reprieve we're experiencing from our Donkey Elephant war. I was recently introduced to René Girard, a French historian, literary critic, and philosopher of social science.[4] Girard is perhaps best known for his work on generative scapegoat mechanism. Lead Pastor Jeremy Duncan of Commons Church, Calgary has developed a YouTube series that makes Girard's expansive work much more accessible to people like me, whose background is in science and religion, not sociology and psychology.

WITHOUT A COMMON ENEMY TO RALLY AGAINST, IT BECOMES EASIER TO TAKE SHOTS AT ONE ANOTHER.

Duncan summarizes the generative scapegoat mechanism cycle this way:[5] tensions rise, resources become limited, somebody makes a wrong move, and all the underlying tensions of the rest of the group get poured out on the designated victim. Girard sees this as the basic human experience, and the only way that humankind grew beyond small tribal groups. Groups need to identify an external scapegoat in order to stay internally cohesive. Despicably referring to COVID-19 as the "Chinese virus" is merely a case study in trying to make an invisible scapegoat visible.

---

4   "René Girard," Wikipedia, April 7, 2020, https://en.wikipedia.org/wiki/Rene_Girard.

5   Jeremy Duncan, "An Introduction to René Girard Part 1: Memetic Desire," published by Commons Church, May 7, 2019, video lesson, 13:12, https://www.youtube.com/watch?v=5SCnonH0Yr4.

Here's what I find even more interesting! Girard taught that religion is how we take the generative scapegoat mechanism and ritualize it, contain it, and minimize it, and he believes that all religions employ a scapegoat. What shocked him was how Christianity ultimately undermines the cycle of violence and scapegoating. The Christ story identifies with the *victim*, eliminating the need for future scapegoating and violence. Christ comes from outside the story and has no debt to violence and scapegoating (i.e. without original sin). His whole teaching is that there is no outsider. This was so unsettling that people turned their latent violence on the One claiming there *was* no outsider. Everyone turned against Jesus—everyone! In that climactic moment, Jesus receives all our violence instead of returning it.[6]

Jesus is ultimately the source of our peace, not a newer, nastier enemy who can unite us in opposition. I grew up Lutheran, and one part of Lutheran worship services is called "passing the peace." It's a ritualized way to greet one another, with people saying, "The peace of the Lord be with you" and responding, "And also with you" instead of something simpler like "hello." Yet that ritualized action symbolizes one of our deepest human longings. We need a peace that's stronger than the storms raging around us. We need a peace that can talk louder than the fears screaming in our ears. We need a peace that transcends the Donkey Elephant war, the COVID-19 war, and whatever war follows those. Jesus, the Prince of Peace, outlasted death itself. I believe Jesus is our answer.

Guidance

This prologue relating to the COVID-19 pandemic follows the same pattern as the rest of the book: identify the problem, seek out root causes, and move toward solutions. So even though this has been the briefest of discussions, let's wrap it up by paying attention to areas that are actually in our control. I find fear knocking on the door when I'm focused on aspects of a crisis over which I have no control, whereas peace settles

---

6   Jeremy Duncan, "An Introduction to René Girard Part 2: Ritual Sacrifice," published by Commons Church, May 14, 2019, video lesson, 11:38, https://www.youtube.com/watch?v=QvBvbGylBMk&t=7s.

in when I'm concentrating on choices that are actually mine to make, and then trusting God with the rest.

How can we live in the "peace of the Lord," instead of merely mouthing the words? When everything around us is shaking, how can we stick close to the Unshaken, Unshakable One? If you're reading this after the pandemic has settled down, save these thoughts for the next crisis, whether global or just in your sphere of influence. Here are a couple of quick recommendations before we even get past the prologue of this book.

- *Consider this season we're in as EGR time.* High stress times are EGR times—"extra grace required." Everyone everywhere is on edge, whether due to financial instability, health fears, or the removal of the activities that used to bring us comfort. Each of those are huge by themselves, but the trifecta of all of them forms a perfect storm. We need to cut one another some slack, because the longer this goes, the more on edge we're likely to be. This is an Extra Grace Required season—we need people around us to overlook some of *our* tension-induced faux pas, and we need to do the same for others.

- *Drop the blame game.* Both Washington and the dining room table would do well to drop the blame game. The Donkeys and Elephants are chomping at the bit to cast the other in a negative light, but who wins when that happens? Nobody. Only losers. Hopefully the seriousness of the pandemic will be sufficient to temper the ill will for as long as these hard times last. But while we can't control Washington, we alone are in control of our own tongues. Even if somebody in your sphere of influence has clearly been in the wrong, ask yourself if dishing out blame will improve the circumstances. There are times when accountability is both necessary and growth-producing. There are other times when grace will get us further than grievances.

- *Grow deeper roots.* In a drought, plants grow deeper roots in search of water. Life is like that, too. Nothing goes to waste with God—no hardships, no tragedies, no circumstances. All the trials and challenges of this season can result in new growth and a deeper relationship with Jesus. If you have no idea where to even start . . . a) ask someone you know who could help you, or b) keep reading (or jump ahead) to the Epilogue. Jesus can and wants to be a living Presence guiding your life and holding your hand through the challenges of each day. Times like these turn words like those into a bright, shining reality.

- *Find something else to focus on.* How much bad news can you watch, really? It's good to be informed, but at some point information becomes deflation, and leaves us depressed. Play a game, go for a walk, or grab a good book. Hmm . . . Learn some new skills during this social distancing season that will put you in better shape for when normalcy returns.

The Donkey Elephant war will flare up again, undoubtedly. In a worst-case scenario, the country will do the opposite of Extra Grace Required, and when pandemic stress is at its peak, we'll crack and double down on the blame game. That would be catastrophic. In a best-case scenario, we'll weather the storm on our collective best behaviors, and not until the next national elections regain the spotlight does bad behavior come out of hiding. Either way, let's be prepared to be part of the solution instead of part of the problem.

PART I

BACKGROUND

INTRODUCTION

*"Acquire a peaceful spirit, and then thousands
around you will be saved."*
—SERAPHIM OF SAROV[1]

P olitics talks . . . and talks, and talks, to the point that many of
us tune it out. Wouldn't it be great if in the middle of all that
political verbiage, another voice could be heard even louder,
the voice of peace? Peace, as we'll see, doesn't just mean the absence
of conflict. Peace is the presence of health and wholeness and relationships and justice. *That* talks. We—you and I—can learn to talk from a
posture of peace instead of partisan politics.

---

1   Seraphim of Sarov, quoted in Matt Woodley, *The Folly of Prayer: Practicing the Presence and Absence
of God* (Downers Grove, IL: InterVarsity Press, 2009), 182. A 19th century Russian monk vener-
ated in both the Eastern Orthodox and the Catholic Church.

Jesus has some surprising priorities, and I'm interested in examining the intersection between Jesus' priorities and passions, and our current political catastrophe. I believe the result is good news, great news in fact, and that's the reason I've chosen to march right into the middle of our Donkey Elephant war.

So there are a few things you ought to know up front...

SURPRISING IRONY

Good news isn't always heard as good news, especially at first. "Your house is on fire" is bad news—unless the hearing of it enables you to save the lives of your family. Then it's the best news you've ever heard in your entire life.

Let's be honest: many in our country aren't seeking peace in the Donkey Elephant wars; they're seeking victory. And for most of those, humiliation or annihilation would be even better than just a narrow victory. For any of you who see yourself in that mirror...for you to read this and find it good news, you'll have to be willing to take a second look at some of your assumptions. For example, if we're all on the same plane, blowing up the other half of the aisle might not be such a good idea. I

MANY IN OUR COUNTRY AREN'T SEEKING PEACE IN THE DONKEY ELEPHANT WARS; THEY'RE SEEKING VICTORY.

believe we're all on the same plane, in the same nation, and our partisanship is hurting all of us, dramatically. After reconsidering some of what you believe and how you've chosen to express it, you'll quite possibly keep many of your convictions the same—but add some new ones. Please at least consider that possibility.

Politics has felt dirty for some time now, since well before the turn of the century, but it's measurably worse today. Our confidence in the very people we elect is at an all-time low,[2] yet we keep electing them. Maybe "them" isn't the problem—maybe it's "us." You're probably familiar with the definition of insanity—when you keep doing the same thing over and over again, while expecting different results. Maybe we need to stop being part of the problem and become part of the solution—not just in which bubbles we fill in (or chads we punch out) at the ballot box, but in how we talk leading up to the next election. If we've given up and stopped talking about anything political whatsoever, maybe it's time we find our voice again. Our voice may be the missing voice of "peace, be still."[3]

It can be hard to take a good look at ourselves personally and nationally. But we must, because our house is on fire.

AUDIENCE

My primary intended audience in this book is people who have an affinity for Jesus, which comprises a majority of Americans. Some might consider themselves fans of Jesus, while others might be followers; some might be part of a church, while others might love Jesus but not want to hang out anywhere near a church. Regardless of how you feel about the label "Christian," if you were asked how you feel about Jesus and your answer would be on the positive side of the spectrum, you're my primary audience, and I'm writing with you in mind.

I recognize that I've just described a huge and wildly diverse audience! There are times where I'll clearly be speaking to people who worship Jesus as Lord and love Him as Savior—Chapter 9 is the clearest example of that. In other parts of the book, like the Epilogue, I'm aiming more toward Jesus' fan-club than His groupies. If it matters more specifically who I'm talking to, I'll try to spell it out, but in most cases, I'm just writing to people, and assuming you won't get offended if I talk about Jesus, too.

---

2   Harry Enten, "Congress' Approval Rating Hasn't Hit 30% in 10 Years. That's a Record," *CNN*, June 1, 2019, cnn.com/2019/06/01/politics/poll-of-the-week-congress-approval-rating.

3   Mark 4:39 (NRSV), "Jesus...rebuked the wind, and said to the sea, 'Peace! Be still!' Then the wind ceased, and there was a dead calm."

If you're an American who either doesn't know who Jesus is or doesn't like who you think Jesus is, you're welcome to follow along, and I hope you will. You picked this up despite the title, so that's something, isn't it? Once some of the muck and grime gets washed off the Jesus story, it's a lot easier to see the good news. Who Jesus is—especially when contrasted with who we are as a country right now—I contend is enormously attractive. The Bible summarizes Jesus as full of grace and truth,[4] and I can't imagine characteristics more necessary yet more rare in the political minefields. My hunch is that much of what I'm asking Jesus-followers to do—meaning things that a majority of us aren't presently doing—may help explain why you feel the way you do.

If you're not American, you're also welcome to join the conversation. If you've ever struggled to understand why America as a "Christian nation"[5] does and says some of the things that it does and says, this may shed some light on it. I maintain that we have an identity crisis, over-identifying with secondary things, which helps to explain some of the behaviors we exhibit that don't fit with the "Christian" label. One whole chapter will be devoted to that topic. You have insights that we need to hear, so please consider yourself invited to the table as well.

ABOUT THE AUTHOR

My full-time job for the last nine years has been encouraging and helping Christians to get along. This book won't help—at least not at first. We're venturing into topics rife with emotional disagreement. I'm breaking all the rules[6] of polite dinner-time conversation, talking about religion AND politics. Sexuality will even make a cameo appearance. Unless I miss my guess, this book will make most people uncomfortable at one point or another. But the end of the story is good news, fully accessible

---

4   John 1:14

5   Many would debate this title today, including Christians lamenting the nation's direction, and non-Christians who might argue that we never were a "Christian nation." Nevertheless, the phrase has been used for most of the nation's history.

6   Reminds me of the best management book ever written (according to my life coach Dennis Watson): *First, Break All the Rules*, by Don Clifton. I never finished reading it. I wasn't made for management. I was made for messages like *this* one.

to everyone reading this, whether my primary intended audience or not, so I invite you to join the journey.

When I say that my paying job is to help Christians get along, that's actually a dim shadow of what Jesus desires. His hopes and dreams for us are way bigger than that, and the rest of this book should help make that clear. These last nine years have brought about realities I wouldn't have believed possible when I started. So I know it can happen for you, too.

MY PRIMARY INTENDED AUDIENCE IS PEOPLE WHO HAVE AN AFFINITY FOR JESUS.

My expertise is as a pastor—both leading a local congregation as well as working in a citywide capacity. I have training as a student of the Bible and a theologian, and have done a lot of work on how the Bible applies to daily life—as well as ways it *doesn't* apply to daily life. I have decades of experience in interpersonal relationships that come with the field of pastoring, and both life experience and training have equipped me with tools to offer to others. Finally, I would also be comfortable with a title of professional unity evangelist, a term that will make more sense as the book progresses.

I do *not* have formal training in psychology or political science, both of which are integral to this book. I approach both as an interested lay person, not a professional. I've done my homework for this project and learned plenty in the process. My goal is simply to apply what I know to areas where others are the experts, and be a voice of peace and unity in the midst of discontent and division.

THE BATTLE PLAN

If you tend to be a "jump around" type of reader, I have a suggestion: skim if you must, but try reading this one in order. Each piece builds on what's gone before. And just because I know some people will jump ahead anyway, I've put some warnings at the start of chapters 6 and 7!

- Part I lays out the background of the Donkey Elephant War.

  - Chapter 1 provides an overview, introducing many of the themes that will be explored later.

  - Chapter 2 looks at the influences of psychology, technology, media, and foreign actors.

  - Chapter 3 explores the contribution our Western worldview has made to our partisanship.

  - Chapter 4 addresses the theological issue of identity, central to the problem.

  - Chapter 5 is the reason I wrote the book—to juxtapose one of Jesus' prayers over against our current challenges as a country.

- Part II, Chapters 6 and 7, will apply those building blocks collectively, looking at several hot-button political issues championed by each party (three each for the Elephants and the Donkeys), hopefully from a fresh vantage point.

- Part III, Chapters 8 and 9 will tie everything together with some conclusions and recommendations for the country and the Church.

- And the Epilogue brings the Good News home in a personal way.

If you're fed up with the partisanship and vitriol streaming out of Washington, flooding the news channels, drowning your social media feeds, and damming up progress, you're due for some good news. If you teach your kindergartners to behave differently than our elected leaders, you could use some hope and restored confidence. If you struggle to understand how the other side thinks, you need some direction.

I believe you've found some.

CHAPTER ONE

CASUALTIES
OF WAR

"War is politics by other means."
—CARL VON CLAUSEWITZ[1]

"Politics is war by other means."
—MICHEL FOUCAULT[2]

L ike other wars, both sides in America's political war are striving desperately to win. "Both sides" refers to the Donkey (Democrats) and the Elephant (Republicans). But unlike other wars, if the battle continues in its present form, there will be no winners. Only losers. And the list of losers is legion and lengthening.

I grew up in an Elephant household. There were very few things we all agreed upon, but this was one of them: we were Elephants. We've

---

1   Carl von Clausewitz, *On War*, trans. Michael Howard and Peter Paret (Princeton, NJ: Princeton University Press, 1989), 752. Early 1800's Prussian general and military strategist.

2   French philosopher Michel Foucault, in the mid 1970's, took von Clausewitz' phrase and flipped it inside out.

been Elephants for generations, as far as I know. We voted Elephant, we cheered for the Elephants and we assumed that nothing good came from Donkeys.

I also grew up in a Christian household. I'm told that before I was old enough to go to school myself, I would on occasion tell the school kids walking by that Jesus loved them. I don't ever remember a time before I was a Christian, though I certainly remember plenty of times when light bulbs came on and faith grew. And I'm still discovering blind spots in my faith and life at age 56.

I don't consider it problematic to grow up in either a Christian home, an Elephant home, or both. The problem is that I thought the two were flip sides of the same coin, conjoined twins, as inseparable as Hansel and Gretel, thunder and lightning, politicians and flags. I don't ever remember being *told* that both were birthrights, that I was as genetically predisposed to one as I was to the other. It was just assumed, which is as common as it is dangerous. (Such assumptions apparently abound. I recently saw an advertisement for a Ford dealership in Alabama that's giving away a Bible, a 12-gauge shotgun, and an American flag with the purchase of every new vehicle. Hmm.)

You're likely familiar with the crass saying about assumptions: when we assume we make an ass (not the donkey kind) out of u and me. I learned by the time I was in middle school Confirmation classes that being Christian wasn't a genetic trait: it had to be owned and personalized. It took decades longer to learn the same about political affiliations.

Hang in there, restless Elephants. I can feel your agitation. The floor is already starting to shake. I could set aside your fears by telling you that I haven't done the unthinkable and become one of *them*, and that would be true. But then I would start the Donkeys braying, so I can't go there quite yet. And dear Donkeys, if I just raised *your* blood pressure, rest assured that I have no intention of declaring your affiliation either unthinkable or unfaithful. I warned you both in the introduction that while my intent isn't to offend, I predict it will happen. If it just did, I'm hoping . . . no, pleading . . . that you will keep reading. Our country is worth the effort.

My lovely bride and I have four wonderful adult children, and when our oldest daughter Amy was a teenager, we tripped over our own political assumptions. Like all good Elephants, we got most of our news from the Elephant news station. We knew that the Donkey news station couldn't be trusted, because we were looking for "fair and balanced," and that's what the Elephant station claimed to be.

War brings with it many casualties, and one of the worst is the collateral damage, shrapnel wounds that injure unsuspecting bystanders. One evening Amy came walking into the living room with great conviction and pain. For my wife the scene is seared into her memory. Amy said, "*Whhhyyyy* are you watching this?" Amy's emotional tremor turned out to be merely a warning sign, with the earlier warning signs having been undetected by her parents, and the bigger quakes yet to come. The war was taking place in our living room, we invited it in, and alienated our own kids in the process. How painful and unnecessarily tragic. We didn't just *talk* politics; we allowed the television to *scream* politics, muzzling questions or alternative perspectives before they were ever uttered. Emotional eruptions in years to come with Amy's younger siblings were dramatically more painful because of how poorly we'd handled the P word, politics. I can't count how many political fights with our kids ended with tears, slammed doors, or dramatic exits. We're still dressing wounds, cleaning up messes, and learning how to navigate the mine fields with fewer injuries. The Donkey Elephant war is personal for me. As a father, let alone a pastor, I should have known better. Now, I do.

In this chapter, my goal is to briefly lay out the problem, introducing a number of topics that will be explored more fully in subsequent chapters. It doesn't take a rocket scientist to point out problems. All of us tend to be quite skilled at noticing things that are wrong, especially in the world around us. It isn't difficult for me to find flaws in others' arguments; it's way harder to look at *my own* erroneous assumptions. Jesus said something similar 2000 years ago:

Why do you look at the speck of sawdust in your brother's eye and pay no attention to the plank in your own
eye? How can you say to your brother, "Let me take the
speck out of your eye," when all the time there is a plank
in your own eye? You hypocrite, first take the plank out
of your own eye, and then you will see clearly to remove
the speck from your brother's eye.[3]

Jesus taught that self-reflection and humility should always precede
confrontation. And it's worth noting that He *didn't* teach that we should
never confront the other person; just that we should start by looking
in the mirror. It's almost as if Jesus knew something about our Donkey
Elephant war 2000 years ago.

One of the richest blessings of my life has been discovering that
Donkeys and Elephants can actually become really dear friends. We
can break the "polite conversation" rule and talk politics AND religion
AND live to tell about it. Even within our own family, we have political
and religious leanings that differ significantly from one another, probably like your own. I'll share some of those stories in subsequent pages.

I don't know of a more effective way to discover my blind spots than
to spend time with people who can lovingly point them out, which is
predicated on hanging out with people from different backgrounds than
my own. Two such people I've met in recent years have given me permission to share some of their stories here. By traveling across the world, we
can get a better picture of our own house. It's my honor to introduce to
you my friends Célestin Musekura and Tass Abu Saada.

African insight to our American problem

I first met Rev. Dr. Célestin Musekura in 2017 in Phoenix. Both of
us were plenary speakers for the International Wholistic Missions
Conference, and he introduced himself to me after I had spoken at the

---

3   Matt. 7:3–5. I find it fascinating that one of the books I read in my research was written by a self-
     described liberal atheist, who begins his book with this same exact quote.

opening session. Within a few minutes, I could tell that we would be doing ministry together in the future, which is proving to be true. His story is riveting.

Musekura was a pastor in Rwanda *before* the genocide in 1994. He tells his Christian audiences that people tend to forget that Rwanda was considered an evangelical success story in the early 1990's. Statistics indicated that as many as 90% of the country had been baptized into Christianity, including both Hutu and Tutsi. All of which makes the genocide even more horrific, if that's even possible, because it means brothers and sisters in Christ were slaughtering one another.

In October 1990 the Tutsi-led Rwandan Patriotic Front (RPF) mobilized and attacked the government of their home country of Rwanda, an incident that began the tribal war between the Tutsi minority and the Hutu-led government and its Rwandan Armed Forces (RAF). Four years later, in the 100 days between April 1994 and June 1994, the unthinkable happened as the government took to the streets, massacring nearly one million people. Another three million fled the country and lived and died in neighboring refugee camps. Even though the genocide was officially brought to a halt by the RPF, revenge killings continued until

"WE WERE HUTU OR TUTSI FIRST, AND CHRISTIAN SECOND."

1998. On Sunday, December 28, 1997, while Musekura was studying at Dallas Theological Seminary, men in uniform invaded his own village and killed about seventy people: some in their homes, some on their farms, and others in the church where they had gathered for morning prayer. Among those killed were Musekura's father, stepbrother, his stepbrother's wife and two children, and a new sister his mother had adopted in the refugee camps in Congo after the first wave of killings in 1994.[4]

---

4   L. Gregory Jones and Célestin Musekura, *Forgiving as We've Been Forgiven* (Downers Grove, IL: IVP Books, 2010), p. 14–21.

At the Phoenix conference where I first was introduced to him, Musekura shared stories of pastors of one tribe willingly turning over their own parishioners of the other tribe to be slaughtered, sometimes even rounding them up in their own church buildings. Other incidences included Hutu pastors bravely sheltering Tutsi parishioners in their own homes, until their own families were threatened if they didn't give up those they were sheltering. Many watched their families get slaughtered anyway, even after turning over their friends to be killed.

"How can this happen?" Musekura posed. How can a country that is 90% Christian experience such a horrific genocide? Answering his own question, Musekura explained that while 90% of the country had been baptized, very few had been discipled, or trained to follow Jesus. "We were a country of baptized pagans." "We were Hutu or Tutsi first, and Christian second."[5]

Musekura founded ALARM, African Leadership and Reconciliation Ministries, in 1994 immediately following the genocide, to engage the church of Rwanda in a radical ministry of forgiveness and reconciliation for their sins of commission and omission.[6] Twenty five years later, ALARM is making a massive difference in multiple East African countries, having trained more than 150,000 Christian leaders in eight countries, focusing especially on high-impact leaders who can change countries.[7]

I've heard Musekura share his story in the United States several times now. Every time he ends with a warning that he seems uniquely qualified to issue. "In America, you have tribes too, it's just that they're called Republican and Democrat instead of Hutu and Tutsi. And your tribes here are at war, too, it's just that you use words instead of machetes."

---

5   Ibid, p. 19.

6   Commission refers to things we've done that we shouldn't have. Omission refers to things we should have done but didn't.

7   Visit ALARM-Inc.org to learn more and consider supporting this amazing world-changing ministry.

Middle Eastern insight to our American problem

I first met Taysir (Tass) Abu Saada in February of 2019, and only because of a series of divine circumstances associated with my full-time job of connecting Christians to one another. The story he shared with the fifty or so of us in the room was so engaging that I boldly requested some additional time with him over lunch. We remain connected due to our common life calling, though our life circumstances couldn't possibly be any different.

Tass was born in a refugee camp in Gaza City in 1951. He was a Palestinian who hated Jews, and his amazing story is told in his book, *Once an Arafat Man: The True Story of How a PLO Sniper Found a New Life.*[8] Displaced from their family's home by the establishment of Israel as a nation, the Saada family suffered the ultimate indignity for an Arab: they owned no land. As Tass said, "A man without land is a man without honor, and a man without honor is better dead." That reality and perspective was the genesis of his hatred for Jews. Tass shared when he was with us in Tucson that the mantra of his friends growing up was "A good Jew is a dead Jew." By age 17, he joined Fatah—a branch of the Palestine Liberation Organization (PLO)—and became a trained assassin. He eventually met Yassir Arafat, even driving for him a few times to dangerous areas. Part One of his book is entitled, "How I Learned to Hate."

At age 23, he moved to the United States, and brought along with him all of his antisemitic baggage. The story of how he came to experience the good news of Jesus through a Christian nanny and a Christian businessman is one of the most unusual and most compelling I've ever read, so rather than retell it, I simply encourage you to read it for yourself in *Once an Arafat Man.* He met and came to love Jesus through a dream/vision he had on March 14, 1993, a common experience in recent years for Muslims around the world. It was only *after* professing allegiance to Jesus that he learned that Jesus was Jewish! He was equally surprised to

---

8   Tass Saada with Dean Merrill, *Once an Arafat Man: The True Story of How a PLO Sniper Found a New Life* (Carol Stream, IL: Tyndale House Publishers, 2008), 256.

discover how positively Ishmael[9] and his family were portrayed in what he had always seen as Jewish propaganda, the Old Testament. The root of the conflict between Arabs and Jews can be traced back to the story of Ishmael and Isaac in Genesis 21. Tass believes (and I agree) that since the root of the conflict is described in the Bible, the root of the solution must be found there as well.

Now Abu Saada, a former PLO hit man, is working for reconciliation between Jews and Arabs. Reconciliation is at the heart of his ministry, Hope for Ishmael,[10] and Abu Saada, like Musekura, has had to practice what he preaches at great personal cost. Hope for Ishmael leads with love, meeting practical needs both in Israel and the West Bank as well as in the United States.[11] His book ends with a Road Map for Reconciliation in the Middle East that goes beyond personal reconciliation to also include reconciliation between warring nations.

> **"THOSE IN THE CHURCH ARE CALLED TO BE PEACEMAKERS, YET OUR OWN DIVISION NEGATES OUR CALL."**

When Tass spoke in Tucson, he said, "We aren't saved just to be Christian. We're saved for a ministry of reconciliation. Those in the Church are called to be peacemakers, yet our own division negates our call. Some Christians love Israel and hate Ishmaelites, while others love the Ishmaelites (Palestinians) and hate the Israelites (Jews)."

From Musekura and an African context, we can see more clearly the speck in our neighbor's eye, the tendency to revert back to tribal identity instead of a common identity that can encompass both tribes. I'll

---

9   Muslims trace their spiritual and physical lineage back to Abraham through his son Ishmael. Christians and Jews trace their spiritual and physical lineage back to Abraham through his son Isaac.

10 Visit hopeforishmael.org to learn more and consider supporting this amazing ministry.

11 Ishmaelites refers to all Arabs, most of whom are Muslim. But the Jew/Arab conflict dates back 4000 years, whereas Mohammed died in 632 A.D., or 1400 years ago.

unpack that statement in Chapter 4. And from Abu Saada and a Middle Eastern context, we can see more clearly the speck in our neighbor's eye, the tendency to view situations from an either/or perspective, even when they have so much in common (i.e. a common father in Abraham to both Ishmael and Isaac). And I'll unpack that one in Chapter 3. But first, how about the plank in our own eyes here in America?

Body count

Pastor David Platt of McLean Bible Church in Washington, DC had just finished preaching his sermon on June 2, 2019 and was preparing to lead his congregation in celebrating Holy Communion, when staff members urgently called him aside. They told him, "President Trump is on his way to our church right now. He'd like you to pray for him in the service." Platt immediately thought of the beginning of 1 Timothy 2 where Christ-followers are urged to pray for all those in authority, and made the impromptu decision to agree to the President's request, knowing that such a decision probably wouldn't be universally popular. His prayer for the President can be googled if you're curious.

The result? A firestorm of controversy both from within and beyond his own congregation. After spending all day Sunday answering questions, the next day he wrote a letter to his church explaining what had happened and why he made the decision he did in agreeing to the request. The result of the letter was that many of those who hadn't been angered by the Sunday service were now upset by his letter. Social media acted like social media regularly does, with machete-words flying all around. And in his sermon to the congregation the next Sunday, June 9, he shared that as a result of praying for and with the President of the United States in a worship service, increased security had become necessary at the congregation.[12]

---

12   Platt's June 9, 2019, sermon can be found at https://radical.net/sermon/on-unity-in-the-church/. It would be a great use of your time to stop reading my words and listen to his. The donkey elephant war threatened to implode his congregation, and he addressed the division phenomenally. I'll be quoting his words later in Chapter 9.

Praying publicly with a politician has become a life-threatening decision?[13] When a decision to accept a President's request to be prayed for during a Sunday service can result in such controversy that additional security becomes necessary, we may not *have become* Rwanda (in 1994) or the Middle East (any time since 1948), but you can certainly see them from here. In fact, "several research studies conclude that our country has not been this polarized and divided since the Civil War."[14] If that doesn't send chills down your spine, it's only because you've become inoculated to it and see no hope of anything changing.

Politics has become so partisan that it's rarer to see one word (politics) without the other (partisan) than to see a peanut butter sandwich minus the jelly. Jonathan Haidt in his book *The Righteous Mind: Why Good People Are Divided by Politics and Religion*, defines partisan as "Reject first, ask rhetorical questions later."[15] Later in his incredibly well-researched book, he shares some historical context to the problem. Prior to the 1990's, friendship and social relationships between Congressional members were more the norm. More time was spent in Washington while Congress was in session, and relationships helped humanize the members of the opposite party. But that all began changing rapidly, arguably in the 90's, as travel became more efficient and more affordable and the Information Age kicked into hyperdrive.

> Friendships and social contacts across party lines were discouraged. Once the human connections were weakened, it became easier to treat members of the other party as the permanent enemy rather than as fellow members of an elite club. Candidates began to spend more time and money on "oppo" (Opposition research), in which staff members or paid consultants dig up dirt on

---

13   Platt explains well in his June 9 sermon that the issue wasn't whether or not to pray for a president, it was whether or not to invite him on stage during a service, and that well-meaning, unity-loving, mature believers could be found on both sides of that argument.

14   Mark Strauss, "It's Been 150 Years Since the U.S. Was This Politically Polarized," *Gizmodo*, June 12, 2014, https://io9.gizmodo.com/its-been-150-years-since-the-u-s-was-this-politically-1590076355.

15   Jonathan Haidt, *The Righteous Mind: Why Good People Are Divided by Politics and Religion* (New York: Vintage Books, 2013), 127.

opponents (sometimes illegally) and then shovel it to the media. As one elder congressman recently put it, "This is not a collegial body anymore. It is more like gang behavior. Members walk into the chamber full of hatred."[16]

Historical changes to what kinds of Washington behavior are encouraged versus discouraged are significant enough to warrant repeating from another source. If we look back over the entire history of our nation, we can easily find that partisanship isn't unique to our era. Nevertheless, the 1990's definitely saw a shift for the worse. Tim Urban writes,

> In 1994, when the Republicans finally won back Congress, Gingrich, now the Speaker of the House, doubled down on the effort to tribalize. He crunched the traditional five-day legislative schedule into three days. According to Haidt and Abrams, "he changed the legislative calendar so that all business was done Tuesday through Thursday, and he encouraged his incoming freshmen not to move to the District. He did not want them to develop personal friendships with Democrats. He did not want their spouses to serve on the same charitable boards." He also helped to do away with the seniority system for committee chairmen, a move which law professor Cynthia Farina says, "many now blame for enhancing extremist voices, punishing defections from the party line, and burying measures with bipartisan support." Whatever the cause, the shift from a standard partisan tone to a fully tribal Us-vs.-Them tone is now ubiquitous in Washington. In 2012, Chris Christie's entire convention speech used the structure, "They believe ____; We believe ____." In her 2015 presidential campaign announcement, Hillary Clinton made

---

16   Haidt, *Righteous Mind*, 320–321. The quote within the quote is from Democratic Congressman Jim Cooper of Tennessee in 2011. Would anyone want to argue that things have improved since 2011? Wait, nobody?

six "They [something bad]" statements in just over a minute. Just a few months ago, Kamala Harris called on voters to not "let the bad guys win."[17]

History can be twisted significantly simply due to who's telling the story—what they choose to include, who they choose to honor and vilify, and so forth. Chapter 2 will address in greater detail the impact of media in the Donkey Elephant war, because unless we're highly intentional, it's impossible to *not* get a skewed view of what's happening in Washington. The morning after President Trump's 2020 State of the Union Address, I went to *FOX News'* website, where the first thing I saw was video of Nancy Pelosi right there on the dais above and behind the President, tearing up a copy of his speech while everyone was watching. How immature! Then I went to *CNN*, where the first thing I saw was video of President Trump handing Nancy Pelosi a copy of his speech, and then snubbing her offer of the traditional handshake. How immature! Both Trump and Pelosi probably had a hard time getting through kindergarten. See what I did there, with my disrespectful language? How immature of me!

If only kindergarten behavior from our leaders were the worst of our problems. Donkeys and Elephants fire away at one another with ever-increasing hostility. Ponder the worst insults or comparisons you can imagine, and I can virtually guarantee that Elephants and Donkeys have plastered such labels on the other one. "Donkeys are Marxists." "Elephants are Nazis." "Donkeys are stupid and reckless." "Elephants are racists and ____phobic (multiple prefix choices)." "Donkeys hate America." "Elephants hate the poor." "Donkeys kill babies." "Elephants kill women." And on and on and on. When both our media and our elected leadership use such hate-filled and incendiary language with such regularity, how on earth can we not expect increased hostility in our classrooms and streets? As I write this, we just endured nationally

---

17   Tim Urban, "A Sick Giant," Chapter 10, The Story of Us, published January 8, 2020, https://wait-butwhy.com/2020/01/sick-giant.html. Urban's blogs are available on his website, but not published elsewhere yet, so the best I can do for a reference is cite the chapter from which the quote is taken.

a weekend with *two* mass shootings, and of course both the Elephants and Donkeys are hard at work blaming the other one.

Sometimes the Donkey Elephant war is about as subtle as an oncoming train. On the day after the Donkeys voted to formalize impeachment inquiry procedures against the lead Elephant, Elephant news columnist David Bossie wrote this: "With House passage Thursday of a resolution formalizing their blatantly partisan impeachment witch hunt against President Trump, House Speaker Nancy Pelosi and her fellow crazed radical Democrats have declared war on the duly elected president of the United States. Now it's time for Republicans to draw up their own declaration of war against Democrats."[18] Not only is the war reference noteworthy, so is the carefully crafted language that's all positive when referring to his own party, and entirely negative when referring to the other party.

"THIS IS NOT A COLLEGIAL BODY ANYMORE. IT IS MORE LIKE GANG BEHAVIOR. MEMBERS WALK INTO THE CHAMBER FULL OF HATRED."

In June of 2019 I heard a U.S. Senator share that Washington only has another month or so to even hope to get anything accomplished, because the more momentum the election cycle gathers, the more motivated the Donkeys and Elephants will be to point to the stalemate as the reason why they need more votes in 2020.[19] Our political parties have ceased working for solutions in favor of working for votes. The average approval rating for Congress in the summer of 2019

---

18   David N. Bossie, "David Bossie: Trump Impeachment Vote Is Democratic Declaration of War—Republicans Must Declare War on Dems," *Fox News*, November 1, 2019, https://www.foxnews.com/opinion/david-bossie-trump-impeachment-vote-is-democratic-declaration-of-war-republicans-must-declare-war-on-dems.

19   I'm not footnoting the specific speech because a) I've taken the sentiment shared and reworded it for this context, and b) if I revealed whether the Senator was a donkey or an elephant, both animals would likely get more agitated.

was 17.6%,[20] and for the first time ever, hasn't been as high as 30% in over a decade.[21] The system is so broken that good people seem incapable of fixing it. The Donkey and Elephant establishments have grown sufficiently strong that it appears the driving question is, "What's best for us Donkeys/Elephants?" instead of "What's best for the land?" We seem to have completely flipped President Kennedy's famous quote inside out. Instead of "Ask not what your country can do for you, but what you can do for your country," it's "Ask not what's best for the country, but what will get our mammal the most votes in the next election."

Americans turning on themselves is not only internally damaging, but externally enticing. Foreign governments who wish us ill see our partisanship as an opportunity to weaken our nation. Speaking last year, FBI Director Christopher Wray said the 2016 Russian influence campaign "has continued pretty much unabated, [through] the use of social media, fake news, propaganda, false personas, et cetera, to spin us up, pit us against each other, sow divisiveness and discord, undermine Americans' faith in democracy. That is not just an election-cycle threat; it's pretty much a 365-days-a-year threat."[22] We'll look more closely at forces fanning the flames of our fight in the next chapter. Our situation is more precarious than I had realized when I began this project.

The Bible has a number of lists of virtues and vices. Here's one: sexual immorality, impurity, lustful pleasures, idolatry, sorcery, hostility, quarreling, jealousy, outbursts of anger, selfish ambition, dissension, division, envy, drunkenness, and wild parties.[23] Doesn't that sound like the evening news when it's covering politics? Several of the items on the list are exactly what each party tries to dig up about their opponents.

---

20 "Polls: Congressional Job Approval," *RealClearPolitics*, August 2, 2019, https://www.realclearpolitics.com/2019/08/02/.

21 Enten, "Approval Rating."

22 Nathan Hodge, "Why Putin Would Want Trump to Win in 2020," *CNN*, February 21, 2020, https://www.cnn.com/2020/02/21/europe/putin-trump-2020-election-analysis-intl/index.html. The interview can be found at https://www.cfr.org/event/conversation-christopher-wray-0.

23 Gal. 5:19–21 (NLT).

But moral failure has become so commonplace[24] that it no longer necessarily disqualifies someone from public office. The worst part is that several of those vices in the middle (hostility, quarreling, outbursts of anger, selfish ambition, dissension, and division) have ceased to be vices politically, and in fact are more seen as virtues—qualities that can get a candidate elected, especially if she/he is successful in getting other members of the team to do the dirty work while the candidate appears to be above the fray.

Washington has become so dysfunctional that many simply choose to ignore it. The problem, though, is that the war isn't confined to Washington. How many of us dread Thanksgiving dinner conversations with the extended family, knowing that Uncle so and so is going to blurt out his partisan views more predictably than the pumpkin pie that follows dinner? How many of us avoid colleagues as much as possible due to their political views and their affinity for sharing them? How many of us have unfriended someone on Facebook or been unfriended ourselves simply because of political differences? How many of us have accepted as fact that half the country is full of idiots and jerks? Or, we wish we didn't react so gutturally to the other side, but the only alternative seems to be to stop caring? We struggle to determine which bad option is worse.

The Big Picture

In case you skipped reading the Introduction like I sometimes do, the reason I'm writing this book is not because of how partisan our politics have become, or how incapable of solving serious problems Washington, DC seems to be. Anyone with an arm can hit the darkness blindfolded. My motivation isn't even to point out how incongruous and unacceptable our situation is in a country where a strong majority (typically 70%[25]) choose to identify positively with Jesus. Collectively, followers

---

24 Quite possibly, moral failure isn't any more common today than in generations past, just more commonly known.

25 "Religious Landscape Study," Pew Research Center, May 12, 2016, https://www.pewforum.org/religious-landscape-study/.

of Jesus have not positively influenced the culture; in fact, we are often part of the problem rather than part of the solution. This despite Jesus' claims that His followers are the salt and light of the world.[26] Salt in ancient cultures functioned as a preservative in addition to its flavoring role. Jesus said, "If the salt loses its saltiness . . . it is no longer good for anything, except to be thrown out and trampled underfoot."

I fear that Musekura is prophetic when he compares our political tribes to the African tribes responsible for massacres. This is a family fight of the worst kind, and the stakes keep getting higher. Families have stopped talking to one another, work environments have been damaged, and the behavior of many of our national leaders virtually guarantees that rage will continue to rise.

Do you ever throw your hands up in the air, turn off the television and radio and their blaring Donkey/Elephant battle cries, and wonder if there's any hope? Can anything reverse a trend where each election cycle seems to get uglier, more personal, and more violent? And where the downhill slide seems to be picking up momentum? If so, I have tremendous news for you, and *this* is the reason I've chosen to wade into the battleground with this book.

The darker the darkness gets, the brighter the light shines. Over the last nine years I've learned that I was put on this Earth to do all I can to see Jesus' prayer for unity[27] answered wherever I have influence. And in a world/country so badly divided, Jesus' prayer is some of the best news we could ever hear or hope for. If you're already hungry for some of that good news, grab a Bible or go online (for instance Biblegateway.com) and read through John 17. Jesus is praying that prayer for us right now, in the midst of our battle against COVID-19, as well as our Donkey Elephant War. Let Jesus' peace speak deeply to your soul.

---

26   Matt. 5:13–16.

27   This prayer, recorded in John 17, also happens to be one of the last recorded prayers of Jesus, and is His longest and most developed prayer by a large margin.

In order to get *out* of the mess we're in, it will help to have a better understanding of how we got *into* the mess. In the next chapter we'll look at some root causes from the vantage points of psychology, technology, and sociology. And I'm excited to introduce my oldest son Mike as our guest author!

CHAPTER TWO

HOW WE
GOT HERE

*"The real war is between humanity and our
new environment, and we are all its victims."*
—MIKE DRUM[1]

Our problem is getting worse, not better. Many people see the last few presidential elections as a pendulum swinging from one side to the other, moving further and further out with each pass. Data backs up that impression. Pew research reveals broad trends over the past 25 years showing Donkeys and Elephants widening the gap on issues across the board. Figure 2.1 provides the details.

---

1   This chapter was primarily written by my son, Mike Drum, including the epigraph above. Mike's background is in computer science and the technology industry. He's an avid learner and has been studying politics and psychology ever since the last election. He volunteered to contribute this chapter due to a shared desire to help guide the conversation in a positive direction, and his deeper understanding of an evolutionary worldview and the scope and impact of technology in recent times. We come from different places spiritually and politically, and he may not even agree with everything in this book, but we've learned how to talk with one another peacefully, and how to work together to create something neither of us could have done independently.

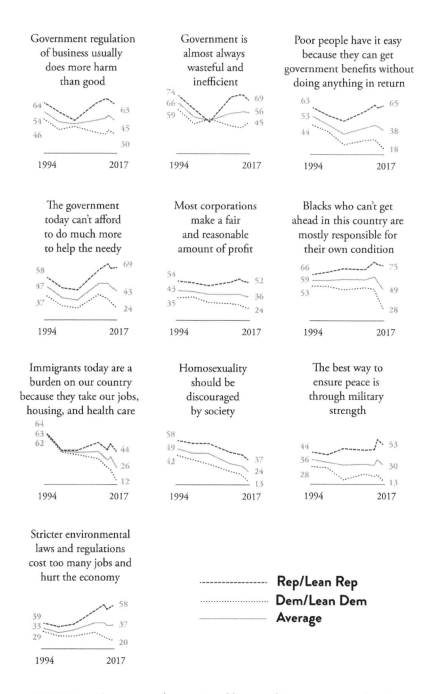

FIGURE 2.1 *Growing gaps between Republicans and Democrats across domains.* Percentage who agree with the 10 statements listed. (Pew Research Center. Source: Survey conducted June 8–18 and June 27–July 9, 2017.)

In all ten examples, the gap between Republicans and Democrats is wider in 2017 than it was in 1994, by a significant margin.[2] Figure 2.2 shows that data again, except combined to show the trend in the distance between the two parties:

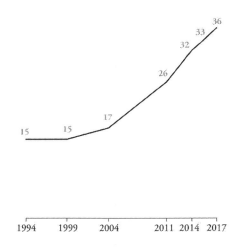

FIGURE 2.2 *Partisan gap in political values continues to grow.* Indicated percentage gap between the share of Republicans/Republican leaners and the share of Democrats/Democrat leaners who take the conservative position across 10 values items that have a traditional "left/right" association. (Pew Research Center. Source: Survey conducted June 8–18 and June 27–July 9, 2017.)

In just 25 years, the gap between the parties has grown from 15% to 36% on a sampling of ten value statements. It doesn't get any better in Congress itself. Figure 2.3 is a chart[3] of the past approximately 140 years showing the ideological differences between the House (light dashed line) and Senate (dark dashed line), based on things like roll-call numbers:[4]

---

2   "The Partisan Divide on Political Values Grows Even Wider: Sharp Shifts Among Democrats on Aid to Needy, Race, Immigration", Pew Research Center, October 5, 2017, https://www.people-press.org/2017/10/05/the-partisan-divide-on-political-values-grows-even-wider/.

3   Jeff Lewis, "Polarization in Congress," Voteview, August 14, 2019, https://voteview.com/articles/party_polarization.

4   "NOMINATE Scaling Method," Wikipedia, last modified April 9, 2020, https://en.wikipedia.org/wiki/NOMINATE_(scaling_method).

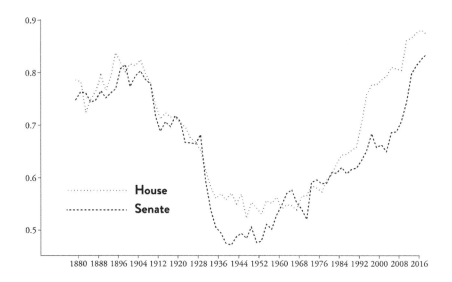

FIGURE 2.3 *Polarization in Congress*. Distance between party means by year. (Voteview.)

The increasing distance between the two parties is matched by the increasing hostility. So how did we get in this mess?

We weren't built for this stuff. Life used to be very different for humans, and it takes a species a bit longer than a few hundred years to adapt to changes of the magnitude that we're seeing. Our brains were originally wired for hunting and gathering with a tribe, not trying to hash out the details of a health care system. Our very survival used to be based on forming tight tribal bonds and being wary of outsiders. Trusting strangers was extremely dangerous, and social acceptance within your group often was the difference between being able to live and raise children, and starvation. You may have heard the saying, "The only constant is change," but the pace of change is accelerating rapidly with the technology age, and even more with the information age. The internet, social media, and cable news have all come about in the last few decades. It's all coming at us pretty fast, and I think the pace is starting to really catch up with us. Our instincts have programmed us for the wrong world.

None of those things are within any of our control, but just because it's not our fault doesn't mean it's not our problem. Examining some of what brought us to this place at a macro level can help make us more alert personally during times when our base tribalistic instincts might be running the game. As for me, the research I've done on this topic has proven to be extraordinarily helpful in re-examining many of the beliefs I thought I held firmly. All that I've learned has allowed me to pull out of some very steep nose-dives into an "us versus them" mentality.[5]

The other value of this chapter and book is to hopefully help us empathize with people on the other side of the battle lines. It's important to remember that our immediate surroundings and upbringing shape who we are and how we think, and everyone has a real reason for having the opinions they do. The "other guys" might even really be wrong, but if we know why they think the way they do, we'll be better equipped to know how to speak to them on their terms. The real war is between humanity and our new environment, and we are all its victims.

Insights from the field of psychology

We're all humans, and these are human problems. Studying the way that we think has completely reshaped how I approach these issues. A few key areas of psychology can offer insight and give us tools going forward to better understand why we get into all of the messes we do. The brain itself hasn't changed much in the last several thousand years, but the outside world sure has. To really grasp the reasons behind our current struggles, we need to start by looking inside.

We all like to think we're open minded, but evidence suggests otherwise when it comes to politics. In 2016, a study was published showing that the more politically sensitive a topic was, the *less* likely any amount

---

5   Dave here—As Mike's father, I too have reexamined many of the assumptions I grew up with—or actually, examined them for the first time. And it's been incredibly lifegiving in our family to pull out of well-worn ruts that have damaged us in the past, and learn how to talk with one another in mutually edifying ways.

of new evidence could change someone's mind.[6] When participants were given new information about benign topics like whether or not multivitamins were helpful, or if Thomas Edison invented the lightbulb, they were far more receptive to changing their mind than when presented with challenges to their beliefs on political issues like abortion or gay marriage. The surprise is what showed up on the MRIs: the parts of the brain responsible for decision making only lit up when presented with challenges to nonpolitical beliefs. When pushed on a political belief, the amygdala and insula, where we experience emotions and fight-or-flight triggers, were the parts that lit up. No wonder "fight or flight" are such common reactions to political topics—that's literally the part of the brain called upon!

One thing is for certain: there are several competing interests going on in our brains, and the battle can be intense. This manifests in little things in our day-to-day where we fight our instincts:

- *"I need calories to survive! Maybe I'll grab that candy bar by the cash register."* "Stay away! They're empty calories, I can get more nutritious food at home."

- *"That coworker is really attractive! I'd better let them know I think so."* "You don't think that would make them or their *spouse* a little uncomfortable?"

- *"Writing this book is too hard! I bet that new video game would be much more fun."* "This book should probably get finished before the next presidential election . . ."

We're made up of a bunch of different neurologic systems that each wants to do its job, and when they all start yelling at us in our internal monologue, contradictions don't matter. This phenomenon is often simplified into two buckets: our emotional and our rational cores. Haidt

---

6   Jonas T. Kaplan, Sarah I. Gimbel, and Sam Harris, "Neural Correlates of Maintaining One's Political Beliefs in the Face of Counterevidence," *Scientific Reports* 6, no. 39589 (December 2016), https://doi.org/10.1038/srep39589.

calls these the "Elephant"[7]—a big brutish mammal that does most of the work at moving us through the world—and the "Rider"—an external force that adds some control and guides the elephant in the right direction.[8] Tim Urban has his own model for this which he calls the "Primitive Mind" and the "High Mind."[9] They're all describing this same idea though: our instincts often mislead us, driven by desires that suited us great ten thousand years ago, but still needing something to rein them in every now and then to keep us out of trouble.

NO WONDER "FIGHT OR FLIGHT" ARE SUCH COMMON REACTIONS TO POLITICAL TOPICS.

Here's where it gets fun: those oft-misguided instincts are largely in charge of how we learn and take in information about the world. As such, we are in fact extremely weak at seeking out ideas that contradict our own. If we encounter an idea that threatens our understanding and worldview, it will trigger our fight-or-flight response, and that's not a pleasant feeling. So instead, our brains have little bouncers guarding the club, preventing any ideas that are too uncomfortable to acknowledge from even reaching our centers for higher reasoning. Of course, it also follows that the opposite is true: we are absolute masters at searching out ideas that reaffirm our beliefs. It just feels so darn good to be told how smart we are, ya know?

This tendency causes us to seek out "echo chambers"—places where we surround ourselves intentionally or subconsciously with voices that echo what we already think. Urban contrasts that with an "idea lab" where different ideas are free to bounce up against one another without threat to the person posing the idea.[10] In an Idea Lab, a healthy environment

---

7   Haidt's "elephant" merely refers to the animal, not the Republican mascot.

8   Haidt, *Righteous Mind*, 2–109.

9   Tim Urban, "The Great Battle of Fire and Light," Chapter 1, The Story of Us, published August 26, 2019, https://waitbutwhy.com/2019/08/fire-light.html.

10   Tim Urban, "Idea Labs and Echo Chambers," Chapter 8, The Story of Us, published October 8, 2019, https://waitbutwhy.com/2019/10/idea-labs-echo-chambers.html.

filled with diverse people and opinions, people and their ideas are treated as separate entities—people are meant to be respected, ideas are meant to be challenged and tested. In echo chambers, a person's ideas are part of their identity; respecting a person and respecting their ideas are one and the same, leading to stunted intellectual and emotional growth.

Another fun thing we do is simplify. Our brains are incredible at pattern-matching, so that we don't have to process the entire world all at once and at all times. This is an absolutely essential skill that makes life possible, but it can have some unfortunate side-effects.

- "The last time I ate something like that I got sick, so let's not do that again."

- "Oh, that looks like a car; I know how that works and how to behave around it."

- "Those dudes remind me of some sketchy characters I saw in a movie, so I'm gonna stay away from them."

- "I've heard this argument about capitalism before, and it was dumb, so you must be dumb."

There's even evidence that our internal monologues can lie to us. The voice in our head isn't actually informing our beliefs as much as we might think. Haidt's studies on moral intuition and reasoning have shown that people will perform "post-ad hoc reasoning" to justify a position that they already hold, even if it doesn't hold up to any scrutiny. In his studies, he presented people with situations that would challenge some moral position they held (for example, an aversion to incest). When the participants offered a reason as to why it was "wrong" (say, genetic defects in offspring), the situation was changed to remove that factor (they are using birth control). In case after case, the majority of participants still kept coming up with reasons it was immoral, or just landed at "I don't know, it just feels wrong." In other words, our morality-based positions have been shown to be embedded in us on a deeper level than our conscious reasoning. We are able to defend these strong beliefs so well because we're really just thinking in reverse: most of the work is just in putting words to our gut feelings, not in actually determining the reasons for those beliefs on the spot.

A great summary of this comes from Tim Urban in the form of the "thinking ladder." He describes four levels that people might find themselves in when thinking and taking in new information: the Scientist, the Sports Fan, the Attorney, and the Zealot.[11] Scientists have no stake in the game; their goal is to challenge their own hypotheses until they can't disprove them. Sports Fans still value the rules of the game, but are rooting for a certain outcome. Attorneys expect a predetermined outcome and are going to go out of their way to downplay any contradictory evidence. Zealots have no interest in other opinions; they *know* the truth, and anyone who doesn't believe it is wrong. As you move down the ladder, the more you're really just interested in reaffirming your beliefs than you are actually searching for the truth. We all move up and down the ladder several times a day without thinking about it, and a little stake in the game isn't the end of the world. However, I believe most people wish they could live higher up on this ladder, and the labels can be a useful tool for examining *why* we might be responding the way we do in any given moment.

The impact of technology

Here is what has changed dramatically in recent times. Remember that graph showing political polarization since 1994? Figure 2.4 is a pretty similar-looking curve, except this time showing the percentage of the U.S. population using the internet, during the exact same time frame:[12]

---

11   Tim Urban, "The Thinking Ladder," Chapter 7, The Story of Us, published September 27, 2019, https://waitbutwhy.com/2019/09/thinking-ladder.html.

12   "Individuals Using the Internet (% of Population)," The World Bank Group, accessed March 10, 2020, https://data.worldbank.org/indicator/it.net.user.zs.

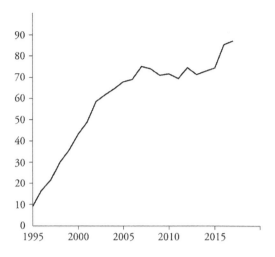

FIGURE 2.4 *Individuals using the internet.* Percentage of US population over time. (The World Bank Group.)

What is now an integral part of our culture barely existed 30 years ago. Internet access is now available to more than 90% of our population. Obviously, polarization can exist without the internet. The similarity of the polarization curve and the internet usage curve is merely a correlation, but I believe there's a strong case to be made that there's an extremely strong influence between the two.

Politics is driven by communication: people communicating their opinions to one another, constituents communicating with their representatives, and representatives communicating with each other on our behalf. Well, communication has gone into overdrive with the creation of the internet and social media. It's one of the most measurable, clearly observable changes in recent history. At the end of 1995, there were 16 million people on the internet—0.4% of the population. By 2019, that number reached 4.5 billion.[13] Social media has gone from being used by just 5% of Americans in 2005 to over 70% today.[14] Facebook alone

13   "History and Growth of the Internet from 1995 till Today," Internet World Stats, accessed March 5, 2020, https://www.internetworldstats.com/emarketing.htm.

14   "Social Media Fact Sheet," Pew Research Center, June 12, 2019, https://www.pewresearch.org/internet/fact-sheet/social-media/.

has almost 2.5 billion monthly active users at time of writing.[15] That's 2.5 billion people actively logging in, posting, and reading every month. The scale is mind-boggling, and the onset has been so rapid that we are still unable to see all the impacts it's having. This is a seismic shift in one of the most fundamental aspects of human interaction, on a timescale that is unprecedented.

Now, I don't actually think technology or the internet is evil. If anything, I'm a bit of a tech enthusiast. It's more of an amoral force—merely reducing the "friction" involved in communicating, allowing people to talk much more frequently and pervasively in our daily lives. This is a miraculous thing in so many ways. It's created entire domains of work that could not have existed before. It allows intimate, instant communication between loved ones no matter how far apart they are. With social distancing mandated during the pandemic, these technological capabilities have been a life-saver both for businesses as well as for family and friends. Answers to any question, and opinions from any point of view, are just a few keystrokes away. A single voice with an important message can now reach the entire world.

COMMUNICATION HAS GONE INTO OVERDRIVE WITH THE CREATION OF THE INTERNET AND SOCIAL MEDIA.

Social networks are the primary technology allowing this explosion in communication. Even if you're not on Facebook, chances are you're either sending or receiving messages or reading posts from one of any number of other apps that specialize in some other form of communication. Twitter is built for real-time, broad-reach messaging. Want something a little more private? Try Snapchat or WhatsApp. How about if you want to share something a little more important, and less time-sensitive? Post to your Instagram grid. Don't want it to last forever?

---

15   J. Clement, "Number of Facebook Users Worldwide 2008-2019," Statista, January 30, 2020, https://www.statista.com/statistics/264810/number-of-monthly-active-facebook-users-worldwide/.

Snapchat and Instagram stories welcome your content. There's always a place for your communication to happen electronically.

Each of these social media platforms have an essentially infinite supply of posts, shares, and other content to show you. The platforms decide what to show you first based on computer algorithms (instructions written in code). These algorithms build models of behavior that are trained and updated over time to learn what kinds of things people engage with the most, and then they give that content more prominence. If you always like the posts of one of your friends, that person's posts will keep coming up first. If you stop scrolling and stare just a little longer than average at some scantily clad ad babe, the app will know what kind of ad to show you next time. If you can't help but comment on some dumb thing your high school classmate keeps posting about the president, guess what the algorithm learns?

ALGORITHMS ON SOCIAL MEDIA ENABLE AND ENCOURAGE ECHO CHAMBERS.

Algorithms on social media enable and encourage echo chambers. They are taught by our own behavior to favor people and topics that we agree with. We will like, comment, and favorite all the same kinds of things, and then the platforms will gladly keep you happy by showing you more of the same. Not only that, but political leanings are directly baked into software; if Facebook thinks you favor a certain political party, you're probably seeing ads from those candidates during elections. It learns this from the websites you visit and the people you talk to, and what *their* political leanings are, which just feeds back into the echo chamber cycle. In many cases, the algorithm isn't even doing most of this isolation; merely by accident, we might simply only be friending and following people in our tribe, and clearing any dissenting voices out of our feed. This one's personal to me,[16] because I found myself in the

---

16   As a reminder, this is Mike Drum speaking.

middle of an echo chamber during the last presidential election, one full of Donkeys who never even took the Elephant-turned-president seriously. It turned out I hadn't been hearing a single voice from the other side, the side that actually won.

Facebook, Instagram, Twitter, Google, and YouTube have been building these algorithmic models of human behavior for a long time, and of course they have gotten very good at amplifying the best and, importantly, worst of us. Facebook has recently even publicly spoken about the issues with sensationalist content: people are naturally drawn to it, and it receives far more engagement. The company has said they are working to change the algorithms to instead downrank it.[17] The problem can never fully go away though, because the platforms are designed to increase engagement: these platforms are simply amplifiers of human behavior, and as discussed earlier . . . human behavior is flawed.

We're not usually at our "highest mind" when browsing social media, so we're susceptible to the classics already discussed: tribalism causing us to fear those in the out-group, writing off any ideas that don't match our worldview without a second thought, and simplifying those views that we do get exposed to into the most extreme, horrible versions of the other side's ideas. This is how we get to the point where the majority of political posts we see are either only reaffirming our existing views, or are the most comically awful versions of those with whom we disagree.

Finally, and perhaps most dangerously: technology physically separates us from the humans we're actually talking to, turning them into words and (sometimes) a picture. It's a lot harder to yell at people when they're standing right in front of you, than when they're a thousand miles away and you might never even meet them. This is called "online disinhibition," and it's a measurable, studied effect.[18] It's why having

---

17   Mark Zuckerberg, "A Blueprint for Content Governance and Enforcement," Facebook, November 15, 2018, https://www.facebook.com/notes/mark-zuckerberg/a-blueprint-for-content-governance-and-enforcement/10156443129621634/. Facebook acknowledging problems with sensationalist content.

18   John Suler, "The Online Disinhibition Effect," *CyberPsychology & Behavior* 7, no. 3 (July 2004), https://doi.org/10.1089/1094931041291295.

hard conversations in person is much more difficult than over text or email. The "text message breakup" is so common now it's a dead meme. We're disinhibited because we don't see the recipient as a full-on person in those moments. It's an unavoidable form of dehumanization, and dehumanization is the dark heart of many of the worst things that have been done throughout history. When the majority of communication is now happening virtually, we've lost many of the social skills and empathy that we would otherwise develop naturally for use in day-to-day discourse. And the tools responsible for a majority of human communication—body language and intonation—are missing altogether.[19] We're still learning to cope with this new reality.

Each of these phenomena has a profound impact on political discourse, and it's not hard to draw a correlate line between the rise in online communication and the shift towards greater polarization. When we can pick our ideological exposure diet a la carte, it's far harder to see things from the other side.

The changing media landscape

Technology's impact extends past just direct person-to-person communication. Certain technological shifts have also allowed for dramatic movement in one of the critical pillars of democracy: the free press. Geography used to be a major constraint in disseminating information to a mass audience; radio and television signals only traveled so far, and newspapers had travel limitations for daily delivery. These limits encouraged the institutions with which many of us grew up: city-based newspapers with their own journalist staff, and local six o'clock news with anchors you would probably run into some day. These regional media companies did actually have the freedom to behave a little more partisan since they were representing more homogenous areas. But their primary focus was covering issues of local importance, while the Donkey Elephant war was left to the big guys.

---

19   The 1967 Merhabian study concluded that 93% of communication is nonverbal. That study has been whittled down in terms of its applicability, but most other studies would concur that a majority of communication is nonverbal.

Only a few major media companies built up the resources to work with local affiliates to get national television broadcasts or newspaper distribution. Covering the entire country was such an investment that costs needed to be recouped by reaching as broad an audience as possible. Therefore, media companies needed to keep everyone happy. The anchors you saw sitting there reading the news needed to become trusted voices by the entire country, not just for the sake of keeping the viewers on board, but more importantly for their real customers: the advertisers. The only advertising that was effective was by big brands that also had their own nationwide distribution channels and were mostly just focused on building brand recognition. This kind of "brand advertising" is still done today mostly with the same broad, family friendly, inoffensive media because it's in their economic interest to not appear to have taken anyone's side. Coca-Cola is for everyone.

Cable news sparked a change in this dynamic, and once the internet came around, that symbiotic relationship was in flames. Something far more effective had appeared: targeted advertising. With this new infrastructure making it more efficient to spin off new branches of media, as well as show different advertisements to different people, the economic incentives shifted. Instead of media needing to go broad and be digestible by everyone, they could go to a smaller market but have a bigger impact, "narrowcasting" instead of "broadcasting." It became possible and even more profitable to go after smaller market segments, because more companies were able to effectively advertise, and their ads were able to be shown to their relevant audiences. This completely exploded in the last decade with online advertising: Google and Facebook redefined the game by building platforms that knew all about its users, thus building individual "ad profiles." Now this kind of advertising is used all over the web, and it allows for ultimate efficiency: advertisers perfectly paired with an audience they know want their product.

Because advertisers were happy, media companies were again able to start building brand loyalty by catering to specific segments of the population with messages they knew they wanted to hear. As mentioned in the section about our psychology, people naturally seek out opinions that reaffirm their world view, and the tides had shifted to allow giant media companies to start filling that role. Companies could build much deeper audience loyalty by filling their 24-hour news cycles with the specific news and opinions they knew their audience would respond to, and even further by pointing out how "one-sided" the other guys were. The truth was, almost every media company had started to shift to one side or the other; the press is arguably where the polarization started.

Partisan media has several really effective tricks up its sleeve, all of which soundproof the walls of our echo chambers. The easiest is simply in what they choose to cover. Even if a news outlet just sticks to the facts with no opinion or embellishment, it can pick only the facts that support the story they are trying to tell, or the stories they believe exemplify it. Likewise, when covering news about the opposition, the argument will be constructed in a way they already know how to defeat. First, there's the "straw man" type of argument: a conversation about illegal immigration becomes one about how "these people think it's okay to put kids in cages," and discussion involving an assault weapons ban turns into "a need to defend the Second Amendment." A more subtle version of this includes the "weak man" fallacy:[20] choosing only to attack the weakest part of the opposing view, (for example, pointing at the Westboro Baptist Church[21] as an example of why

PARTISAN MEDIA HAS SEVERAL REALLY EFFECTIVE TRICKS UP ITS SLEEVE, ALL OF WHICH SOUNDPROOF THE WALLS OF OUR ECHO CHAMBERS.

---

20 Yvonne Raley and Robert Talisse, "Getting Duped: How the Media Messes with Your Mind," *Scientific American*, February 1, 2008, https://www.scientificamerican.com/article/getting-duped/. On fallacies in the media.

21 Westboro Baptist Church is largely the extended family of the late Fred Phelps, and is well-known for its hate speech against homosexuals.

Christianity should be rejected). Finally, there's the "hollow man": completely fabricating an opinion or untrue set of assumptions that the other guys might hold, constructing an argument based on that, and then tearing that argument apart. In my[22] opinion, there really aren't many people out there who believe that women should kill babies or rich people shouldn't pay taxes, but those are the views that the media focus on, because it's outrageous and effective.

Communication gets further muddled by the rise of online, ad-funded articles and videos. You probably know the term "click-bait": an especially juicy title or thumbnail that triggers all those lovely emotions like anger, lust, or fear. We're all but helpless to click the link and see what it's all about (and, of course, look at some ads). Once we've clicked, though, it's far more beneficial to the website if you either keep scrolling and viewing more ads, or just get clicking onto the next thing as fast as possible. This means publishers are incentivized to either bloat out the story and bury the lede[23] way down the page, or oversimplify everything and get you to share it on your own social media without even digging into the claim being made. Either way, clearly communicating the truth is sacrificed for getting the click.

None of this is some big conspiracy though. We're all just people, with people problems. We all want to feel surrounded by people with whom we feel comfortable. We'd rather feel passionate than bored. Headlines tend to try and stir emotion because it's impossible to be nuanced in six-to-eight words. Many in the media believe it's their duty to reach as many people as possible, since it's the job of the free press to inform the public. News has shifted into an entertainment industry, because that's where the money is. Journalists are just as human as the rest of us, with the same pattern-matching skills and filter bubbles and hopes and fears. We can only hope that they spend more time as

---

22 Mike is speaking here.

23 This actually is the correct spelling. Lede is a journalistic word meaning, "the opening sentence or paragraph of a news article, summarizing the most important aspects of the story." https://www.lexico.com/en/definition/lede.

Scientists and maybe sometimes Sports Fans, than they do as Lawyers or Zealots.

The history and threat of continued foreign interference

All of this has also culminated in a uniquely powerful set of tools enabling foreign powers to interfere with our elections. In 2016, Russia capitalized on our already-growing political tensions, and used social media to spread messages of polarization.[24] The Senate report is clear: this was a long-running campaign that began in at least 2014 to gather intelligence about our cultural and political situation, and exploit it for their ends. The belief is that this was mostly done to deliberately sow discord among the American people and undermine our trust in democracy. Allow me to quote from the report directly [italics mine]:

> Analysis of the behavior of the IRA[25]-associated social media accounts makes clear that while the Russian information warfare campaign exploited the context of the election and election-related issues in 2016, the preponderance of the operational focus, as reflected repeatedly in content, account names, and audiences targeted, was on *socially divisive issues—such as race, immigration, and Second Amendment rights—in an attempt to pit Americans against one another* and against their government. The Committee found that IRA influence operatives consistently used hot-button, societal divisions in the United States as fodder for the content *they published through social media in order to stoke anger, provoke outrage and protest, push Americans further away from one another, and foment distrust in government institutions.* The divisive

---

24 Direct from the opening lines of the report from the U.S. Senate Intelligence Committee: Russian Active Measures Campaigns and Interference in the 2016 U.S. Election (p. 3). I'll be citing this a few more times with links.

25 IRA: Internet Research Agency, the name of the Russian business responsible for these online influence operations.

> 2016 U.S. presidential election was just an additional feature of a much more expansive, target-rich landscape of potential ideological and societal sensitivities.[26]

Just let that sink in—re-read it if you must. This is a group of people that learned which issues are most sensitive to us, and used psychological tricks triggering tribalism, when they had absolutely no stake in either tribe. This new kind of ideological warfare is uniquely enabled by the time in which we live: the internet and social media allow anonymous actors to have a voice in our democracy. As more of our communication occurs online, it is also visible to those who wish to use it against us. There are no gatekeepers for disseminating information to the public anymore. The press also played a part: it's believed that Russia was responsible for hacking documents from the DNC,[27] which they then leaked out to media organizations who were more than happy to report on juicy material during the election season. Polarization is the new weapon on the battleground of the digital domain. It erodes civility and prevents the ability to compromise, grinding progress to a halt; this was their goal, and it sure seems to be working.

This new battlefield is taking place not in public under the jurisdiction of the government, but on the platforms of private companies. This complicates things even further, since it largely falls to individual corporations to fight back. They often either lack the resources or the incentives to do much about it; it's making them money, after all. In this case, accounts originating in Russia were even buying targeted advertisements on Facebook and other platforms. Below is an example that an election interference team purchased during the Trump/Hillary presidential race:[28]

---

26 Russian Active Measures Campaigns and Interference in the 2016 U.S. Election, Volume 2: Russia's Use of Social Media, I.2 page 6, https://www.intelligence.senate.gov/sites/default/files/documents/Report_Volume2.pdf.

27 Katelyn Polantz and Stephen Collinson, "12 Russians indicted in Mueller investigation," *CNN*, July 14, 2018, https://www.cnn.com/2018/07/13/politics/russia-investigation-indictments/index.html.

28 Scott Shane, "These Are the Ads Russia Bought on Facebook in 2016," *The New York Times*, November 1, 2017, https://www.nytimes.com/2017/11/01/us/politics/russia-2016-election-facebook.html.

FIGURE 2.5 *Foreign interference via Facebook*. The text of the post reads, "Today Americans are able to elect a president with godly moral principles. Hillary is a Satan, and her crimes and lies had proved just how evil she is. And even though Donald Trump isn't a saint by any means, he's at least an honest man and he cares deeply for this country. My vote goes for him!" (Facebook.)

Facebook allows ads to be sent to people of any demographics of the purchaser's choosing, and this one was meant for Christians. There were hundreds of ads placed just by this fake "Army of Jesus" account.[29] These were not advertisements meant to sell a product or make money; they were purely there to affect divisions and influence an election by targeting us.

This is something that even the CEO of Facebook refused to accept at the time.[30] Not only were these advertisements being placed, but

---

29 UsHadrons (@ushadrons), "This space is a repository for content from the Russian social media account 'Army of Jesus,'" Medium post, October 18, 2017, https://medium.com/@ushadrons/this-space-is-a-repository-for-content-from-the-russian-social-media-group-army-of-jesus-553c6aa74fea. Compilation of ads placed by Army of Jesus, a known entity owned by Russian operatives.

30 Olivia Solon, "Facebook's Fake News: Mark Zuckerberg Rejects 'Crazy Idea' That It Swayed Voters," *The Guardian*, November 10, 2016, https://www.theguardian.com/technology/2016/nov/10/facebook-fake-news-us-election-mark-zuckerberg-donald-trump.

there were also deliberately fake news stories being circulated on the platform. If you ever saw and believed the news that the Pope endorsed Donald Trump,[31] you fell for the most successful of these. (Fun fact: the term "fake news" was popularized initially during 2016 to refer to these fabricated stories that were generally *supporting* Donald Trump.) That fake news story received 960,000 total shares, reactions and comments; it outperformed the top news stories from every major news outlet.[32] Since then, Facebook has added preventative measures and released data on foreign-placed ads meant to influence elections.[33] In order to keep up, Facebook is deleting around 3.4 billion accounts every six months.[34] It's a battle on an entirely new domain that cannot be won, only managed; it's also largely being fought by private companies instead of a military.

This will continue to happen: there were no effective consequences or counterattack from our government, and our adversaries are emboldened. Vladimir Putin has openly joked about Russia's intent to meddle in 2020.[35] Much like Facebook is conflicted in fighting back as it makes money from this, why would a presidential administration want to prevent someone from helping their campaign? Others will join in the fun, too; we've been alerted to similar campaigns from China and Iran.[36]

There are proven effective strategies for inciting polarization, but their goals also include attacking our election infrastructure and ultimately undermining our ability to even trust the outcome of an election.

---

31 Dan Evon, "Pope Francis Shocks World, Endorses Donald Trump for President," *Snopes*, July 10, 2016, https://www.snopes.com/fact-check/pope-francis-donald-trump-endorsement/.

32 U.S. Senate Intelligence, "Report on Russia," 9.

33 Mark Zuckerberg, "Preparing for Elections," Facebook, September 12, 2018, https://www.facebook.com/notes/mark-zuckerberg/preparing-for-elections/10156300047606634/.

34 Vanessa Romo and Amy Held, "Facebook Removed Nearly 3.4 Billion Fake Accounts in 6 Months," *NPR*, May 23, 2019, https://www.npr.org/2019/05/23/726353723/facebook-removed-nearly-3-2-billion-fake-accounts-in-last-six-months.

35 "I'll tell you a secret: Yes, we'll definitely do it [interfere]. Just don't tell anyone." As quoted in Nathan Hodge, Olga Pavlova, and Mary Ilyushina, "Putin Jokes That Russia Will Meddle in 2020 U.S. Elections," *CNN*, October 3, 2019, https://www.cnn.com/2019/10/02/politics/putin-2020-us-presidential-election-joke-intl/index.html.

36 Jordan Fabian, "U.S. Warns of 'Ongoing' Election Interference by Russia, China, Iran," *The Hill*, October 19, 2018, https://thehill.com/policy/national-security/412292-us-warns-of-ongoing-election-interference-by-russia-china-iran.

Imagine the true consequences of this: if we become much more polarized and distrustful of one another, any anomaly in November 2020 could fundamentally prevent us from agreeing on the outcome. For nearly a week after the 2020 Iowa caucus, we were still unsure of the final outcome due to technical issues.[37] Imagine this on a nationwide scale; could America today handle an even more extreme version of the Bush-Gore election of 2000? The Supreme Court effectively had to decide the outcome, since the Florida counts were not agreed upon. We are measurably more polarized now than we were twenty years ago, and our global adversaries know just how to destroy our trust in the system.

The flames of the Donkey Elephant war are being fed not only by our own failure to find unity, but by foreign actors intent on keeping it that way.

In the next chapter, we'll continue with some of the psychological background, looking at a key contributing factor from our Western worldview.

---

37   Nate Cohn, Josh Katz, Denise Lu, Charlie Smart, Ben Smithgall, and Andrew Fischer, "Iowa Caucus Riddled with Errors and Inconsistencies," *The New York Times*, February 6, 2020, https://www.nytimes.com/2020/02/06/upshot/iowa-caucuses-errors-results.html.

CHAPTER THREE

OUR WESTERN WORLDVIEW PROBLEM

"This isn't either/or, this is both/and."
—ANDY STANLEY[1]

Not only are foreign influences stoking the discontent, our own Western way of thinking is fueling the Donkey Elephant war. Western thought operates in either/or paradigms, not both/and, and that's a significant part of our problem.

One of the primary books I read as part of my research was *The Righteous Mind: Why Good People Are Divided by Politics and Religion*, by Jonathan Haidt. I introduced my son Mike to Haidt's book, and he introduced Tim Urban's work to me. Suffice it to say that as a life-long Christian with a bachelor's degree in science and a master's degree

---

1   Andy Stanley, "The Separation of Church and Hate," sermon audio, published by North Point Community Church, https://store.northpoint.org/products/the-separation-of-church-hate.

in divinity, I hadn't spent much time reading evolutionary psychology. Putting all my cards on the table, I didn't even know evolutionary psychology was a thing. Haidt self-identifies as a liberal, atheist evolutionary psychologist, so to say that his and my worldviews are a world apart would be not only safe, but an understatement. And that's exactly why I read the book and other similar material, since worldview clashes are a significant part of the Donkey Elephant war. As C.S. Lewis taught in *Mere Christianity*, truth is truth wherever you find it.[2] I learned plenty, found much of it a fascinating read, and ended up quite encouraged in an odd sort of way, which I'll fully explain later in my concluding chapters.

Here are Haidt's own words:[3]

> The first principle of moral psychology is *intuition comes first, strategic reasoning second*, [which is Haidt's elephant and rider analogy that my son introduced in the last chapter.] . . .

- We are obsessively concerned about what others think of us, although much of the concern is unconscious and invisible to us.

- Conscious reasoning functions like a press secretary who automatically justifies any position taken by the president.

- With the help of our press secretary, we are able to lie and cheat often, and then cover it up so effectively that we convince even ourselves.[4]

---

2   Not a direct quote, but in line with the beginning of Book 2 of *Mere Christianity* by C.S. Lewis.

3   Haidt, *Righteous Mind*, 106–7.

4   I don't know about you, but I always find it encouraging when people arrive at Biblical truth through other means. Compare Haidt's conclusion with Jeremiah 17:9, "The heart is deceitful above all things, and beyond cure. Who can understand it?"

- Reasoning can take us to almost any conclusion we want to reach, because we ask "*Can* I believe it?" when we want to believe something, but "*Must* I believe it?" when we don't want to believe. The answer is almost always yes to the first question and no to the second. [italics mine]

- In moral and political matters we are often groupish, rather than selfish. We deploy our reasoning skills to support our team, and to demonstrate commitment to our team.

I believe Haidt's insights above match a Biblical understanding of human nature. Haidt helps us see some of what's likely going on beneath the conscious mind. No wonder our political landscape is such a mess!

I was familiar with the concept of natural selection developed by Charles Darwin, but unfamiliar with the concept of group selection, which Haidt's last bullet begins to point toward. My reason for including his work here draws more from the rest of his book, starting with the concept of group selection. What follows is my very brief summary of Haidt's writing on an evolutionary view of social development.

- Individuals compete with individuals, and that competition rewards selfishness, but simultaneously groups compete with groups, and the tribes that are more cohesive (team players who cooperate and work for the good of the group) generally win.

- Group selection happens when individuals find ways to suppress selfishness and work as a team, in competition with other teams. For example, one person pulls down a branch while the other plucks the fruit, and they both share the meal. Interestingly, chimpanzees, widely believed to be the closest to humans in terms of brain development, never do this. [5]

---

5   Haidt, *Righteous Mind*, 238.

- Humans construct moral communities out of shared norms, institutions, and gods that they will fight, kill, and die to defend.[6]

- The coevolution of tribal minds and tribal cultures didn't just prepare us for war; it also prepared us for far more peaceful coexistence within our groups, and in modern times, for cooperation on a vast scale as well.[7]

- Groupishness is focused on improving the welfare of the in-group, not on harming an out-group.[8]

Tribal identity is central to understanding our Donkey Elephant war. Republicans and Democrats can't just be viewed individually, but must be seen as groups. Urban comes from a similar place as Haidt, and even quotes Haidt's work occasionally. Urban writes,

> On the ancient landscape—the one we were designed for—the human being wasn't really the independent life form of the human race. The tribe was. In the human world, we think of "Me vs. You" selfishness and "Us vs. Them" tribalism as different concepts, but they're actually just the same phenomenon.[9] . . . Tribalism generates peer pressure to conform and a fear of being labeled a secret member of Them and ostracized (or worse).[10]

Haidt goes into great detail describing the development of groups or tribes, and some of the moral foundations that underpin their viewpoints. I am only giving tribalism the briefest of overviews here, so some readers may want to check out either of the primary sources I've cited (Haidt

---

6   Ibid, 240. Clearly, here is a place where our worldviews clash, as I do not believe that we created God, but rather that God created us.

7   Ibid, 246.

8   Ibid, 253. Perhaps we've devolved?

9   Tim Urban, "A Game of Giants," Chapter 2, The Story of Us, published August 29, 2019, https://waitbutwhy.com/2019/08/giants.html.

10   Tim Urban, "A Story of Stories," Chapter 3, The Story of Us, published September 4, 2019, https://waitbutwhy.com/2019/09/stories.html.

or Urban). Remember that with no reference to evolutionary psychology whatsoever, Rwandan Pastor Célestin Musekura arrived at the same conclusion in his observations of America: Republicans and Democrats function just like the African tribes Hutu and Tutsi. I'll explore further the related issue of identity in the next chapter.

Another influence on Western culture came from the 3rd century Persian prophet Mani, after whom the religion Manichaeism is named. Arguably the most influential bishop of the Catholic Church, Augustine, spent ten years of his life in Manichaeism, and while he later rejected those roots, others have noted Manichaeistic themes showing up in his writings.[11] Part of the larger Gnostic movement, Mani preached that the visible world is the battleground between the forces of light (absolute goodness) and the forces of darkness (absolute evil). You must pick one side and fight for it. "If you think about politics in a Manichaean way, then compromise is a sin. God and the devil don't issue many bipartisan proclamations, and neither should you."[12]

"ON THE ANCIENT LANDSCAPE, THE HUMAN BEING WASN'T REALLY THE INDEPENDENT LIFE FORM OF THE HUMAN RACE. THE TRIBE WAS."

This either/or mentality has deeply affected our political landscape, which has carried over into some most fascinating arenas, like where people live and shop! The Civil Rights Act of 1964 led to significant realignment, as many in the South who had been conservative Democrats since the Civil War left the Democratic party and became Republican. Before the realignment, there had been liberals and conservatives in both

---

11 Johannes van Oort, "Manichaeism: Its Sources and Influences on Western Christianity," *Verbum et Ecclesia* 30, no. 2 (December 2009), http://www.scielo.org.za/pdf/vee/v30n2/20.pdf.

12 Haidt, *Righteous Mind*, 362.

parties, but after the exodus, there was very little overlap.[13] "Cross-party friendships are disappearing; Manichaeism and scorched Earth politics are increasing."[14] In 1976, only 27% of Americans lived in "landslide counties" (defined as a county that voted Republican or Democrat with greater than a 20% margin). In 2008, 48% of Americans lived in a landslide county. If there's a Whole Foods store in your county, there's an 89% chance the county voted for Obama in the 2008 election; if there's a Cracker Barrel restaurant in your county, there's a 62% chance the county voted for McCain.[15] When the neighborhoods we live in are more and more politically homogenous, the echo chamber effect is further magnified. Yet again from a different lens, we're becoming more polarized and isolated, not less, and that does not bode well for the future.

Are you WEIRD? "WEIRD is an acronym for Western, educated, industrialized, rich, and democratic. The WEIRDer you are, the more you see a world full of separate objects, rather than relationships."[16] Haidt identifies this Western worldview as part of our political challenge, arguing for more of a group view to moral psychological development than an individual view. Haidt refers regularly to French sociologist Émile Durkheim, who argued "that Homo sapiens was really Homo duplex, a creature who exists at two levels: as an individual and as part of the larger society."[17] From a psychological point of view, we simply cannot understand why humans act and react the way they do, politically and otherwise, if we only view them individually. And the tribal tendency to view groups as either/or instead of both/and is at the root of many of our struggles.[18]

---

13   Ibid, 362.

14   Ibid, 363.

15   Ibid, 364.

16   Ibid, 112.

17   Ibid, 261.

18   If you're noticing an apparent contradiction spotlighted by the story of my Rwandan Pastor friend (who can be described as very non-Western), I believe that's because the next chapter on identity was even more at play than the either/or thinking. Tribalism is an identity issue.

Biblical worldview

It would be hard to overestimate the power of worldview. It's like a lens that automatically and subconsciously filters out anything that doesn't match expectations. One of the most incredible illustrations I've seen of the power of worldview is a simple, grainy video of teams of people passing a basketball to one another. If you've never seen it, do yourself a favor right now and join the 24 million who've taken the one minute test by googling "Test Your Awareness: Do the Test." Worldviews cause us to interpret the world around us without all the data, because we simply filter out what we don't want or expect to see.

Even though my target audience for this book is people who already have an affinity for Jesus, I'm not assuming a Biblical worldview as the norm. Barna research reveals that less than 10% of American adults have a Biblical worldview, and it's dropping by the year: from 10% in 2016 to 9% in 2017 and only 7% in 2018.[19] While Barna's definition of a Biblical worldview is quite specific, identifying six different tenets,[20] I'm using the term more loosely to simply mean a view of the world consistent with the overarching themes of the Bible. Since about 70% of the country self-identifies as Christian, but only 7% has a Biblical worldview, it's safe to assume that what I'm presenting here will be new information for many.

Using an evolutionary worldview as his lens, Haidt identifies some challenges with the Western worldview that contribute to our poisoned partisan political landscape, the either/or tribalism being chief among them. Now, let's start from scratch and see where the Bible might cause

---

19   George Barna, "Survey Reveals That Fewer Adults Have a Biblical Worldview Now Than Two Years Ago," released October 18, 2018, http://www.georgebarna.com/research-flow/2018/10/17/survey-reveals-that-fewer-adults-have-a-biblical-worldview-now-than-two-years-ago.

20   "For the purposes of the survey, a 'biblical worldview' was defined as believing that absolute moral truth exists; the Bible is totally accurate in all of the principles it teaches; Satan is considered to be a real being or force, not merely symbolic; a person cannot earn their way into Heaven by trying to be good or do good works; Jesus Christ lived a sinless life on earth; and God is the all-knowing, all-powerful creator of the world who still rules the universe today. In the research, anyone who held all of those beliefs was said to have a biblical worldview." [Reprinted, by permission, "Changes in Worldview Among Christians over the Past 13 Years," The Barna Group, accessed October 19, 2019, https://www.barna.com/research/barna-survey-examines-changes-in-worldview-among-christians-over-the-past-13-years/.]

us to land on the same topic, and let's use one of the most well-known stories of the Old Testament to illustrate. I'm sharing quite a bit of the backstory as it relates to multiple themes in this book, not just the either/or issue.

Moses is one of the Old Testament's most well-known heroes. He was born to Jewish parents at a time when Pharaoh had enslaved all the Jews and felt threatened by their growing population. He had ordered the midwives to kill the male Jewish babies, but when that didn't work, he ordered all baby boys to be drowned in the Nile. When Moses' mother could hide Moses no longer, she placed him in a basket, floated him down the river, and prayed like crazy. In what must go down in history as a candidate for "best day ever," Pharaoh's daughter found the basket with Moses in it, asked Moses' older sister Miriam to "find someone to nurse the baby," and by the end of the day, Moses was back home and his mother was being paid to nurse her own son.[21]

> **WORLDVIEW IS LIKE A LENS THAT AUTOMATICALLY AND SUBCONSCIOUSLY FILTERS OUT ANYTHING THAT DOESN'T MATCH EXPECTATIONS.**

I'm certain Moses' early years were 1) stretched out as long as possible, and 2) filled with his parents drilling into him who he really was. Fast-forwarding through the next 75 years of Moses' life, he grew up in the palace as if he were Pharaoh's daughter's own son. As an adult, when he saw an Egyptian taskmaster beating a Hebrew slave, he looked around, thought nobody was paying attention, and killed the Egyptian—his Hebrew identity overriding his Egyptian identity. News spread quickly, and Moses fled Egypt, where he lived as a shepherd in the wilderness of

---

21   Ex. 1:6 – 2:10.

Midian for 40 years. At age 80,[22] God called Moses to return to Egypt to "set My people free." Moses was reluctant, to say the least (see Exodus 3–4 for his long list of excuses,) but he finally agreed when God promised to be with him every step of the way.[23]

Every time Moses (and his brother Aaron) told Pharaoh to let the Israelites go, Pharaoh said no, and God inflicted a plague, with each one more painful than the last.[24] The tenth and final plague resulted in the first-born male of every Egyptian household dying. The Israelites were instructed to kill and eat a lamb without blemish and put some of the blood on the doorposts of their homes so that the angel of death would pass over them.[25] Hence, the "Passover" meal that Jews still celebrate today, and the reason that "Lamb of God" became a title for Jesus, who came to save all of us from eternal death.

With pressure from all the grieving Egyptians who were still alive, Pharaoh not only let the Israelites go, but kicked them out of the country. Exodus chapters 13–14 tell those stories, including the odd path God chose for them to take, right up to the edge of the Red Sea. By this time Pharaoh had unwisely changed his mind and decided he really didn't want to see his free labor force evaporate, so he called for his best chariots and best army to go get the Israelites and force them to return back to slavery. By the end of Exodus 14, the Israelites are pinned between a rock and a hard place, with the Red Sea on one side and the Egyptians breathing down their necks on the other side.

Have you ever been there? Most of us have been in such a predicament at one point or another in our lives: a place where we can see no way out,

---

22 If you find it either distracting or troubling that Moses was 80 years old when God called him to liberate the Israelites from slavery, consider the following. In Genesis 6:3, God declares that from that point on, people's normal lifespan would not exceed 120 years. That's still significantly more than today, but many of today's primary causes for death (cancer, car accidents, suicide) might not have been issues in Moses' time. Deuteronomy 34:7 says, "Moses was 120 years old when he died, yet his eyes were not weak nor his strength gone." He would have been at the 2/3 point in life when God changed his life direction.

23 Ex. 3–4.

24 Ex. 5–10.

25 Ex. 11–12.

and unless God parts the "Sea" in front of us, we're toast. At times our problems seem so large, that unless God solves them, they won't get solved. One might argue that our Donkey Elephant war is one such situation.

There are two questions we can ask of this Exodus story that unless you've read Exodus 1–15 closely, you likely won't be able to answer correctly. The first is, "Who parted the Red Sea—God or Moses?" And the answer is not one or the other, but "yes"—both. Clearly there was nothing Moses could do *on his own* to cause the waters of the Red Sea to pile up on both sides, dry land to appear in the middle for the Israelites to cross, and then the Sea to close back up at just the right time in order to protect them from the Egyptians in hot pursuit.[26] Yet God told Moses to hold out his staff in the direction of the body of water, and God waited to part the Sea until Moses obeyed. It strikes me as similar to a young boy begging his dad to let him help fix the car, so the dad says, "Sure, child, you can hold the wrench." Our part compared to God's part is usually miniscule. But more often than not, God waits to do His part until we've done ours, whatever big or little thing that might turn out to be. When it comes to God's part/our part in the twists and turns of life, it's usually a both/and, not an either/or.[27] Our part pales compared to God's part, but God will usually patiently wait for us to do what He's invited us to do before He does the heavy lifting. We can and should pray for God's help in ending the Donkey Elephant war. We just need to be prepared to do what He tells us to do in answer to our prayer.

---

26   I've read articles by modern scientists trying to explain the phenomena of the plagues and the parting of the Red Sea, including the suggestion that perhaps a well-timed earthquake could have caused the Sea to part. It makes no difference to me whether or not we understand *how* God does the "miraculous" things He does. Our understanding of how God does something miraculous should simply add to the gratitude, not diminish it.

27   My seminary training was Lutheran, and I can hear all my theology profs braying and stomping louder than any donkeys or elephants. When it comes to salvation, it's all God. There's nothing I can do to save myself, and no contribution I can make gets me any closer to the finish line of salvation. The hard-core Lutherans would want the paragraph to stop there, and I understand why. It's grace, grace, and all grace. AND, unless one wants to take a universalist position that I find hard to justify Biblically, some of us receive/acknowledge/cooperate with/align ourselves toward such a gift from God, and others don't. That's "our part," such as it were.

The other question addresses one of the many hard-to-understand statements in the Bible. The question is, "Who hardened Pharaoh's heart—God, or Pharaoh?" If you've ever read Moses' biography from the first half of the book of Exodus, it's highly likely you stumbled over verses like this one: "The Lord said to Moses, 'When you return to Egypt, see that you perform before Pharaoh all the wonders I have given you the power to do. But I will harden his heart so that he will not let the people go.'"[28] That seems so unfair to a modern reader that it probably caught your attention. And it would be bad enough if it were in the Bible just once, but it's in there a whole bunch of times. In fact, Pharaoh's arteriosclerosis is mentioned 17 times in the book of Exodus. Case closed: God did it, right? Well, not so fast. Ten of the 17 times say that God hardened Pharaoh's heart; four times it simply says that his heart became hard with no further commentary; and three times it says that Pharaoh hardened his own heart. So the correct answer to the question, "Who hardened Pharaoh's heart: God or Pharaoh?" is "Yes," just like the last question. It isn't one or the other, but both. Here's what makes this all the more significant. All of the references that say Pharaoh hardened his own heart are found embedded in the middle of the story. At the beginning and the end, God's in charge. I find both parts of that observation incredibly comforting. I'm glad I have a part to play, but I'm even more glad that I don't have the *ultimate* part to play. God gets things started and decides when (and how) they're finished, with my part of the story landing somewhere in between. We completely miss those kinds of truth-nuggets when our worldview insists we choose one side or the other—or when our worldview causes us to filter out anything that doesn't fit without even noticing it. We have a part to play in ending the Donkey Elephant war, but we aren't flying solo.

The Bible consistently proclaims that God is all-loving and that God is all-powerful. We're so Western in our thinking that when those two attributes seem to crash into each other, we're quick to jump to an either/or instead of a both/and. Most of us seem to be more comfortable with a God who's all loving, so we'll hedge our bets on the all-powerful part. But the Bible appears to be quite content to let the clash just

---

28   Ex. 4:21.

happen rather than try to resolve it one way or the other. And that's because the Bible is very Eastern (Hebrew) in its worldview, from cover to cover.[29] In my last nine years working full time to see Jesus' John 17 prayer answered in my hometown, I've observed over and over again that a high percentage of unnecessary conflict simply comes from turning something God intends as a both/and into an either/or.[30]

Followers of Jesus are surrounded by both/ands. We believe that Jesus is both fully human and fully God. We believe that we are both saints (set apart by and for God) and sinners (falling short of who we are) at the same time, all the time. We live in both the now and the not yet—that the Kingdom of God has arrived, but not as fully as it will at the end of time. The Christian life is packed full of both/ands, and when we revert back to a Western either/or worldview, it's like settling for grainy black and white when high resolution color is available. Both/and thinking values the contribution of each part, while recognizing that those parts must be held together for the whole package to reach its full potential.

I have a friend, Evan Davis, who produced the documentary, *It's a Girl: The Three Deadliest Words in the World*. The movie is simultaneously pro-female and pro-life. That's the kind of both/and we need to see so much more regularly. I'll share some other similar examples later in Part III. We miss out on so much of what God intends when we settle for either/or in a both/and world. Either/or is a poverty mindset, but God is a God of abundance. He's over-the-top extravagant in His love and mercy.[31]

29　Some people, knowing that the Old Testament was originally written in Hebrew and the New Testament in Greek, might find this confusing. But while the New Testament was written in the Greek language, every single author was Jewish, and spoke from a Jewish both/and worldview.

30　The examples are nearly endless, and my last book took a good part of a chapter fleshing them out, but here are a few, the answer to each being "yes": Does God want worship to be emotional and expressive, or quiet and reverent? Does God heal by miracles or medicine? Does God speak through reason or revelation? Did Jesus come full of grace or truth? Is racism an individual or a systemic issue?

31　This could be an entire book, but as just one example, when Jesus miraculously fed a crowd of over 10,000 (5000 men plus women and children) with only five loaves of bread and two fish (not whales, either), there were 12 baskets of leftovers afterward. See Matthew 14:13–21 for one rendering of the story. When you pick up more leftovers than you started with, you're clearly in both/and abundance land.

Abu Saada, introduced in Chapter 1, laments that Christians in the West tend to take an either/or approach to the Middle Eastern conflict, siding either with Israel or the Palestinians, and failing to see the possibilities of embracing both. And Musekura, also introduced in Chapter 1, is working hard to address the tribal mentalities in Rwanda and other East African countries that so closely mirror the either/or partisanship we're suffering with in American politics.

Summarizing Western cultural assets and liabilities

America is a melting pot, and so not everyone who's American has a Western mindset. Americans with European descent, as well as anyone who's breathed American air for a few generations, will likely have adopted several Western viewpoints. Both evolutionary psychology and Biblical theology landed at the same conclusion, that our WEIRD thinking contributes to our either/or partisanship. We can summarize what we've learned from both wildly diverse starting points into a few broad themes. Western culture:

- *Divides the whole into parts, and focuses on the parts.* Ancient Greeks brought us the sundial, for instance, dividing time into measurable increments. Productivity can increase in a Western approach to time, but at the expense of relationships unless we're conscious of the need for a wholistic both/and approach to time. There's value to focusing on the parts, but we will misread the picture unless we also focus on the whole.

- *Views the world individualistically.* Western culture looks at individuals while Eastern culture looks at larger entities: families, villages, or tribes. The most famous verse in the Bible, "For God so loved the world that He gave His one and only Son..."[32] takes on added value when we understand that God doesn't just love the world generically, but me specifically. Yet many of the

---

32   John 3:16.

statements in the Bible that westerners read individualistically were intended collectively. For instance, "You are the light of the world"[33] is a statement to a whole community, not just each individual.

- *Makes us especially prone to the "inner press secretary" syndrome due to its hyper focus on the individual.* We can convince ourselves of just about anything, and if we only surround ourselves with others who view the world the same way we do (the "echo chamber" concept from the last chapter), we're highly unlikely to be enlightened or repent (pick your word based on your worldview).

- *Defaults to an either/or mindset, not a both/and mindset.* And here is where the application to our Donkey Elephant war becomes the most pronounced. We aren't forced to choose between voting all Republican and voting all Democrat, as if those were the only options. We shouldn't have to choose between protecting the unborn and protecting the immigrant, promoting healthy marriage relationships and promoting healthy race relationships. Our political parties, when they're functioning as they were designed, should be seen as both/and, not either/or. Peace *talks*, and it uses the language of both/and.

Moses' successor, Joshua, had an encounter that perfectly summarizes the both/and perspective we need if we are to rise above the din of battle. We read,

> When Joshua was near the town of Jericho, he looked up and saw a man standing in front of him with a sword in hand. Joshua went up to him and demanded, "Are you friend or foe?" "Neither one," he replied. "I am the commander of the Lord's army." At this Joshua fell with his face to the ground in reverence. "I am at Your command," Joshua said. "What do You want me to do?"[34]

---

33 Matt. 5:14.

34 Josh. 5:13–14 (NLT).

Joshua asked an "either/or" question: "Are you friend or foe?" The "man" he encountered answered with a both/and response: "Neither one. I am the commander of the Lord's army." Who was this "man"? There are many Biblical instances like this when an angel[35] or some other messenger from God appears to people. Often by the end of the story the messenger's identity has morphed into the Lord Himself. What's unique here is that typically if people bow down and worship an angel, the angel quickly brings a halt to the worship service, since only God Himself is worthy of worship. Therefore, some have speculated that this might have been a pre-incarnate Jesus.[36]

I believe if we were to ask Jesus, "Are you Republican or Democrat?" we'd get exactly the same answer Joshua got. "Neither one. I am the commander of the Lord's army, a Kingdom that is far above the Donkey/Elephant perspective in which you're stuck." We'll explore this more fully in Chapter 5: the unity Jesus is praying for *transcends* political unity, but that doesn't mean it can't *include* political unity. Jesus said, "Give to Caesar what is Caesar's, and to God what is God's,"[37] recognizing that political authority has its place here on Earth, just not an ultimate place. Is God interested in politics or spiritual things? Yes.

The next chapter will help explain why we so quickly act like Elephants and Donkeys destined for mortal combat.

---

35   The word "angel" literally means messenger.

36   Jesus existed before he took on flesh (literal definition of "incarnate").

37   Mark 12:17.

CHAPTER FOUR

IDENTITY THEFT

*"If you deify the Donkey or the Elephant,
you're not aligned with the Kingdom."*
—RANDY REYNOLDS[1]

Any time we place our identity in anything secondary, tragedy results. When we try to ask of something more than it's equipped to provide, a letdown is inevitable.

When I was in transition between jobs in 2018, I had an incredible opportunity to spend two full days of "life planning" with a mentor, Michael Gray, who guided me through a very detailed and methodical process. One of the highlights was a life map, where I listed key events or turning points in my life along the top of some newsprint, in chronological order. Some of those events were obviously significant, while

---

1   Randy Reynolds, personal email correspondence to author, November 18, 2019. Tucson Pastor and leader.

others were a misspoken word or an unexpected health issue that had much greater impact than perhaps it should. Along the left column we listed different quadrants of life, and we then identified how those events affected me in each of the areas. When we were all done, we put a data point for my own sense of spiritual health at each stage of life, and drew a red line connecting each dot. My red line looked like a stretched-out EKG reading! My greatest Eureka moments in those two days came from examining what was happening when I was healthy and getting healthier, versus what was happening when my wellbeing was plummeting. Here's my story, which I believe can help us identify the other chief contributor to the Donkey Elephant war.

Childhood

Nobody comes out of the womb with a heart and soul already surrendered to God. We all enter the world selfish, focused on what we want and when we want it, and willing to do what it takes to get it. I'm sure my self-centered nature equals or surpasses everyone else's. Nevertheless, I was raised in a Christian home, and I don't remember the time when I first started loving and caring about God. My parents told me that as a preschooler I would sometimes wait out on the street corner as kids walked home from school to tell them God loved them. I guess this preacher thing started rather early for me.

I grew up in a Lutheran tradition that baptizes babies. Invitation: For those of you ready to write me off over the error of my (parents'?) ways, please keep reading. For children raised in this tradition, Confirmation was the opportunity to make our parents' faith our own.[2] Confirmation for me was meaningful—I wasn't there because I had to be, I was there

---

2   All Christian churches believe that God saves us apart from anything we do to earn it, and that we have some role to play in receiving/acknowledging that gift. Churches that emphasize God's part often baptize babies (who obviously aren't doing anything except receiving) and confirm youth/adults when they're older (so they can make faith their own). Churches that emphasize our part typically dedicate babies (so parents can promise God and others to share faith with their children) and baptize youth/adults when they're older. I'm not minimizing the difference, but I don't think it has to be another dividing wall—which, of course, means that I potentially caused a rift right now with *both* sides. And yes, for many Confirmation is an empty ritual. For some, so is going forward for altar calls. We can ruin any good gift if we work hard enough at it!

because I wanted to be. I wanted to learn more about this amazing God, and when the process was complete, I was grateful to profess my faith and receive the prayers of others.

"So you're saying you had it altogether as a kid, huh?" Hardly. Faith was a compartment in my life. An important compartment—one that I'd have argued with you about if you had tried to take it or demean it— but a compartment, nevertheless. In seventh grade I desperately longed to be a pro basketball player when I grew up. I could have made it, too, except for a couple tiny problems: my height (I was the shortest kid in junior high); my asthma (I struggled to run the length of the court); and my allergies (I often had to wear sunglasses indoors due to my over-sensitive eyes). To say that I was an easy target for bullying would be to state the obvious. "But God helped you through all that, right?" Well, if you mean "Did I survive adolescence?" I'm still around, so yeah, I guess so. But my solution for bullying was to become the king of the cut down. I used words to fight back, and I fought back hard. Making other kids feel worse only helped me feel better for the briefest and sick-est of moments, but that didn't stop me from trying. My wit and words simply weren't weighty enough to carry my sense of self-worth, and my faith (which *could* have helped) was locked away over in the Sunday morning and Wednesday night boxes.

So as a sophomore in high school, when I heard a speaker proclaim, "There's no such thing as a Sunday Christian," it was even better than making a three-pointer. (I could only dream of slam dunks.) And to complete what this man's declaration had begun in me, a woman at church offered to meet weekly with six of us sophomores in order to help us learn how to live life together as people loved by God. God used those two people—Kevin Murphy and Diane Scholinski—to dramati-cally change the direction of my life. My red line was on a steep upward incline, as compartments kept being dismantled and I started caring more and more about what God thought regarding all kinds of things: how I viewed myself, how I viewed others, how I viewed sex and marriage, my choice of words, my choice of friends, and on and on. In college the sharp upward trajectory continued because I finally burst out of my

Lutheran bubble and started hanging out with Christ-followers from all different denominational backgrounds. I probably grew more between age 15 and 22 than any season of my life, with the possible exception of the one I'm currently in.

Young adulthood

If you remember how EKG lines look, you might anticipate the question: what caused mine to fall precipitously? I can answer that in one word: seminary. Even though I went to Lutheran seminary with my guard up, fully aware that some of the things I would be taught weren't Biblical and must be rejected,[3] some garbage slipped in the back door anyway. Chief among them was an overemphasis on being Lutheran.[4] Anytime we place our identity in anything secondary, problems await. Denominations cannot bear the full weight of our identity in Christ.

I've had fellow unity-fans tell me many times that they've always believed that denominations were a problem.[5] Much to their surprise, I usually share my disagreement. The Body of Christ has been incredibly diverse from the beginning of the Church; whether or not we apply labels to all the differences matters little. And these differences aren't merely a function of sin; they're inherent to God's creation. God created us with various preferences and personalities, and all of us tend to hang out with people with whom we have much in common. The problem comes when we forget that our part is just one part of a bigger Body. When our identity is wrapped up in a denominational label instead of Jesus the head, the term for that is idolatry. References to Lutheran

---

3   Why, a reader might ask, would I invest time and money in a seminary I knew not to trust? Because I was Lutheran, that's why, and so attending a Lutheran seminary run by my tribe was my only choice, or so I assumed. If I knew then what I know now, I would have done things differently.

4   I won't go into all the other issues here. I'm not an anti-academic, but suffice it to say that putting faith under a microscope, in an academic environment largely removed from the Church, seems like a bad idea from the outset. Faith is meant to be practiced more than scrutinized. Ph.Ds mean little (nothing?) in the Kingdom of God. They aren't inherently wrong, but neither are they inherently helpful.

5   Denominations refers to subsets of Christianity, like Lutheran, Baptist, Methodist, Assembly of God, etc. People who voice their opposition to denominations usually identify as non-denominational, which in my experience is usually just one more grouping within the Body of Christ. If it walks like a duck…

superiority made me sick every time I heard about them at the seminary, and I was often labeled a heretic by the faculty for saying so. Nevertheless, what did I do when I got out of seminary? Spend all my time with Lutherans. And sadly, even that's an exaggeration, because there were the right Lutherans and the wrong Lutherans. I still tried to convince myself that I had the same beliefs I did prior to seminary, but my calendar would argue otherwise. And the more insular I became, the more my blind spots stayed hidden.

My parents' conflicted marriage had given me plenty of reason to value unity on a deeply personal level. But even when my head and heart are in alignment, my hands and feet might need an adjustment. I told every membership class I taught that if they were looking for a congregation that was going to emphasize Lutheran distinctives and why we as Lutherans were right, there were plenty of those, but ours wouldn't be one of them. Yet when non-Lutheran pastors around town would invite me to citywide events, I was always too busy (or so I thought). When we're too busy to prioritize what Jesus prioritizes, well, Houston, we have a problem.

ANYTIME WE OVER-IDENTIFY WITH SOMETHING NOT BUILT TO HANDLE THE WEIGHT WE'RE PLACING ON IT, A COLLAPSE IS INEVITABLE.

The 1996 Promise Keepers International Clergy Conference in Atlanta, Georgia was the event that woke me up from my seminary-induced coma. Over 40,000 pastors filled one end of the Georgia Dome, and the gathering was monumental in every way. The highlight for me was when Max Lucado preached on John 17, and I was cut to the quick. Lucado said, "Of all the world problems Jesus could have chosen to address as He prayed fervently the day before He knew He would die, He thought the most important issue was whether or not Christians in future generations would get along." I started weeping, literally (which is saying something for me), and called my wife later that night with an urgent message for my home congregation. "Tell them they need to be there this coming Sunday, because I need to repent. From here on, we'll be doing things differently." She did, they did, I did, and we did.

My spiritual health-meter started rising once again as we built relationships with other congregations different from our own. We formed our own CIA with two African American churches: "Christians in Action," not spies. We exchanged pulpits and choirs, we served in the community, and we spent a lot of time growing in relationship and in prayer. Simultaneously I started hanging out with some other parts of the Body that could teach me more about the Holy Spirit. By the time I took my first planned sabbatical after nearly eight years as a pastor, I had a wealth of relationships to draw from in order to keep learning and growing. It was immediately *after* my sabbatical ended that I was first officially diagnosed with depression...

Depression

With all those exciting things happening, how on earth could I be struggling with depression? Tell me if you've heard this before, but anytime we place the weight of our identity in anything secondary, we're knocking on the door of trouble. I had repented of my denominationalism and made the necessary changes to get my actions better aligned to my heart. But I had another idol that went largely unrecognized: ministry. Ministry became my mistress. I loved my wife and my four children, but they got the leftovers of my energy and passion for Jesus. I found it a hundred times easier to pray with other pastors or with various groups at church than to pray at home with my wife and kids. When life at home was messy and challenging, I could retreat to church where I felt more competent. I believed that it was my job to build the Church, and I asked God to take care of my family while I was "away." That's exactly backwards. It's God's job to build His Church, and my job to make my family my first field of ministry.

Workaholism is particularly seductive for those of us whose paycheck is signed by some ministry organization. It's hard to say no when we've convinced ourselves that God is asking us to say yes. And there will always be people ready to stroke our egos for all the sacrifices we're making for God. Ministry is never finished—there's always another person to call, another book to read, another sentence to be reworked in Sunday's sermon, another prayer to be prayed. You either learn healthy Sabbath rhythms,[6] or you develop a Messiah complex. You either learn how to put the work down and trust God, or you work yourself (or your family) to death.

Over-identifying with work isn't limited to religious professionals, of course. Workaholism is particularly seductive to ministry folk, but it isn't exclusively so. Work is what we do, not who we are. How can you tell if you've errantly mixed up your identity in your work? Well, the way most of us figure it out is if we get laid off, disabled, or retire. In other words, when we no longer have that job, that's when we discover how enmeshed we'd become in it. A job change or a change in seasons (from employed to retired) is stressful enough without our very identity being wrapped up in it, too. If you're still employed but wondering if this might be a problem, ask yourself a few questions: How hard is it for you to put work down—when the shift is over, on a day off, and for a vacation? What gets your best energy and what gets your leftovers? Do you compulsively check your work email? You get the idea...

If the last chapter on both/and, not either/or is still fresh in your mind, you might have already noticed that there are two different ways our Western worldview is coming into play here. First, ministry isn't *either at church or at home*, it's both. And second, my depression wasn't being caused by either my choices or my biochemistry, but both. Since my depression was first diagnosed *after* the longest stretch of time away from work I'd ever taken, timing is a pretty good indicator that biochemistry is involved. The help I've experienced from antidepressants proves it.

---

6   Sabbath is an Old Testament term that literally meant Saturday, the seventh day, and was intended to be a day to rest from our labors and worship God. "Sabbath rhythm" refers to the need for a time of rest and worship daily, weekly, monthly, quarterly, annually, and about every seven years (sabbatical).

Furthermore, anytime sin is involved, whether it's my own sin or somebody sinning against me, Satan is quick to pile on. Our problems can rarely be explained simply by either personal sin or spiritual warfare; both are usually in play. Satan never plays fair, so the more vulnerable we are, the more he pounces. The Holy Spirit convicts us—He helps us feel appropriate guilt when we're doing something wrong. The Holy Spirit's conviction is similar to how properly functioning nerve endings will let us know if we're touching a hot stove. Something's wrong, so move. Satan doesn't convict; he condemns. Conviction focuses on what we've done or failed to do; condemnation focuses on who we are. Conviction is always hopeful, pointing to a solution. Condemnation is always hopeless, lying to us by telling us there is no solution for the likes of us. Conviction is focused on our actions and attitudes; condemnation is focused on our identity.

Other pitfalls

Anytime we over-identify with something not built to handle the weight we're placing on it, a collapse is inevitable. In telling some of my own story, I've identified my junior high wit and words, my denomination, and my ministry as three areas at different stages of life that functioned as idols. If you'd asked me in any of those seasons who I was, I might have said something like, "I'm the cutdown king," or "I'm a Lutheran pastor" or simply "I'm a pastor." Unless I recognized the question as a religious test, it's unlikely that I would have answered more accurately, "I'm a child of God. I was handcrafted by a loving God, who then came and gave everything He had so I could discover who I really am. Everything else is just details."

There are plenty of pitfalls we can unwittingly fall into around the question of identity. My job got more of my attention than my marriage and family did for many years, but it's just as easy to trip and land in the ditch on the other side of the road, turning family into an idol. Our marriages weren't designed to carry the full weight of our identity. When our spouse is our only friend, when we rely on our spouse predominantly or even exclusively for encouragement or validation, or simply when we can't imagine any length of time apart from our spouse, it should be obvious that we're asking for trouble. At best, our spouse is mortal. And not just mortal, but imperfect, too—just like we are. It's unfair to the person we married to put that much weight on something not built to carry it. Same with our kids. It's a sad sight indeed when parents are living vicariously through their kids—at a sporting event, an academic contest, or some fine arts performance. Let your kids be your kids, and don't require them to live the life you wished you could have lived.

> ## "IDOLS CANNOT SIMPLY BE REMOVED. THEY MUST BE REPLACED."

The pitfall possibilities are endless! We can overidentify with our ethnicity. My son Mike pointed out how I identify lots of other leaders by their ethnicity when their ethnicity isn't the same as mine. Caught red-handed! Proceeding . . . I'll never forget my Latino pastor friend correctly and healthily saying one day, "My Hispanic heritage didn't die for me; Jesus did." We can overidentify with our image or reputation or accomplishments. We can overidentify with our hobbies, our entertainment, or anything else that shows up on our calendars. The Biblical/theological term for this overidentification is idolatry. An idol isn't simply a statue we handcrafted; no, we've become far more creative than that. As Tim Keller says, "An idol is anything more important to you than God, anything that absorbs your heart and imagination more than God, anything you seek to give you what only God can give you."[7] Later, Keller adds, "Idols cannot simply be removed. They must be replaced. If you only try to uproot them, they grow back."[8]

Identity lost

Of course, the reason this entire chapter is in this book is my contention that a very high percentage of voters who self-identify as Christian have their identity too melded to their political party. There are several ways

---

7   Tim Keller, *Counterfeit Gods: The Empty Promises of Money, Sex, Power, and the Only Hope That Matters* (New York: Dutton, 2009), xvii.

8   Ibid, 155.

we can tell if this has happened to us. How emotional is our reaction when our party or one of our party's platforms gets mischaracterized? How defensive are we when that happens? How different is our reaction when it happens to the other side of the aisle? When what ought to be a civil discussion of political ideas and philosophies turns personal, that's the very definition of overidentifying with politics.

When Rwandan Pastor Musekura prophetically says that we have tribes in American, too, referring to our political parties, what he's saying is that we have a whole host of people on both sides of the political aisle who have overidentified with their political party. When we place our identity or a major portion of it in something secondary, we damage not only ourselves but the object of our affection. We're hurting not only ourselves but the country when our identity gets wrapped up in political parties. A case of stolen identity is the best explanation I have for many of the Facebook posts I've read from Christian leaders from both persuasions. Moreover, I can't think of anything else than politics that would inspire the same kind of behavior from people who should know better.

My friend and Tucson colleague Randy Reynolds says, "If you deify the Donkey or the Elephant, you're not aligned with the Kingdom."[9] And of course, if you deify your own party, you're highly likely to demonize the other one. My friend and Washington, DC colleague Steve King says, "Our ultimate identity is not as Elephants or Donkeys but sheep who belong to the utmost King, Jesus Christ. Our supreme citizenship is the kingdom of heaven and we bring its values into all our political engagements for the glory of The King of all kings!"[10]

Americans love competition—it's built into our free enterprise system, and it dominates much of our entertainment, whether sports, musical shows like *American Idol*, or reality shows like *Survivor* or *The Bachelor* or *Shark Tank*. I'm as competitive as they come, so for me to argue against competition would be hypocrisy of the highest order. The

---

9   Randy Reynolds, personal email correspondence with author, November 18, 2019.

10   Steve King, personal email correspondence to author, November 19, 2019.

problem isn't competition; it's in misunderstanding the opponent. The other political party isn't an enemy to be demonized.[11] Healthy sports competition brings out the best in all involved. Political "competition" is supposed to do the same—in a healthy exchange of ideas, new and stronger possibilities emerge. Wishing the worst for the other party is like passengers on an airplane hoping for a wing to fall off. When "declaration of war" is the language used to describe the relationship between the Donkeys and Elephants,[12] we're engaged in another Civil War—words for now, but what comes next?

I used to eagerly anticipate flipping news channels on the first Tuesday evening in November with the same thrill I got out of a University of Arizona basketball game when the season was on the line. Who's winning, red or blue? By how much? If my team was winning, I went to bed happy; if not, the sky was falling. Winning by a little was good; winning by a wipeout was better. "The Donkeys must go down!" I thought. I was a victim of stolen identity, as evidenced by my emotional euphoria or depression, either of which were grossly out of proportion to the circumstances, but I had nobody to blame but myself.

Identity restored

Then I met some Donkeys. Not just met, but really got to know them. My full-time job since the summer of 2011 has been working for greater unity within the Body of Christ. In that capacity, I've proactively built bridges to networks of pastors identified by their ethnicity, theological persuasion, or particular interests or passions. My passion for unity only grows every time I meet another facet to the diamond known as the Body of Christ.

In the height of the Presidential election campaign of 2012, African American Apostle Warren Anderson called me with a question.

---

11 Ironically, the Bible in Ephesians 6:12 says that there is a demonic enemy, but it's not other people in other political parties or any other group, for that matter. "For we are not fighting against flesh-and-blood enemies, but against evil rulers and authorities of the unseen world, against mighty powers in this dark world, and against evil spirits in the heavenly places." (NLT).

12 Bossie, "Trump Impeachment." As quoted on page 29.

"It seems to us," he began, and I knew that meant fellow African American pastors, "that there were a lot more Evangelicals praying for the president back when the president was Bush than now that it's Obama. Could we talk about that?"

There's this filter in our heads between our brains and our mouths, and I've rarely been more thankful for that filter than right then. We aren't required to voice every thought that crosses our mind! I was still an Elephant News junkie back then, so my initial thoughts were all defensive. I'd been in training, you see—just the wrong kind. I literally started rifling through the files in my brain for the best comebacks. But thankfully, the filter kicked in, and what came out of my mouth *instead* was, "That sounds like a great idea." Disaster averted. A tremendous flight could have been aborted before it ever left the ground if I'd taken the enemy's bait and responded defensively. Instead, this flight not only took off but soared to worlds previously unknown to many of us. Pastor Partners was born, and eight years later we're still meeting monthly. Pastor Partners didn't start as a program; it started as a group of black and white pastors eager to get to know one another better. It's become a treasured tool for multicultural and spiritual growth in our city.

OUR RELATIONSHIPS WERE WHAT MADE HARD POLITICAL CONVERSATIONS POSSIBLE.

The upfront out-in-the-open question of Pastor Partners was this: Was our unity in Christ as fellow Christian pastors sufficient that we could actually talk politics and live to tell about it? Many of us had met one another at citywide prayer or service events, so we weren't complete strangers. But neither were we friends . . . yet. We may not have been strangers, but I believe a majority of us would have seen the other side's political persuasions as strange at best. Early on we all agreed to what we knew to be true in our heads: we're here as brothers[13] in

---

13   The group started with all men. Some women have joined us in subsequent years.

Christ first, and Elephants and Donkeys a distant second. Our *primary* identity is children of God; political affiliations need to be way down the identity list. But that right-answer-on-a-religion-test had to be tested by entering into the hard conversations. Our first meetings began with one or two of us simply telling our stories, highlighting the parts where racial identity and assumptions may have been birthed. We prayed together regularly and learned that while we might not use the same words, we were voicing the same passions. When we started talking about Donkey concerns and Elephant concerns, we made liberal (no pun intended) use of the statement, "Help me understand." By this point we *knew* that we were in the company of brothers in Christ. We knew we'd be spending eternity together, so we actually cared what made the other person tick.

Our relationships were what made hard political conversations possible. Haidt writes,

> The main way that we change our minds on moral issues is by interacting with other people. We are terrible at seeking evidence that challenges our own beliefs. . . . When discussions are hostile, the odds of change are slight. . . . But if there is affection, admiration, or a desire to please the other person, then . . . [we] try to find truth in the other person's arguments.[14]

Keep in mind, Haidt is an evolutionary social psychologist, and a self-described atheist. He's not starting from a Christian worldview at all, but rather basing his statements on 25 years of research on moral psychology. Yet his conclusions describe what ought to and actually could be a common experience among a unified Body of Christ. He continues,

> Each individual reasoner is really good at one thing: finding evidence to support the position he or she already holds. But if you put individuals together in the right

---

14   Haidt, *Righteous Mind*, 79.

way, such that some individuals can use their reasoning powers to disconfirm the claims of others, and all individuals feel some common bond or shared fate that allows them to interact civilly, you can create a group that ends up producing good reasoning as an emergent property of the social system.[15]

He's describing the Church, at least when it's healthy!

In another gathering called Tucson Ministry Alliance, we dedicated time back in 2013 to discussing the hot potato of immigration—a particularly challenging topic in our border community of Tucson, AZ. Afterwards several people confirmed the same observation, stating that because the people sharing opposite viewpoints from their own were fellow brothers and sisters in Christ, they actually heard and considered perspectives that in other contexts they would have rejected out of hand. Pastor Partners and other similar experiences like Tucson Ministry Alliance are the reasons my last nine years have led to the greatest growth of my life. Assumptions I'd held for decades were exposed and challenged—and I loved it! Now we have dinners at one another's homes, celebrate one another's victories, exchange pulpits, attend sporting events together, and watch movies together that present racial themes and talk about them afterward. I would go to war with those Donkeys—*with* them, not *against* them. We view our experience as the country's best hope—perhaps its only hope.

We have learned that it takes something larger than the gap to bridge the gap. The gap between cultures ethnically and politically is massive. But the Cross is bigger—big enough to bridge the gap. And now we like to say that regardless of how we vote, we don't see ourselves as belonging to the party of the Elephant or the party of the Donkey, but the party of the Lamb.[16] The Lamb is in the foreground; the Donkey and Elephant at some distance behind.

---

15   Ibid, 105.

16   Lamb of God is a common title in the Bible for Jesus. It dates back to the Old Testament Exodus, when the Passover Lamb was sacrificed, leading the Israelites to freedom from slavery. Reverend Amos Lewis is the first person I heard coin the phrase, "Party of the Lamb."

Identity protected

Jesus said, "My Kingdom is not of this world."[17] His statement could stand on its own in any setting, but it's worth noting that the context of His comment was right in the midst of a 1st century version of our Donkey Elephant war. Jesus was caught in the middle of *two* political struggles: one between the Jews and the occupying Romans; and the other between the Jewish religious leaders who had plenty of power, and the average Jewish citizen. It would have been so easy for Jesus to take sides. He could have played the ultimate trump card (no pun intended) and revealed His divinity in a massive power display, ending all conversation once and for all. Instead, Jesus chose to respect human freedom, even freedom run amok, and reveal His Kingship in the most unexpected way: by laying down His life. Jesus chose a cross for His throne.[18]

Through all the cross-cultural work I've had the privilege of engaging in over the last couple of decades, the most powerful truth was right in front of me the whole time, and I'd missed it. The best way to make progress cross culturally is through the culture of the cross. At the cross we lay down our rights rather than assert them. The cross is the ultimate valuing of others over our own selves. King Jesus' cross-throne is the path not only toward cultural reconciliation but political progress as well. Cross-cultural unity (whether the cultures are ethnic or political or otherwise) starts with the culture of the cross: listening more than we speak, seeking to understand more than to be understood, placing others in the best light possible.

"My Kingdom is not of this world." With such a clear statement from our Savior, I wouldn't expect it to be so easy to mess it up. Yet if we pay attention to politics at all, it's so stinking easy to over-identify and jump right into the competitive melee. Well-meaning people can so easily become part of the problem once they enter the political arena. Should the answer be to disengage from politics? Does "My Kingdom is not of this world" mean that Jesus doesn't care what happens down here,

---

17   John 18:36.

18   Unwittingly, the Roman leaders in a sarcastic slam on the Jews posted a sign over Jesus' head on the cross that read, "This is Jesus: The King of the Jews" (Matt. 27:37).

so neither should we? No, and no. Jesus cares greatly about what happens here where we live out our lives. His statement isn't an invitation to escape. His own life bears witness to that quite clearly: He left the safe confines of heaven to enter our messy world. As God, surely He could have invented some other way to do business if His ultimate message was, "Abandon ship. This world's going down." He *entered* the world, out of *love* for the world. He's merely inviting us to recognize that our ultimate identity is elsewhere.

Jesus is inviting us to invest in the eternal, rather than merely good and temporal things that can't deliver beyond the grave.[19]

WE'LL BE MOST EFFECTIVE IN CARING FOR THIS WORLD IF OUR IDENTITY IS *OUT* OF THIS WORLD.

As we'll see even more in what follows, political engagement is the goal. Political identity is the fumble. Being politically inclined is positive, but being partisan identified is not. "My Kingdom is not of this world" is a both/and statement, not an either/or. We'll be most effective in caring for this world if our identity is *out* of this world.

As I've illustrated from my own life, keeping our identity rooted where it belongs is no one-time task. We acknowledge Jesus as Lord when we accept Him as our Savior, but unlike the playground days of my childhood where "No takebacks!" was the ultimate argument-ender, we take back control all the time, putting all kinds of substitutes in the place that belongs to Jesus.

The very first invitation I received to speak about the contents of this book came from a most unlikely place. An African refugee congregation in Tucson was preparing to celebrate their fourth anniversary, and they invited me to speak at the occasion. Jean Steven Parfait Mfuranzima,

---

19   Jesus said in Matt. 6:19–20, "Do not store up for yourselves treasures on earth, where moths and vermin destroy, and where thieves break in and steal. But store up for yourselves treasures in heaven, where moths and vermin do not destroy, and where thieves do not break in and steal."

one of the leaders of the congregation and a Burundian refugee, was my point person. When we got together to plan for the service, we started by catching up with one another. I shared about this new ministry (J17 Ministries) that I had started and this writing project that was on my heart. He looked at me awkwardly, thinking of literal Donkeys and Elephants at war, and not knowing what I meant at first. When I explained, his look was even more surprising—one of utter astonishment. He said, "Pastor David, that is what you must speak about when you come to our congregation." I said, "Really? American politics?" But then he explained that many of the people in their congregation had been very engaged in their faith back in Africa, but that in America, it was very hard to stay engaged. There was so much to learn—English, American culture and customs, new job skills, and so forth—that Christian faith was slipping into the back seat, while the American Dream took over the driver's seat. He said, "You must talk to us about our primary identity, because we're losing ours in pursuit of the American Dream."

Identity in Christ

Identity is key. Satan knows this as well. When Jesus launched His ministry, Satan launched his counterattack. And every temptation started with, "If you are the Son of God . . ." If Satan could steal Jesus' identity, all would be lost. Satan tempted Jesus with power—power over hunger, power over angels, and power over people. Ironically, Jesus actually had all that power and more, far more than the one tempting Him.[20] But He was secure enough in His identity that He took no shortcuts, exercising phenomenal restraint.[21] This was good practice, as He would need even more self-restraint in His last hours on Earth pre-resurrection.[22] At any point in time He could have ended the suffering, but He chose not to. Surely every demon around was whispering in His ear perpetually, "Take a shortcut, Jesus. Compromise your identity, and 'come

---

20   You might have noticed that I'm capitalizing all the "he, him, his" references to Jesus, even though the Bible doesn't always do that itself—capitalization is an editor's decision. I believe Jesus is who He said He is, so I capitalize pronouns referring to Him.

21   Matt. 4:1–11.

22   Matt. 26–27, Mark 14–15, Luke 22–23, John 18–19.

down from the cross.'"[23] Nails weren't what held Him there—it was His love for you and me.

The same Satan who tempted Jesus tempts us, too, and much of it goes straight to our identity. For five days near the end of May 2019, my wife Valerie and I joined a few other couples for a retreat/seminar called Potter's Wheel.[24] Potter's Wheel is designed to help us better understand why we do some of the things we do, as well as equip us to help others in that same endeavor. I'd love to tell you that I signed up out of my great courage and desire to learn more about myself. The truth is that I had made a mess of things yet again, and pain (both my own and the pain I'd caused by wife) is what prompted us to sign up. The developers of Potter's Wheel are a Tucson couple, John and Patti Cepin. Patti says, "Every time I get to know another image-bearer,[25] I get to see/know another aspect of the face of God." And so the better we get to know ourselves and who God made us to be as His image-bearers, the more we learn of God, too. She also says, "The very thing the enemy tells us is the opposite of what God has uniquely equipped us for." How true I have found that to be. When the enemy points out my cowardice, it's precisely in the areas where God is calling and enabling me to act with courage. One more quote from Patti: "God is grieved by our sin, but He isn't disappointed in us. To be disappointed implies that He's surprised by what He sees!" He knows us fully and loves us completely. That's the source of our truest identity, and nothing else can hold a candle to it.

Power is the primary pull of partisan politics. Politics itself isn't the problem, even though for many the word has been so dirtied by its practice that it can hardly be uttered without disdain. But when politics becomes about power instead of public service, partisanship is evident everywhere. In power struggles, there are winners and losers, a reality

---

23 Matt. 27:41–44. Satan loves little more than when he can get humans to give utterance to his own temptations.

24 http://journeycompanionsministries.org/offer/potters.

25 "Image-bearer" refers to Genesis 1:27, where we come to understand that every human being is created in the image of God, and therefore has infinite worth.

which stokes the competitive fires so deeply inherent in many of us. The pursuit of more power for our favorite Mammal can cause all we might otherwise know and value to be tossed out the window—manners, morals, common sense, clear thinking, and the like. Power isn't a new issue; it's been a struggle as long as there have been people. Richard Foster wrote a book back in 1985 called *Money, Sex & Power: The Challenge of the Disciplined Life.*[26] The temptation is to turn money and sex into power pursuits also, such that the title could just as easily be "Power, Power, and more Power."

POWER IN THE KINGDOM OF GOD IS ABOUT SERVICE.

The answer for Jesus is the same as for us: be secure in your identity in Christ. For Jesus, knowing that He was the Messiah[27] didn't lead Him to a power trip; it led Him to a path of service: unmatched public service. Earlier the same evening that He prayed the John 17 prayer for our unity, He set the tone for His coming sacrifice on the cross through a most unexpected plot twist. There's a verse that reads, "Jesus knew that the Father had put all things under His power, and that He had come from God and was returning to God; so He got up from the meal..." What would you expect to follow such a sentence?[28] Some display of power, right? Or at least a powerful speech of some kind. But no, He got up from the meal to begin washing the feet of His followers. Power in the Kingdom of God is about service.

For us, too, the answer to our partisan politics fiasco is to be secure in our identity in Christ. Our struggles with power all go back to the Fall, where we rebelled against giving God His rightful place in our lives.[29] Instead of being content as literal children of God, we took

---

26   Similar to Keller's book in 2009 of a similar title, quoted on page 81.

27   The words "Messiah" in Hebrew and "Christ" in Greek both literally mean "the anointed one," referring to the long-promised Savior.

28   John 13:3–4.

29   Gen. 3.

the enemy's bait and wanted to be our own gods.[30] Instead of gaining a more powerful identity, we ended up losing the very powerful identity we already had. Dutch Sheets wrote an entire book about all that was lost and how to regain it, entitled, *Becoming Who You Are*. Sheets rightfully declares, "The created cannot look to itself for definition; this understanding is found only in its Creator."[31] As Deb Waterbury penned, "Don't let a confused and frustrated world identify who you are, even if that confused and frustrated world consists of confused and frustrated Christians. Your identity is in Jesus."[32] When we know who we are in Christ, we have a security and refuge that can withstand any attacks (political or otherwise), and instead of responding in kind and escalating the war, we may not need to respond at all. When we know who we are in Christ, we discover a peace, a meaning, a significance that can weather any storm. Peace talks, and it talks powerfully.

We'll return to these concepts in the Epilogue. But for now, we have one more chapter of background information to go, taking a close look at exactly what Jesus prayed and how it applies to our current situation.

---

30 I say "we" instead of Adam and Eve because if Adam and Eve had remained sinless, and their kids sinless, all the way down to me, I would have likely been the one to blow it. Their issues look remarkably like our own.

31 Dutch Sheets, *Becoming Who You Are: Embracing the Power of Your Identity in Christ* (Bloomington, MN: Bethany House Publishers, 2007), 18.

32 Reprinted, with permission, from Dr. Deborah Waterbury, *The Lies That Bind: And the Truth That Sets You Free* (Tucson, AZ: DebWaterbury, Inc.), 79.

CHAPTER FIVE

JESUS' SURPRISING PRIORITY

*"How good and pleasant it is when God's
people live together in unity."*
—PSALM 133:1 [1]

G ood news is when someone knows and cares about our challenges. *Great* news is when that same person also has the power to make a difference.

So, I have some good news: Jesus knows and cares about the Donkey Elephant war that's raging. And I have some great news: He has the power to make a difference.

My favorite way of describing what I do is that my full-time job is to see Jesus' John 17 prayer answered, starting in my hometown and

---

1   King David, Ps. 133:1.

anywhere else God chooses to grant me influence. If you don't already know what John 17 is, you likely won't guess, even if I tell you that it's a chapter in the Bible recording what Jesus prayed right before He gave His life on the cross.

To illustrate how Jesus' prayer can be experienced as great news, here's a true story from a year ago.

Great News breaks into bank, steals boredom

The ministry I lead, J17 Ministries (referring to Jesus' prayer in John 17), started as a DBA[2] of a local church in Tucson. When I went to the bank to open our checking account, the church had already started the process and seen the teller I met with earlier in the day. She had been told about a retreat we offer called a John 17 Weekend, and so the conversation started with her politely asking me to tell her more about these John 17 Weekends.

"Well," I said, "We have people from over 60 different Christian congregations in Tucson all coming together for 72 hours to experience more of God's endless love and learn better how to share that with others."

"That sounds amazing," she said, and then continued, "I grew up Catholic—is that Christian?" I paused for a second before answering, balancing out the need for this to be a *brief* conversation with a bank teller, and the reality that the answer is somewhat complicated.

"Yes," I said.[3]

---

2   DBA is shorthand for Doing Business As. It's a legal entity by which a corporation or non-profit can work in a related field under a different name.

3   Basic Catholic doctrine aligns with basic Protestant doctrine in its understanding of who Jesus is and how we're saved. Some Catholic *practice* focuses on works, downplays a personal relationship with Jesus, and places more emphasis on Roman Catholic distinctives than on broader Christian commonalities. Latin American Catholicism, which is what many of the Hispanic pastors in my hometown grew up with, mixes in (the theological term is syncretism) a variety of religious practices that most Christians would find objectionable. I have a friend, Gary Kinnaman, who regularly says, "Our unity is based on Jesus Christ plus nothing. Not Jesus Christ plus the pope, and not Jesus Christ plus not-the-pope (in other words, unity based on a dislike for the Catholic church)."

"I've heard of Methodists, too. Are they Christian?" she asked.

"Yes," I said.

She continued, "And I see on your application that it's a Lutheran church that owns the account. I have no idea what a Lutheran is. Is that Christian too?" When I answered yes once again, she replied, "I don't understand."

I told her that the Bible uses the analogy of a body, and that all of those groups are just different parts in the same body. Then I said, "We just have to get better at acting that way."

"What a great idea!" she exclaimed exuberantly. "Why hasn't anyone thought of this before?" I chuckled before quickly pointing out that I can't take credit for the "idea." (Plagiarizing Jesus sounds like a patently bad idea!) I asked her if she knew what John 17 was, and she didn't. So I told her that it's both a chapter in the Bible and a prayer that Jesus prayed right before giving His life for us on the cross.

"This is His idea, not mine."

At her leading, the conversation turned more personal as she shared about her family, spiritual questions her son was raising, and so forth. She then mentioned that she and her boyfriend had been talking about their need for a Bible study, and asked if I knew of any that she could join. I did. Forty five minutes after we started the paperwork for the new account, I thanked her for her help and left, thanking God for the good news of Jesus.[4] (No, there wasn't anyone in line behind me this whole time, hearing the conversation and cursing religion.)

Few people are fans of division. Most people appreciate unity, at least in theory, even if they're blindly or intentionally contributing to division in some aspects of their lives. I believe a chief reason that over

---

4   If a woman asking about a Bible study doesn't strike you as good news, perhaps because you're not a fan of the Bible at all, please see Chapter 10 where I briefly address that concern.

80% of the country disapproves of the work Congress is doing is because we recognize how division ultimately hurts us, even if we're less clear or unified on the solution. Just like the bank-teller needed a vision of unity for her to engage some of her spiritual longings, I believe a vision of unity can help us as a nation forge a pathway through our political war zone. We need clarity of vision all the more since the Church has done a terrible job living that vision out, both by how we've treated those outside the Christian faith (i.e. the Crusades), as well as other Christ-followers (since the Reformation).[5]

This chapter is unique for this book, in that we'll be examining Jesus' words closely, all from one section of the Bible. If Bible study isn't your forte, two pieces of encouragement: one, you don't even need to own a Bible to understand what's coming; and two, this chapter is the only one of its kind in this book. Jesus paints a clear picture of what kind of unity we need, and the Bible is our source document for examining that picture. This is the final chapter in Part I because it's "background" for me—Jesus' prayer in John 17 is the reason I wrote this book. If this material is familiar to you, the political application angle may be new.

What *Jesus prayed*

The more divided our world gets, the better news John 17 appears as it reveals the heart of God through the prayer of Jesus.[6] Discovering John 17 is like spotting a lighthouse when you're at sea and being battered mercilessly and perilously by a storm, especially if the storm is one of partisan politics.

If you have a red-letter version of the Bible, where the words of Jesus are in red, the reddest section of the entire Bible is the thirteenth through seventeenth chapters of the Gospel of John. The only black-letter parts are questions that the befuddled disciples kept asking. All

---

5   The Protestant Reformation in the early 1500's involved groups breaking away from the Catholic Church. The breaking away continues into smaller and smaller fragments.

6   *John 17: The Heart of God*, ed. Joseph Tosini (Hyde Park, NY: New City Press, 2018), 170. A collection of essays.

of it took place Thursday night before Good Friday, the day Jesus gave His life for us by hanging from a cross. The entire evening is surreal, starting with Jesus donning a towel and washing the feet of His own followers, including Judas, who Jesus *knew in advance* would betray Him before the evening was up.[7] No political betrayal will trump Judas' betrayal. Jesus and his followers had gathered to celebrate the Jewish Passover, and throughout the evening, Jesus reinterpreted and even heightened the urgency of the Passover meal. As the evening continued Peter would boast that if Jesus couldn't count on the rest of His buddies, He could certainly count on him, to which Jesus replied that before the night was up, Peter would cowardly deny that he even knew Jesus.[8] No political boasting will trump Peter's.

IF YOU READ JOHN 17 EVEN ONCE, YOU CAN'T MISS ITS CENTRAL THEME—THAT WE, HIS FOLLOWERS, WOULD BE UNITED.

In previous months leading up to this night, when Jesus had predicted His upcoming betrayal and crucifixion, the gang of twelve in response started arguing about which one of them was the greatest. Aye aye aye . . . Add in the differing political backgrounds and personalities of the disciples, and perhaps it shouldn't strike us as such a surprise that Jesus would pray what He did. These wouldn't appear to even be reliable teammates, let alone Hall of Fame Christ-followers. If you read John 17 even once, you can't miss its central theme—that we, His followers, would be united. If it was easy, Jesus wouldn't have prayed for it.

Keep in mind that Jesus could have prayed about anything He wanted to. He knew exactly what was coming, why it was necessary, and what the result would be. His prayer begins, "Father, the time has come."

---

7   Even if you know very little of this story, I'm willing to bet you haven't named any of your kids Judas.

8   One of my favorite spots on my wife's and my recent (and first) trip to the Holy Land was a Church called St Peter in Gallicantu, or "St Peter of the Crowing Rooster," marking the spot of Peter's prophesied denial of Jesus.

So it's not like John 17 catches Jesus daydreaming. Further, there are three times in the prayer where He specifically points out what He's *not* praying. Jesus was so intensely focused on His central theme that He disallowed anything to sidetrack Him. Who could guess that our unity as His followers was *that* important?

Taking a closer look

Let's look a little closer at this diamond in the rough, this gem of a prayer that addresses the painful divisions that tear apart families, groups, and nations. There are five very specific descriptors that we can unpack from John 17.[9]

1. *Unity, not uniformity.* "...[T]hat they may be one as We are one." (Verse 11)

2. *Public, not private.* "My prayer is not that You take them out of the world..." (Verse 15)

3. *Substantive, not spineless.* "Sanctify them by the truth; Your Word is truth." (Verse 17)

4. *Timeless, not timebound.* "My prayer is not for them alone. I pray also for those who will believe in Me through their message." (Verse 20)

5. *The means to an end, not the end.* "...[T]hat they may be brought to complete unity. Then the world will know that You sent Me and have loved them even as You have loved Me." (Verse 23)

I've intentionally chosen to end each section with a reflection question, since the intersection of Jesus' prayer and our political mess is the whole reason for this book. I'll unpack my thoughts in subsequent

---

9   Both my previous books, *Jesus' Surprising Strategy* and *If It Was Easy, Jesus Wouldn't Have Prayed For It*, go into greater detail regarding applying this prayer to the Church. Here I'm focusing the application on the political landscape.

chapters, but I encourage you to beat me to the punch and reflect right as you read.

Jesus' immediate context for His prayer is the small group of followers surrounding Him, and the prayer begins focused on them. But this prayer stands the test of time, which He specifically articulates in verse 20, so I believe it's appropriate to apply it to our current Donkey Elephant war, especially with the reminder that my primary intended audience for this project is those Americans who self-identify as having an affinity for Jesus. Jesus is praying for His followers to unite and love one another wherever we might be found.

1. UNITY, NOT UNIFORMITY[10]

When Jesus prays that we would be one, or unified, in the same manner as He is with His heavenly Father, He's making it clear that He isn't praying for uniformity. Jesus had taken on flesh, and as a man was limited in time and space. His Father remained a spirit, unlimited in time and space. That alone makes the two of them enormously different from one another. Jesus doesn't pray that we all be *alike*; He prays that we would all be *aligned* for greater purposes.

Taking Jesus' prayer seriously and applying it to our political conflict, I don't think Jesus is praying that all labels get wiped out. Differences don't necessitate division, and God is not only a huge fan of diversity, He's the author of it. One of mankind's very first acts, even before the train came off the tracks, was naming the things God had created, with God's watching approval.[11] So names and labels aren't inherently evil. The fact that we're different from one another isn't a problem. Jesus isn't praying for a new hybrid animal, a donkephant. Different perspectives and different priorities are part of the asset side of the equation, not the liability side. The problem comes when we tear apart what God joins together, what God sees as parts of a whole. The problem is demonizing

---

10   John 17:11. "That they may be one even as We are one."

11   Gen. 2:19.

the other side, rather than recognizing that we share common goals and each bring valuable ideas to the table.[12]

Since Jesus prays that our differences wouldn't divide us, how can we turn our differences into assets instead of liabilities?

2. PUBLIC, NOT PRIVATE[13]

Jesus specifically states that He isn't praying for Christians to escape the world. I'm sorry that we've so often given that impression! Unlike some other religions, Christianity is all about the intersection of the spiritual and the physical, both in its central claim that Jesus is the Son of God who entered our world, as well as in how we're called to live our lives as His followers. Jesus isn't praying for an "other-worldly" unity, where Christians escape into sanctuaries and have a holy love fest that nobody outside the Church ever sees. Even the word "sanctuary" implies being set apart from the world, for better and worse.

As I write this, I'm thinking of devoted Christ-followers who I love, admire, and respect, some of whom happen to be registered Donkeys and others of whom are registered Elephants. Does Jesus want unity within each of the various congregations throughout the land? Yes, but that's not what He prays for here. He wants our unity as brothers and sisters in Christ to go public, to show the world around us what a unified, serving Church looks like. I am sure there are some readers who've adopted the viewpoint that "religion should be private." That's a bigger discussion than this paragraph warrants, and which Chapter 6 will partially address.

CIVILITY AND TOLERANCE DON'T GO NEARLY FAR ENOUGH.

---

12   I'm not papering over opposing positions in direct conflict with one another. I'm saying that as followers of Jesus on both sides of the political aisle, we can dialogue with people of good will, recognizing that the whole is greater than the sum of its parts. Much more on this in the remainder of the book…

13   John 17:15. "My prayer is not that you take them out of the world…" Verse 18 specifically states that Jesus sends His followers out into the world.

Since there are followers of Christ who claim to be both Elephants and Donkeys, what would it look like for us to find ways to drink from the same watering hole, worshiping and serving in unity?

3. SUBSTANTIVE, NOT SPINELESS[14]

Jesus includes a prayer for truth in His prayer for unity! You may have heard or even said, "It doesn't matter what you believe as long as you're sincere." I don't think Jesus would agree. And frankly, I don't think we really believe it either. September 11 in our country is a permanent reminder that beliefs matter. Nobody can accuse the terrorists of unbelief; they gave their lives for their beliefs. So Jesus is appealing to a higher authority and praying that we would all be influenced by the Truth—right in the middle of His prayer for unity. For Jesus, truth and unity are on the same team.

I've read numerous calls for a civility pledge in response to our current, toxic environment. I don't think that's the solution. I'm not calling for an *uncivility* pledge: "More fiery rhetoric and cheap shots, please." Not at all. I'm just saying that civility and tolerance don't go nearly far enough. Hard conversations must be undertaken. Areas of extreme disagreement must be examined. And unless people who have a higher allegiance than their political party lead the charge, I see little hope of that ending well.

Do you believe there is such a thing as Truth? If so, where do you find it? And how might the search impact your approach to politics?

4. TIMELESS, NOT TIMEBOUND[15]

Jesus specifically says that this is His prayer and heartbeat for every generation, in every nation and locale. In identifying those who will believe in Jesus through the disciples' message, He's addressing today's Christians, because we're literally reading and examining the words of

---

14   John 17:17. "Sanctify them by the truth; Your word is truth."

15   John 17:20. "My prayer is not for them alone. I pray also for those who will believe in me through their message." Jesus specifically mentions that this prayer is for His followers in every future generation and every neighborhood.

one of those twelve, John. I personally believe that some of His divinity came to the surface at this point, and He stepped out of time and actually was thinking about every generation and every future situation. What a breathtaking thought! He was thinking of our political mess and family squabbles right at that moment.

Just like I told the bank-teller who thought that John 17 was my idea, the notion that this prayer could actually address the Donkey Elephant war comes straight from Jesus' own words. Nowhere does Jesus compartmentalize, as if our unity were only meant to apply to spiritual things, leaving us to fight with our spouses and name call our political adversaries to our little hearts' content. Jesus prays that our love for one another would point to God's love for all of us, and there aren't any footnoted or small print exceptions.

Where do you most need more unity right now? How are you encouraged by realizing that Jesus was praying specifically for your/our needs?

5. MEANS, NOT END[16]

Jesus adds a "so that" to His prayer for unity. This is the fourth time in the prayer that He prays that we would be one or united. But here He adds a greater purpose to the prayer, that through the public witness of our love for one another as His followers, people might recognize Jesus' identity and God's love for each of them. That's a mouthful...but it's also where I'll wrap things up in the epilogue.

Jesus is aiming for something higher than just Donkeys and Elephants at the same dinner parties. That alone would be a lovely outcome, and while I believe He's including that thought in His prayer, He isn't stopping there. If you recall the earlier discussion of my friends Célestin and Tass and the work they're doing in East Africa and the Middle East, respectively, their methodology draws straight from the ultimate purpose

---

16   John 17:23 (NLT). "May they experience such perfect unity that the world will know that you sent me and that you love them as much as you love me." Unity has a purpose that runs way deeper than just more unity.

of Jesus' prayer for unity: that through His prayer being answered we all might come to know who Jesus is and how much God loves us.

Can you imagine how powerful a witness it would be if Jesus Himself were the common rallying cry that ended the logjam and ceased the hostilities?

Practicing what He prayed

As a child growing up in the Sonoran Desert, I would regularly pray for snow when it would get cold enough for there to be a snowball's chance in Tucson. And I would regularly be disappointed—my earliest crises of faith. There was nothing I could do to be an answer to my own prayer, nothing at all. Unless God brought the snow to Tucson . . . no snow.[17]

In weightier matters, though, God sometimes marks our prayers "returned to sender." Examples include praying for a job but not applying for one, or praying for a neighbor to come to know the love of God but doing nothing to share the love of God with our neighbor. Jesus didn't pray for unity but live for division. Jesus' prayer for unity matched His lifestyle.

You're probably familiar with the term Samaritan, as in the Good one, even if only from a legal standpoint like the Good Samaritan laws that protect a well-meaning neighbor from getting sued for their kindness. But did you know that Samaritan is a more loaded political term than Republican or Democrat ever will be?

When ancient kingdoms would be victorious in battle, they would often transport the captives into exile, and displace some other people to live in the newly conquered territory. That's exactly what happened to Samaria—after they were conquered, foreigners were transported into the land. Those foreigners stayed for generations. When Jews in Jesus' day looked at Samaritans, they didn't see them as the real deal, either

---

17   I still remember December 8, 1971, when we got 6.8 inches of snow, the largest ever recorded in Tucson. Proof that there is a God, haha.

ethnically or religiously. The animosity between the two groups rivals anything the Donkeys and Elephants have achieved.

In an earlier chapter in the gospel of John, Chapter 4, we read this simple little statement that Jesus "*had* to go through Samaria."[18] Jesus' need to travel through Samaria was less one of geography than it was of purpose. Jesus looks for dividing walls of hostility[19] and like President Reagan addressing the Berlin Wall in 1987, Jesus seeks to tear down such walls wherever He finds them. In the story of a Samaritan woman whom Jesus encounters at a well in the heat of the day in John 4, Jesus not only tears down the dividing wall between Jews and Samaritans, but additional walls between men and women, and between those who've apparently lived faithful lives and those who obviously haven't.

JESUS DIDN'T PRAY FOR UNITY BUT LIVE FOR DIVISION. JESUS' PRAYER FOR UNITY MATCHED HIS LIFESTYLE.

Jesus went straight after the Donkey Elephant war of His day, the Jews/Samaritans, regularly choosing Samaritans to be the heroes of His stories. And the political and religious tension between Jews and Samaritans wasn't the only tension He addressed. When Jesus put His team together, He intentionally invited people from all fragments of the farm. There were uneducated fishermen, a tax collector (probably significantly more well-off financially, but relationally challenged, since the occupying Roman empire was his employer), a revolutionary (literally Zealot), and more just among the twelve.

The Jewish political leaders, the Sadducees and the Pharisees, had limited authority, since the whole area was under the control of Rome. So when the Sadducees and Pharisees decided that Jesus was too much of a threat to their status, they had to get permission from Rome to put

---

18   John 4:4, italics mine.

19   Eph. 2:14, referring to Jesus, says, "For he himself is our peace, who has made the two groups one and has destroyed the barrier, the dividing wall of hostility."

Him to death. The political tensions between Roman leaders Pilate and Herod, as well as between both of them and Caiaphas, the High Priest of the Jews, form quite the backdrop to Jesus' final hours pre-resurrection. When Jesus says from the cross, "Father, forgive them, for they do not know what they are doing,"[20] I believe He was speaking to the entire mess and everyone who had a part in it. Wherever there are dividing walls of hostility, you can spot Jesus with a sledgehammer. Father, forgive us, all of us, because we're clueless.

Jesus continues this mission *after* His resurrection from the dead. One of the Pharisees likely present and shouting for Jesus' death was Saul of Tarsus. When reports came that Jesus was now alive again, Saul was determined to stamp out such a ridiculous idea before it gained any traction. While on his way to Damascus to arrest some more of these first Christians (or Followers of the Way as they were first called[21]), Saul was literally stopped in his tracks by the resurrected Jesus. And in a powerful picture of how far Jesus goes in breaking down the dividing walls of hostility, Jesus asks Ananias, one of the very men that Saul is hunting down, to go and lay hands on[22] Saul and heal him of his new physical blindness which reflected his previous spiritual blindness. Ananias obeys after a brief discussion with Jesus, and this same Saul became better known as the Apostle Paul, one of the greatest "foe becomes friend" stories in history.[23] In subsequent years Paul, too, would address newly surfacing political tensions within Christianity.[24]

Not only did Jesus live an integrated life, with his prayer priorities and his actions aligned, but so did those who ministered in His name.

---

20 Luke 23:34.

21 In Acts 22:4 Saul/Paul speaks of his persecution of the Followers of the Way. Jesus says in John 14:6, "I am the Way, the Truth, and the Life…", so that's likely the source of the title. In Acts 11:26 we learn that followers of Jesus were first referred to as Christian in Antioch of Syria.

22 "Laying hands on" doesn't mean what it sounds like! In the Bible it's regularly a form of prayer, often resulting in healing and commissioning for a specific task.

23 The entire story is gripping and can be read in Acts 9.

24 The biggest one was between those who argued that Christians had to become Jewish first by following Jewish law. Acts 15 reveals the resolution of this tension. This sounds like a religious tension to us, but it was as much political as religious in first century Palestine.

And such is our call in our day, penetrating walls of division, bitterness, exclusion, and contempt to become voices of peace.

Taking a closer look, take two

We already saw how intentional Jesus was in describing and clarifying the subject of His prayer, our unity as His followers. It turns out that He was just as intentional in modeling how that same unity is achieved. And "practicing what He prayed" is the pattern here, too.

My friend Dennis Fuqua first introduced me to this very well-developed pattern in Jesus' prayer in John 17. It looks like this:

- There are four different requests that Jesus makes in the prayer.

- Each one is repeated. (The last one, that we as His followers would be one, shows up four times; the other requests each show up twice.)

- Before Jesus repeats each request, He shows specifically how He had practiced what He prayed.

While the application of this prayer is much larger than America's divided political landscape, let's briefly see how it applies politically.

GLORIFY THE SON[25]

"Glorify Your Son, that Your Son may glorify You." Unity starts by lifting up Jesus. This principle applies in every setting. If I'm in the middle of a disagreement with my wife and I ask the question, "What would glorify Jesus right now?" half the conflict is solved, because much of our conflict comes from asking a different question, "What would glorify me?" I don't even have to ask the question out loud; if the "What would glorify Jesus" question even crosses my mind, the likelihood of the conflict ending well just dramatically increased.

---

25 The request is made in verses 1 and 5. Verse 4 shows how Jesus practiced what He prayed.

I don't expect either political party to ask the "What would bring glory to Jesus?" question. Both are interested in a different question: "What will bring us more votes?" But as followers of Jesus in both parties, *we* can ask that question. It honors Jesus when His followers cross the aisle and befriend what the world sees as a political enemy. It takes something larger than the gap to bridge the gap, and that something is a Person, Jesus. "What would glorify Jesus?" in any political discourse is a great question, one that would immediately change the tenor of the debate.

"JESUS IS EITHER WHO HE SAID HE WAS, OR A NARCISSIST OF THE HIGHEST ORDER."

If you're wondering what kind of egomaniac would pray that he would get more glory for himself, it's likely because you're thinking of Jesus merely as a man. Jesus is often thought of as a "good man," but "good men" don't talk like Jesus talked. As C.S. Lewis is most famous for pointing out, Jesus is either who He said He was, or a narcissist of the highest order. This prayer request only makes sense if we're referring to Someone who is both God and human. Furthermore, Jesus isn't seeking glory for His own benefit, but for ours. We're actually much healthier when we live in a right relationship with the One who created us, because He helps right our relationships with one another as well.

PROTECT US FROM THE ENEMY[26]

"Protect them from the evil one." I don't believe in the red cartoon character with the pitchfork, but the more we hear of mass shootings, genocides, abductions, human trafficking...it's becoming easier all the time to believe there's an enemy that goes beyond mere flesh and blood.[27] The Bible describes his motives as stealing, killing, and destroying,[28] and his fingerprints are all over the news. We don't need to fear him, but we dare not forget about him. Jesus' prayer of protection is to be our prayer,

---

26   The request is made in verses 11 and 15. Verse 12 shows how Jesus practiced what He prayed.

27   Additional titles in the Bible for the enemy are Satan, the devil, and even Beelzebub.

28   John 10:10.

too; not only when we encounter the darkness perpetrated by the evil one, but in times of calm when the enemy is merely lurking.

The enemy's chief strategy is to divide and conquer, which explains why Jesus would pray (and encourages us to pray) for protection. When we're conscious of the divisive work being constantly sown, we're less likely to be part of that same work. Jesus is the one who first said, "A house divided against itself will not stand;"[29] President Lincoln was quoting Jesus in his famous "house divided" speech. The more contentiously divided our country becomes, the weaker it becomes.

The word "Satan" literally means "accuser." Satan does nothing in the spiritual realm but hurl out accusations against people. If he can find a human mouthpiece to do his work, all the better from his perspective.[30] My goodness, is he having a field day in the arena of politics. Knowing that we're playing on the devil's playground every time we accuse others maliciously should give us pause before firing off or forwarding the next social media slander.

SANCTIFY US IN THE TRUTH[31]
"Sanctify them by the truth; Your Word is truth." Think back over the last several conflicts you were involved in. What's the common denominator? Bad news—it's you! You were in every conflict you were in. We have a tendency to drag our baggage with us wherever we go. The third request Jesus makes in His prayer for unity is that each of us would be sanctified in the truth—that we would mature and grow up.

We can't control the way other people behave. But "other people" aren't what prompted me to write this in the first place. It's us—the various ways we forget who we are, make assumptions, invite the war into our living rooms, and Facebook firebomb our "friends." If instead of being part of the problem, we matured and became part of the solution, how much healthier would we be—in our families, workplaces, and nation.

---

29 Matt. 12:25 (NKJV).

30 Rev. 12:10.

31 The request is made in verses 17 and 19, and verse 19 also shows how Jesus practiced what He prayed.

If you look back over those three petitions, they form an amazing acronym without any manipulation on my part at all—in fact, it works in Spanish just like it does in English.

G̲lorify the Son
P̲rotect us from the enemy
S̲anctify us in the truth

It's our GPS for unity, which is the fourth petition in the prayer. The first three requests Jesus prayed are how the last one, the main focus, comes to pass. The first three are the road map for unity.

The GPS pattern in prayer has helped me navigate through local Donkey Elephant skirmishes more times than I can count. When I'm tempted to get defensive or fire off a political zinger, I can ask, "Jesus, what would glorify You right now?" When division is rampant and tempers are on edge, I can cry out, "Jesus, protect us from the enemy who's trying to divide and destroy us." I can call on God to "sanctify me," meaning that I'm asking Him to reveal my blind spots and help me grow and mature. Such a hopeful and helpful prayer in times like these!

Christmas in November, and always

Let's take a step back, away from a heavy emphasis on Jesus words recorded in one chapter of the Bible, and look at the bigger picture. In John 17, Jesus, whom most of us admire if not worship, is mere steps and minutes away from His crucifixion. And surprisingly, He's picked out unity as the most important need to pray about. The prayer isn't focused on our *political* unity, but neither does it refer to everything *except* political unity. There aren't any footnotes or small print saying that Jesus was only talking about how we treat one another in church. In fact, if you know Jesus, you know that the very last thing He would have done would be to separate churchy things from everyday life. He's imminently practical, and desires to be Lord of all of life, not just the spiritual compartments. A strong majority of our country claims to admire/believe in/follow Jesus according to a wide variety of sources.[32] That means Jesus-admirers are in both political parties, and Jesus' prayer has something to say about our mess.

And let's move from the end of Jesus' life to the beginning of it.[33] On that very first Christmas, the sky filled up with angels who proclaimed at the birth of Jesus, "Glory to God in the highest, And on earth peace, goodwill toward men!"[34] Isn't peace and goodwill the very thing we need as an antidote to our Donkey Elephant war?

Our culture has been preaching tolerance for decades. How's that working out? I, for one, don't aspire to be tolerated. "Honey, how was your day?" "It was a great day, dear. I felt thoroughly and consistently tolerated." Peace, especially the Biblical kind, is what we need far more than tolerance. The Hebrew word for peace is *shalom*, and it implies wholeness and justice, that wrongs have been righted. Shalom peace is far more than a temporary ceasefire. As a friend suggested over lunch yesterday, perhaps one of the reasons our calls for tolerance have led us to even greater hostility is that they've just buried the conflicts deeper. If I believe I must tolerate something or someone that I'm inclined to react negatively toward, I most likely simply suppress my thoughts and feelings. Like tamping down gunpowder, that simply makes the future explosion bigger.

Peace, Jesus' peace, talks, and we need to listen to what He has to say. In His final thoughts before giving His life, Jesus didn't pray for greater tolerance. He prayed for deeper love. Not only did Jesus address the culture's deepest conflicts, He absorbed them in His body on a cross. From birth to death, Jesus was the Prince of Peace, and exactly

---

32   Wikipedia ("Christianity") puts it at 65%, Pew Research Center ("Religious Landscape") at 70.6%, and Gallup ("Key Findings") at 74%. ["Christianity in the United States," Wikipedia, last modified April 11, 2020, https://en.wikipedia.org/wiki/Christianity_in_the_United_States.] [Frank Newport, "Five Key Findings on Religion in the U.S.," Gallup, December 23, 2016, https://news.gallup.com/poll/200186/five-key-findings-religion.aspx.]

33   Rather, the beginning of His human life here on earth. The Bible proclaims that Jesus is eternal and "took on flesh" (John 1:1,14).

34   Luke 2:14 (NKJV).

the influence we need in our day. Ironically, that exact title was spoken prophetically of Jesus some 700 years earlier by the prophet Isaiah. Tell me if this doesn't sound like Good News, not just on the first Tuesday in November or on December 25 but all year round:

> For to us a child is born, to us a son is given,
> And the government will be on his shoulders.
> And he will be called Wonderful Counselor
> Mighty God, Everlasting Father, Prince of Peace.
> Of the increase of his government and peace
> There will be no end.[35]

Oh Prince of Peace, come and speak to and through us.

We're ready to dive into the battleground. The next two chapters will address three issues per party that I believe Jesus likely supports. We don't have to choose one or the other—we can have both! And as long as our identity isn't too tied up in one party, it won't feel like betrayal to adopt some of the values of the other side.

---

35   Isa. 9:6–7.

PART II

BATTLEGROUND

CHAPTER SIX

ELEPHANT FAVORITES

Republican Priorities that Jesus Probably Likes

S ummarizing what's come before, I believe our hearts are so over-identified with the political animal of our choice, and our lungs so filled with Western either/or air, that our brains simply shut down. I'm assuming I'm not the only one, but as I shared in the first chapter, that's certainly been true for me personally in the past. I adopted a Republican worldview with a Manichaean approach.[1] Republicans were my tribe, my people, my homies. And so anything that came from the other party had to be bad.

---

1   If you've forgotten the Chapter 3 material on the prophet Mani, or simply jumped ahead to the controversial stuff, Mani was the king of either/or thinking. My favorite quote from Haidt is this one: "If you think about politics in a Manichaean way, then compromise is a sin. God and the devil don't issue many bipartisan proclamations, and neither should you" (*Righteous Mind*, 362).

HERE'S MY INVITATION

Even if you're taking things out of order and reading this chapter before the earlier stuff, commit that if you're reading this chapter, you'll read the next one, too. And recognize that the predictable yet unhelpful reaction of cheering for one and booing for the other one is why I wrote the first half of the book! Knee-jerk reactions are evidence of echo chambers—which are *not* our friends if we want peace to talk.

Remember, too, who my primary intended audience is—those who already have an affinity for Jesus. My hope and prayer is that since you already like Jesus, you care what He thinks. I'm going to give my best shot at persuading you that Jesus supports the political platforms in this chapter *and* the next one. All of them. Simultaneously. Like the person/angel/pre-incarnate Jesus who confronted Joshua and answered his question "Friend of Foe?" with "Neither,"[2] I am going to argue that Jesus transcends political parties and actually likes some of the favorite talking points from BOTH parties.

KNEE-JERK REACTIONS ARE EVIDENCE OF ECHO CHAMBERS—WHICH ARE *NOT* OUR FRIENDS IF WE WANT PEACE TO TALK.

I'm simply an American who wants what's best for, in no particular order: a) every American and person living in America, b) our country, and c) the world. My training is in Biblical interpretation, pastoring, etc., so allow me to cut off a possible objection right up front. Yes, Jesus shows up by name only in the New Testament,[3] and yes, the "Bible" He would have read consisted more or less of what we call the Old Testament today. Jesus is eternal—older than any of the Bible. He "took on flesh" in approximately 4 B.C.,[4] and He's currently alive

---

2   Josh. 5:13–14.

3   Although something like 300 Old Testament prophecies can be seen in hindsight as painting a breathtakingly accurate picture of Jesus of Nazareth.

4   Based on what we know of the historical figures referenced in the New Testament, as well as the astronomy behind the star over Bethlehem.

and well in heaven.[5] Jesus affirmed the authority of the Old Testament, and He *is* the main point of the New Testament, so when I suggest that Jesus might have approved of something, the whole Bible is fair game as source material.

You don't have to be convinced *yet*—you haven't read the stuff! You may still be certain, even after the last five brilliant chapters of preparation (haha), that the other Mammal is the mortal enemy who must be destroyed. So my invitation is just this: will you at least consider what you read? If you have a Biblical objection—meaning you think I haven't handled the Biblical material well enough, or left out some key verses/passages that would change the argument—you could be right. Let's dialogue. I'll be creating an ongoing platform for dialogue moving forward. But if you find yourself merely rehearsing your party's talking points, please STOP. Just stop. Step out of the echo chamber where all you hear are the same voices over and over again, and be willing to learn something new, even at the risk of . . . changing your mind.

Alrighty, here we go. Entire books have been written on each of these topics, so what follows will be merely an overview.

Protecting religious liberty

Over the last decade, Pew Trusts states that the United States has moved from a country of "low" religious freedom restrictions to "moderate" restrictions.[6] That sentence right there ought to scare us significantly, especially if you've done any substantive reading on our country's history. Freedom and liberty are our bedrock in the United States. We describe ourselves in song as "the land of the free and the home of the brave."[7] In the Declaration of Independence we read, "We hold these truths to

---

5   That's the best I can do with attempting to talk about timelessness and eternal life in a few words, given the limitations of language.

6   "Rising Tide of Restrictions on Religion," Pew Research Center, September 20, 2012, https://www.pewforum.org/2012/09/20/rising-tide-of-restrictions-on-religion-findings/.

7   "The Star-Spangled Banner: The Flag That Inspired the National Anthem," Smithsonian National Museum of American History, accessed September 21, 2019, https://amhistory.si.edu/starspangledbanner/the-lyrics.aspx.

be self-evident, that all men are created equal, that they are endowed by their Creator with certain unalienable Rights, that among these are Life, Liberty and the pursuit of Happiness."[8] And in the Preamble to the Constitution we read, "We the People of the United States, in order to form a more perfect Union, establish justice, insure domestic tranquility, provide for the common defense, promote the general welfare, and secure the blessings of liberty to ourselves and our posterity..."[9] When a research center reports that we Americans are losing our liberty and watching our freedom flee, that should rattle everyone's cages, not just the Elephant cages.

As before, let's approach this from two different starting places. Tim Urban in *Wait But Why* analyzes the amazing genius of the founding of the country this way. Most other countries of the world operated by the principle, "Everyone can do whatever they want, if they have the power to pull it off." The U.S., however, was the first country to choose to operate on sets of values instead of merely a power game. Instead of bullying opponents to get what we want, we have to convince them by using a carrot instead of a cudgel.[10] And in a brilliant division of authority, the Constitution lays out the rules, the citizenry functions as the brain, and the government has the cudgel. Urban summarizes: the net result is a country where "people are free to do whatever they want, as long as it doesn't harm someone else."[11]

Now from a Biblical worldview starting point. Dutch Sheets writes,

> Our founding fathers were all about liberty. It wasn't
> that they woke up one day and were suddenly patriotic
> and nationally-focused. They were largely Christians.

---

8   "Declaration of Independence: A Transcription," The National Archives and Records Administration, accessed September 21, 2019, https://www.archives.gov/founding-docs/declaration-transcript.

9   "The Constitution of the United States," The National Archives and Records Administration, accessed September 21, 2019, https://www.archives.gov/founding-docs/constitution.

10   A short, thick stick used as a weapon. Urban ("The Story of Us") uses "cudgel" as a symbol for power or brute force.

11   Tim Urban, "The Enlightenment Kids," Chapter 4, The Story of Us, published September 10, 2019, https://waitbutwhy.com/2019/09/enlightenment-kids.html.

They understood from their Bible readings and common study of the Word that liberty was very important to God. Liberty and freedom are used almost interchangeably in the Bible. The meaning in the Greek is to be free of anything that would enslave us. . . . The founders saw liberty as a key freedom; as a right given to them by God, their Maker. For whom the Son sets free is free indeed![12] And, where the Spirit of the Lord is, there is liberty![13] In their world, the Spirit of the Lord was involved in every aspect of their daily lives. They looked to God for everything and acknowledged Him in leading them daily. Our government was even formed as they sought Him for Divine guidance.[14]

God values freedom so highly that He risked everything in order to secure it for us. From the Garden of Eden on, people have been free to choose God and His ways or not. Most of the answers to life's thorniest questions, like "Why is there so much suffering in the world?" trace back to human free will. Urban says "we're free to do whatever we want as long as nobody gets hurt," but we hurt one another all the time—sometimes intentionally, often accidentally. As C.S. Lewis points out, God apparently thought it was worth the risk to give us freedom to reject Him, because He desires our love, and love must be freely expressed. "Free will, though it makes evil possible, is also the only thing that makes possible any love or goodness or joy worth having."[15] Jesus came along and invited people to follow Him, but He didn't compel any to do so. And when we are rightly troubled by the depths of evil and depravity expressed by humans, we do well to remember that Jesus chose to pay that cost personally to as high or higher a degree than any of us ever will.

Moving from the value of freedom in general to that of freedom of religion more specifically, Jesus said, "Render therefore to Caesar the

---

12 John 8:36.

13 2 Cor. 3:17.

14 Dutch Sheets, "Thankful for Liberty," Give Him 15, November 22, 2019, http://givehim15.com/.

15 C.S. Lewis, *The Case for Christianity* (Nashville, TN: B&H Publishing Group, 2000), 64.

things that are Caesar's, and to God the things that are God's."[16] "In this statement Jesus established the principle of a distinct realm of 'things that belong to God' that should not be regulated or constrained by the government (or 'Caesar'). This means that people's religious convictions and religious activities should clearly be an area in which government gives citizens complete freedom."[17] Government should not pick a religion and require people to adopt it.

The Constitution addresses this theme in the First Amendment, where we read "Congress shall make no law respecting an establishment of religion, or prohibiting the exercise thereof."[18] The phrase "separation of church and state," to the surprise of many, is not found in the foundational documents of our country anywhere, but rather became popular due to some Supreme Court decisions in recent decades that go beyond what the founders intended, in the opinion of many. The founders never intended to keep God out of everything except religion; their concern was the other direction, that the government would step into the religion business.

The rub comes from a trend in recent years to distinguish between freedom of religion and freedom of worship, arguing *for* the latter but *against* the former. Freedom of worship recognizes the rights of Americans to believe and worship what and how they so desire in the privacy of their own homes or places of worship. Freedom of worship is much narrower than freedom of religion, because without the broader *religious* freedom, religious expression can be essentially excluded from the public square. This shift can be seen in numerous controversies today:

- Whether or not business owners and medical professionals are allowed to carry out their profession in ways consistent with their religious beliefs

---

16   Matt. 22:21 (NKJV).

17   Wayne Grudem, *Politics According to the Bible* (Grand Rapids, MI: Zondervan, 2010), 499.

18   "First Amendment, United States Constitution," The National Constitution Center, accessed September 24, 2019, https://constitutioncenter.org/interactive-constitution/amendment/amendment-i.

- Whether or not prayer can occur in city council meetings, sports team huddles, graduation ceremonies and so forth

- Whether or not religious symbols such as The Ten Commandments or manger scenes or a Menorah can adorn public spaces

- Whether or not students or teachers can include expressions of their faith in the classroom

- Whether or not faith-based non-profits can apply on equal footing with non-faith-based organizations for government grants

- Whether or not churches can advocate for public policy that is consistent with their religion

- Whether or not churches should be tax-exempt

All of the above items don't merely relate to the freedom of religion; they also relate to the freedom of speech. As Urban writes, free speech is often referred to as not just *a* right but *the* fundamental right on which all other rights are based. "Free speech gives citizens a way to resolve conflicts with words instead of violence. When ideas can go to battle against each other, people don't have to."[19] In protecting citizens from the government's encroachment on our ability to speak, the First Amendment paves the way for peace talks.

I've chosen to use language like "faith-based" because it's common vernacular in these discussions, but it's a misleading term. We all have faith in something. Every human alive is faith-based. We might place our ultimate faith in God, or we might place it in human reasoning, education, or any number of other things. Some would appear to place their ultimate faith in a political party, though I can't for the life of me understand why. The effort to scrub the public square free of all "religion"

---

19   Tim Urban, "The American Brain," Chapter 6, The Story of Us, published September 18, 2019, https://waitbutwhy.com/2019/09/american-brain.html.

actually amounts to endorsing one religion (humanism) over others—the very thing the Constitution forbids.

And it runs deeper than that. Identity in Christ isn't an "add-on," one more value added on top of all the rest we might hold. Reducing freedom of religion to freedom of worship is the same thing as a frontal attack on religion, because we take our identity with us wherever we go.

It should be clear from the list above that how much religious liberty we should enjoy is an open question, a concern that the party of the Elephants typically trumpets. This dramatic shift is occurring while a huge majority of the public still professes belief in God. Since many of these questions end up in the Supreme Court, five out of nine judges are all it takes to enact sweeping change in the country. This helps to explain why for many Republicans, at or near the top of their list of priorities is going to be who the presidential candidate will nominate to the Supreme Court, and who the congressional candidates will confirm.

While it isn't hard to assign blame, the Bible has a principle that "judgment starts with the house of God."[20] Jesus said we should examine ourselves before finding fault with others.[21] When the most common words associated with Christians are "judgmental" and "hypocritical," it's no wonder that religious liberty is being threatened.[22] Or, closer to the theme of this book, "When our organizations embody a rugged individualism and fuel division between people intended to be united in mission, we deserve the world's skepticism."[23] We, meaning Christians, have earned much of the baggage associated with us. We would be much better served by focusing our attention on getting our own house in order than by marshalling all our energy against the forces who oppose us.

---

20   See 1 Peter 4:17.

21   Matt. 7:3–5.

22   David Kinnaman, *UnChristian: What a New Generation Really Thinks about Christianity...And Why It Matters* (Grand Rapids, MI: Baker Books, 2007), 41–66, 181–204.

23   Peter Greer, Chris Horst, and Jill Heisey, *Rooting for Rivals: How Collaboration and Generosity Increase the Impact of Leaders, Charities, and Churches* (Bloomington, MN: Bethany House Publishers, 2018), 30.

In the days of the early church, the opposition was quite a bit nastier than anything American Christians currently experience. All but two of the original twelve disciples gave their lives for what they believed.[24] Within months of Jesus' own crucifixion, Peter and John were arrested for following Jesus, for preaching His word and doing His works. After being threatened by the same leaders who had killed Jesus, Peter and John responded, "Judge for yourselves whether it is right in God's sight to obey you rather than God. For we cannot help speaking about what we have seen and heard."[25] Peter and John recognized the government's authority to punish lawbreakers, and yet boldly announced that they answered to a higher authority. They weren't advocating anarchy and lawlessness; they submitted to the law of the land at risk of their lives. And when they were released, rather than praying "Throw the bums out of office, God," they prayed for even greater courage and boldness. The first Christians focused their time and energy and prayers on what was within their control—their own attitudes and actions.

THE EFFORT TO SCRUB THE PUBLIC SQUARE FREE OF ALL "RELIGION" ACTUALLY AMOUNTS TO ENDORSING ONE RELIGION (HUMANISM) OVER OTHERS.

They weren't living in a democracy, however. We are, meaning we have some direct control over who governs us and how they go about it. Christ-followers today also answer to a higher authority, and at some point we may eventually find ourselves in situations just like the first followers of Jesus did, and like many do today around the world. In the meantime, we have the responsibility to live out our faith both in private and in public. For Christians to withdraw from the public arena is to compartmentalize our faith in unhealthy and unbiblical ways. We can follow the example

---

24 And the two who didn't were Judas who committed suicide after betraying Jesus, and John who lived out his life banished to the island of Patmos because of his faith.

25 Acts 4:19–20 (BSB).

of Jesus and His first followers, serving, loving, and speaking the truth boldly and humbly.

I believe we also have a window of opportunity where we can still humbly attempt to remind others (both voters and elected officials) of the value added to our culture by followers of Jesus, both individually and collectively. "In an age where there's a growing belief that religion is not a positive for American society, adding up the numbers is a tangible reminder of the impact of religion," said Dr. Brian Grim, scholar at the Religious Liberty Project at Georgetown University. "Every single day individuals and organizations of faith quietly serve their communities as part of religious congregations, faith-based charities, and businesses inspired by religion."[26] In American cities where there are more faith-based homeless shelters, there is a smaller homeless population.[27] The average church contributes approximately $150,000 of social services to their communities annually.[28] Twenty of the top fifty American charities are faith-based.[29] Across all sectors, churches and faith-based organizations create $1.2 trillion in economic value annually in the United States

FOR CHRISTIANS TO WITHDRAW FROM THE PUBLIC ARENA IS TO COMPARTMENTALIZE OUR FAITH IN UNHEALTHY AND UNBIBLICAL WAYS.

---

26   Faith Counts, "New Study Values Faith in America Over One Trillion Dollars," *PR Newswire*, September 14, 2016, https://www.prnewswire.com/news-releases/new-study-values-faith-in-america-over-one-trillion-dollars-300328315.html.

27   Andy Hallmark and Terry Goodrich, "Faith-Based Organizations Shoulder Majority of Crucial Services and Develop Creative Solutions for Homelessness, New Baylor University Study Says," Baylor University, February 1, 2017, https://www.baylor.edu/mediacommunications/news.php?action=story&story=176953.

28   "The Halo Effect and the Economic Value of Faith-Based Organizations," Brookings, November 29, 2016, https://www.brookings.edu/events/the-halo-effect-and-the-economic-value-of-faith-based-organizations/.

29   Brian J. Grim and Melissa E. Grim, "The Socio-Economic Contributions of Religion to American Society: An Empirical Analysis," *Interdisciplinary Journal of Research on Religion* 12 (2016), http://www.religjournal.com/pdf/ijrr12003.pdf.

alone.[30] For these reasons and others, the government has traditionally made churches and non-profits tax exempt because of the value they bring to their communities. Whether that value continues to be recognized or not remains to be seen.

Advocating pro-life (unborn)

The irony of a phrase like "pro-life" is that each party has parts of the picture, but neither party seems to do a very good job of seeing how all the pieces are part of the same puzzle. "The tragedy is that in America today, one can't vote for a consistent ethic of life."[31] This is the Republican chapter of the book, and the Elephants' strongest pro-life advocacy is in the area of the unborn, so that's where this section will start.

In the interest of transparency, this is an issue of high priority for me. The ultimate issue at hand for the pro-life position is whether or not the baby in the womb is a person.[32] If personhood applies to the unborn, a position held by most Elephants and some Donkeys, then it isn't hard to see why this topic generates such passion. There can be no harsher form of discrimination than to decide that a block of people has no right to live, and then proceed to carry out the death sentence. If only one person were to be so victimized, it would be of utmost importance, but the fact that we're talking about nearly 1,000,000 people a year in the United States alone, year after year, merely heightens the urgency.[33] Based on a survey of a number of different websites, conservative numbers tell us that well over 50,000,000 babies have been aborted in the U.S. since 1973, and well over 1 billion globally since 1980.[34] We

---

30 Grim and Grim, "Socio-Economic Contributions."

31 Jim Wallis, *God's Politics: Why the Right Gets It Wrong and the Left Doesn't Get It* (New York: Harper Collins, 2005), 301.

32 Yes, I will also address the needs of the mothers.

33 Approximately 862,320 abortions were performed in 2017, down 7% from 926,190 in 2014. The abortion rate in 2017 was 13.5 abortions per 1000 women aged 15–44, down 8% from 14.6 per 1000 in 2014. Thankfully, this is the lowest rate ever observed in the United States. ["Induced Abortion in the United States," Guttmacher Institute, accessed November 19, 2019, https://www.guttmacher.org/fact-sheet/induced-abortion-united-states.]

34 1973 is when *Roe v. Wade* decision was made in the U.S. These statistics are shared after having looked at multiple sites.

are rightfully horrified when innocent life is snuffed out in a terror attack. Yet if we add up all the Americans who've died in every war the country has fought (from the Revolutionary War through the current Global War on Terror), the total number of Americans killed by war or terror in the country's entire history is approximately equal to the number killed by abortion in our nation every single year.[35] And just in case the above statistics don't already have your attention, the U.S. is one of only seven countries in the world that allows for abortion after 20 weeks gestation, linking us with China and North Korea as two of the remaining six.[36] If you consider yourself pro-choice rather than pro-life, the above should help shed some light on the perspectives that motivate the other side of the divide.

Jesus consistently attributed value to those the culture devalued, such as slaves, Roman oppressors, women, Samaritans, and children. When Peter cut off the ear of a slave in an attempt to keep Jesus from being arrested, Jesus picked up the severed ear and healed it.[37] When a Roman centurion came seeking healing for his servant, not only did Jesus heal the servant, but lauded the centurion's faith as being greater than anyone in Israel.[38] Women weren't considered credible witnesses in Roman courts of law, yet all four gospels record that women were entrusted as the first witnesses to the most important event in the Bible, Jesus' resurrection.[39] Jesus consistently treated women with respect and love.[40] Jesus personally interacted with Samaritans and gave them respect, and He also used

---

35   1,196,554 Americans have died in all wars combined. [Megan Crigger and Laura Santhanam, "How many Americans have died in U.S. wars?," *PBS*, last modified May 27, 2019, https://www.pbs.org/newshour/nation/many-americans-died-u-s-wars.]

36   Michelle Ye Hee Leeb, "Is the United States One of Seven Countries That 'Allow Elective Abortions After 20 Weeks of Pregnancy?,'" *The Washington Post*, October 9, 2017, https://www.washingtonpost.com/news/fact-checker/wp/2017/10/09/is-the-united-states-one-of-seven-countries-that-allow-elective-abortions-after-20-weeks-of-pregnancy/.

37   Luke 22:47–51.

38   Matt. 8:5–13.

39   Matt. 28, Mark 16, Luke 24, John 20.

40   "It is also clear that Jesus did not treat women as others in His culture did; He treated them with dignity, as people with worth." *Life Application Study Bible: New Living Translation* (Wheaton, IL: Tyndale House), 1797.

them as positive examples and role models in His stories.[41] Most pertinent of all were Jesus' interactions with children. The disciples tried to dismiss the children coming to see Jesus, and Jesus rebuked His followers for doing so.[42] The clear witness of Jesus' life is that He valued all human life equally, and particularly highlighted those slighted or oppressed by the culture.

THERE CAN BE NO HARSHER FORM OF DISCRIMINATION THAN TO DECIDE THAT A BLOCK OF PEOPLE HAS NO RIGHT TO LIVE.

The Bible consistently views human life as starting at conception. When Mary, pregnant with Jesus, went to visit her pregnant cousin Elizabeth, the baby Elizabeth was carrying (John the Baptist) responded to Jesus' presence by leaping in the womb.[43] Both Jesus and John had not been born yet, and personhood is attributed to both. Of particular significance is the fact that the Greek word Elizabeth used to describe her preborn child, *brephos*, is the same word used for a baby before and after birth. In Psalm 51, David speaks of birth and conception equally, referring to both in very human terms.[44] Later, David writes, "For You created my inmost being; You knit me together in my mother's womb."[45] Isaac's wife Rebekah was pregnant with twins, and their rivalry didn't wait for them to see the light of day.[46] And elsewhere in the Old Testament, laws designed to protect life, such as if a baby in the womb were injured or killed, show the value of that unborn baby was the same as any adult.[47]

---

41   Luke 10:25–37.

42   Mark 10:13–16.

43   Luke 1:41–44.

44   Ps. 51:5.

45   Ps. 139:13.

46   Gen. 25:22–23. Isaac was Abraham's son. One of the twins born to Isaac was Jacob, later renamed Israel.

47   Ex. 21:22–25.

Medically, the moment a female's egg is fertilized by a sperm, a genetically unique, whole, living human being begins to exist. Dr. Dianne Irving, a biochemist, biologist, and former professor at Georgetown University writes, "Upon fertilization, parts of human beings (egg and sperm) have actually been transformed into something very different from what they were before; they have been changed into a single, whole human being. The product of fertilization is a living human being with 46 chromosomes (plus or minus, as in the case of Down's or Turner's syndromes)."[48] The argument that we aren't talking about full human beings since they're dependent on their mothers for life is weak, since children remain fully dependent on adults to stay alive for years after they're born. The advent of sonography has made what has always been the case more visible, so that a mother can now see the child in her womb. Once a mother does see the baby she's carrying, a high percentage of abortion-minded mothers change their mind. Our largest Tucson crisis pregnancy center, Hands of Hope, reports that 87% of clients who see the ultrasound choose to continue their pregnancy.[49] As medical technology advances, we're learning more and more about the miracle taking place inside a mother's womb, and arguments that dehumanize these preborn children become harder and harder to support.

As discussed in Chapter 3, the question of caring for the mothers and caring for the babies is a classic both/and, not an either/or misunderstanding that is at the root of this cultural struggle. There may have been a time when those advocating for the life of children yet-to-be-born did so with little apparent concern for the mother, but that time is significantly fading into the past. The organizations I'm familiar with show nothing but unconditional love and concern for the mothers, regardless of whether or not they decide to carry or abort, and for an unlimited number of years after such decisions. The needs of the mother—physical, emotional, financial, material, and spiritual—are given front-and-center attention. My wife has a bumper sticker from a Tucson ministry, Pro-Love Tucson, that simply says "Love them both." Based on a host of stories I'm familiar with, the care and concern shown to the mothers by abortion

48   Wayne Grudem, *Politics According to the Bible* (Grand Rapids, MI: Zondervan, 2010), 161–2.

49   Elisa Medina, Hands of Hope Executive Director, personal email correspondence, January 15, 2020.

clinics pales in comparison to the care and concern shown by crisis pregnancy centers. It isn't necessary to attack the child in order to defend the mother. It's a both/and. Is there room for improvement? Absolutely, and it will take both perspectives to complete the picture.

What about the tougher cases? Let's take the most common ones one at a time. When the life of the mother is at stake, as in an ectopic pregnancy, there are two lives in jeopardy, not one. If the life of the mother can be saved by ending the pregnancy, that would be a thoroughly Biblical option. Unless intervention happens (either divine or human), both lives will be lost, so saving one is better than saving none. In many cases where the mother's life is threatened, once the baby reaches viability, pitting the two against one another is a false choice, because the quickest way to save the mother would be a C-section, not an abortion. Often the question isn't saving one or the other, since saving both is the most logical solution.

Significantly less than 1% of all abortions consist of pregnancies caused by rape or incest,[50] yet those instances deserve attention. Some would argue that a thoroughly consistent ethic would recognize that the innocent human life in the womb should not be sacrificed no matter what the cause of the pregnancy, any more than we would attempt to justify taking the life of a child after being born due to the sin/crime of a parent. Others would argue that to require a traumatized woman to carry a baby to term would be cruel and inhumane, and that if abortion were made completely illegal except where the life of the mother was at risk, these same traumatized women might seek out far more dangerous illegal abortions. Speaking only for myself, my advocacy would be to tackle the >99% of abortions first, and cross this bridge later. In other words, make an exception for instances of rape or incest at least until the 99+% of abortions are adequately addressed, and then tackle the tougher question with great care and concern for all involved.

---

50   Abort73.com, "U.S. Abortion Statistics: Facts and Figures Relating to the Frequency of Abortion in the United States," Loxafamosity Ministries, last modified January 21, 2020, https://abort73.com/abortion_facts/us_abortion_statistics/. Citing studies from both the Guttmacher Institute and the state of Florida.

In a country founded on freedom, such as the freedom of religion, is it right to impose one set of morals on everyone? That's a fair question, but what the question seems to miss is that all laws impose a set of standards on everybody. Law by its very nature is a cultural statement on what's right and what's wrong. Laws against murder, theft, polygamy, sexual harassment, pedophilia, and every other law that could be named are all taking a set of standards and making them more universal. Unless one is going to argue for lawless anarchy, the question isn't whether or not standards should be imposed on others, but *which* standards and in what circumstances. It seems to me that one of the highest functions of law is to protect innocent life—especially life that needs protection, life that would be highly vulnerable to attack without legal protection. I can think of no clearer example than the unborn.

A CONSISTENT LIFE ETHIC OPPOSES ABORTION, EUTHANASIA, AND CAPITAL PUNISHMENT.

The critique that rings the truest to me of Republican advocacy protecting life in the womb is that the Elephants are inconsistent in their ethic for life. That critique says nothing about the validity of a position attempting to protect the unborn; rather, it argues for equal protection for other categories of human life. Some of those will show up in the Donkey chapter, since those tend to be priorities for the other side of the political aisle. But let's briefly address euthanasia and capital punishment. Regarding euthanasia, a distinction must be made between medical procedures that sustain life and medical procedures that intervene in order to end life. Refusing further cancer treatment is a far cry from suicide, self-induced or physician-assisted. Do-not-resuscitate orders are not euthanasia. We aren't required to avail ourselves of everything medically possible. All life matters to God, from the unborn to the elderly, and both need legal protection. Where euthanasia is legalized, it's a guarantee that at some point, some greedy inheritors will pressure their ancestors to speed up the process.

Regarding capital punishment, a consistent Biblical ethic of life would seem to argue against capital punishment. While the Old Testament calls for capital punishment in a variety of situations, Jesus' words and actions would appear to many, myself included, to overturn those Old Testament passages.[51] The counter-argument to this is that the Bible clearly supports governmental authority, and that authority could include capital punishment for murder cases, for instance. My counter-arguments to the counter-argument are more practical in nature. The number of death-row candidates exonerated by DNA evidence, for example, is frightening. For the government to wrongly execute someone for a crime he/she didn't actually commit only compounds one tragedy with another. Furthermore, it's well documented that ethnicity and socio-economic standing affect both the severity of punishments meted out and the quality of the legal defense employed. The death penalty is not administered equally to the population. Finally, the legal costs associated with capital punishment in the U.S. make it more costly than life sentences without parole. For all these reasons, I agree with the critique, and believe a consistent life ethic opposes abortion, euthanasia, and capital punishment.

Promoting marriage

"The world we find ourselves in has made sexuality central to our identity."[52] So says Jackie Hill Perry in her book, *Gay Girl, Good God*. Over-identifying with politics is a root cause of our Donkey Elephant war, and over-identifying with our sexuality is a root cause of much of the ethical turmoil in which our culture finds itself. Perry grew up in the Church, but also grew up same sex attracted (SSA). When she truly surrendered to God and became a Christ-follower, her same sex attraction did not immediately diminish. Rather, as her love for God grew, other things became less important. The majority of her book is simply telling her own story, with Part 1 entitled "Who I Was," and Part 2 entitled "Who I Became." Part 3 has some phenomenal insights under such

---

51   For instance, John 8:1–11, Matt. 5:38–42.

52   Jackie Hill Perry, *Gay Girl, Good God: The Story of Who I Was and Who God Has Always Been* (Nashville: B&H Publishing Group, 2018), 149.

chapter titles as "SSA and Identity," "SSA and Endurance," and "SSA and the Heterosexual Gospel."

On June 26, 2015 the Supreme Court ruled 5–4 in the *Obergefell v. Hodges* case that the 14th Amendment to the United States Constitution requires all 50 states to recognize same sex marriage.[53] Prior to that ruling, the political issue of same-sex marriage was one of the most common battlefields in the Donkey Elephant war. Unlike the 1973 *Roe v. Wade* decision that is still a lightning rod politically, I do not get the sense that much political energy is being spent on trying to get this decision reversed, even by those who vehemently disagree with it. Rather, the battleground has shifted to one of religious liberty. Now that same sex marriage has been normalized by the Supreme Court, what religious liberties do individuals have, both personally and as they conduct their businesses?

I was asked recently by a millennial what the Bible actually has to say on the topic of homosexuality. The place I first went to in response was John 1:14, which says, "The Word became flesh and made His dwelling among us. We have seen His glory, the glory of the One and only Son, who came from the Father, full of grace and truth."[54] Grace and Truth constitute another critical both/and that we have so often turned into either/or. In other words, I don't believe we can even talk about the content of Biblical truth on controversial topics without also talking about how that truth is handled . . . or even more significantly, how we interact with the people directly impacted by the topic. Truth without grace is no more Biblical than grace without truth. Jesus lived His life in such a way that nobody ever accused Him of waffling on the truth, and yet those whose lives seemed the furthest from the truth, the "sinners" as the Bible often puts it, flocked to Jesus like a rock star. Considering that Truth is a title for Jesus,[55] the fact that He also earned the nickname "friend of sinners"[56] says a lot about the uncommon combination of grace and truth.

---

53   Accessed January 2, 2020, https://www.supremecourt.gov/opinions/14pdf/14-556_3204.pdf.

54   "The Word" is a title for Jesus. This passage could be called the Christmas story from the Gospel of John. "Full of grace and truth" is my favorite description of Jesus.

55   John 14:6.

56   Matt. 11:19.

The issue of homosexuality is actually an issue of the role the Bible plays in an individual's and group's life. The culture has moved enough in recent years that adhering to the Bible's guidance is likely the only rationale that would cause Americans to hold to traditional views of marriage. So let's do a brief overview of the Biblical material, what Jesus thought about the topic, and then return to the political questions at hand.

In all my conversations on the topic over the years, one of the first statements made by those arguing for contemporary views instead of traditional ones is that Jesus never mentioned homosexuality. That's true, but Jesus never mentioned nuclear war or pedophilia either, for example, and yet I don't know anyone who would use that fact to conclude that we should all be fans of nuclear war and pedophilia. Jesus did define marriage as between one man and one woman on more than one occasion.[57] Anything different from that definition would be out of bounds according to Jesus, which would include sex before or outside of marriage, virtual sex (pornography), multiple partners, etc. Jesus' standards for marriage were *stronger* than those of the Old Testament, not more lenient.[58] The most developed instruction on marriage starts with "submit to one another out of reverence for Christ," and includes instruction for husbands to "love their wives just as Christ loved the Church." Incredibly high standards that none of us fully attain.

Yet when Jesus interacted with those who fell far short of the truth He upheld, His demeanor was full of grace. The Samaritan woman who had been married and divorced five times and was currently living with a man she wasn't married to experienced Jesus' grace and truth in powerful combination.[59] A woman caught in the act of adultery experienced the same thing, with Jesus explicitly telling her that He didn't condemn her, while also setting her free to "go and sin no more."[60] The Roman culture had a notoriously loose sexual ethic that included homosexuality, yet Jesus is never recorded as blasting the culture. Summarizing: Jesus'

---

57   Matt. 19:3–9, Mark 10:2–12, Luke 16:18.

58   Matt. 5:27–28.

59   John 4:4–42.

60   John 8:1–11.

standard for marriage was between one man and one woman for life, with each joyfully putting the needs of the other above their own, and we all fall short of the standard. Thank God for His grace!

Expanding our study to beyond the four gospels, the direct Biblical references to same sex sexual activity are all negative. I agree with the commentators who argue that the Old Testament reference to Sodom is not referring to people who are attracted to others of the same gender, but rather condemning rape. There is nothing even remotely mutual in the horrific story of Sodom in Genesis 19.[61] The "abomination" passages[62] are in a part of the Bible known as the Holiness Code, which cannot be simply applied universally, nor can it be summarily dismissed. Why? Because Jesus specifically overturned some of the Holiness Code once its purpose had been fulfilled;[63] yet the early Church recognized that the laws bringing order to sexuality still applied.[64] So, while the passages seem clear enough on face value, and clearly speak negatively about homosexual activity, the context includes plenty of topics that the New Testament overturns, making their application to present day much more complicated.

Two New Testament passages[65] use technical terms that get translated in a variety of ways depending on who's doing the translating; one of these passages addresses those who were once homosexual but later are no longer.[66] The possibility of changing orientation is highly unpopular, yet both Biblically and experientially it happens more often than the culture would lead you to believe.[67] The strongest and most universally applicable statement against homosexual activity comes from the book

---

61 Genesis 19:1–29, and a similar story in Judges 19:1–30. In Ezekiel 16:49, the sin of Sodom is said to be neglecting those experiencing poverty, so to claim that Sodom was destroyed because of homosexuality is not Biblically accurate.

62 Lev. 18:22 and 20:13.

63 For example, Mark 7:19, Luke 11:41, and Acts 10:9–16.

64 Acts 15:1–29.

65 1 Tim. 1:8–11 and 1 Cor. 6:9–11.

66 1 Cor. 6:11.

67 Three happily married (male/female) couples in the congregation I led for 21 years included a partner who had previously been homosexual in orientation and practice.

of Romans, and addresses both gay and lesbian activity.[68] The passage discusses what's natural not according to one's personal preferences—this would be a very foreign Western individualistic reading contrary to the author's intentions[69]—but what's natural according to Creation.

Thanks for hanging in there for more of a Bible study than you probably signed up for! Let's return to the political questions at hand. The culture has moved on this topic dramatically. As recently as 2008, both *Democratic* candidates for President, Barack Obama and Hillary Clinton, argued *against* a redefinition of marriage to include same sex couples. Needless to say, the Republican candidates were also opposed to same sex marriage. With the Supreme Court weighing in and public opinion continuing to shift in favor of LGBTQ+ priorities, I don't see the cultural winds reversing direction any time soon. I firmly believe that the primary fault[70] for this lies with the Church, not with the culture. We took grace and truth and split them in half. Some opted for grace at the expense of truth, preaching a "gospel" that actually is a very different gospel than the one in the Bible, one that says instead, "God wants to affirm whatever you want to do." This approach leaves me firmly on the throne of my own life, which is a bad idea. Others reacted against this assault on truth, and in so doing have shown very little grace. And *that* is undoubtedly an even worse approach. Almost never do you see people responding like Jesus did. A graceless truth is even less attractive than a truthless grace. So . . . no wonder the culture rejected Jesus on this topic; they weren't encountering a whole Jesus!

"WE ARE MORE THAN OUR SEXUALITY."

The political issue at hand in this regard is now one of religious liberty. Will Christian parents be allowed to teach their children what they believe about how God created sexuality as a good gift with a

---

68   Rom. 1:24–27.

69   See Chapter 3 for further discussion of this topic.

70   As mentioned above, absent Biblical authority, readers likely wouldn't be looking for "fault," but rather who deserves the "credit."

helpful owners' manual? Will pastors be allowed to teach that to their congregations? Will Christian schools continue to be allowed to teach the Bible? If we want to preserve these freedoms, we Christians with a Biblical worldview would do well to concentrate our efforts on strengthening *heterosexual* marriages. The Supreme Court decision doesn't do anything to discourage healthy traditional marriages! Again, the high divorce rate both in and outside the Church is a significant contributing factor to the cultural shift. Nobody is opposing the Church when we do all we can to strengthen marriage, so let's be known more for what we support than what we oppose.

And whenever we do teach what the Bible has to say about sexuality, we would do well to start with the fact that it's a good gift,[71] and that since all of us fall short of the Bible's standards, we live by grace.[72] To be judgmental doesn't mean to make judgments—all of us do that all the time, and we must. To be judgmental is to distance ourselves from others—and we've been guilty of that regularly, too. If we're going to speak *against* a particular action or behavior or attitude, we need to do it while moving *toward* those same people in love. The voice we desire to engage is the voice of peace, not conflict or condemnation.

Finally, one more caution and reason for including this section in the Elephant chapter. Once a standard that has been in place for millennia has changed, the "slippery slope" means it's hard to find a new place to stand firm. We're already seeing this with all the conversation about gender fluidity and gender dysphoria, and the conundrums we're going to continue to discover as a result.[73] Is it child abuse for parents to administer sex change hormonal therapy to their nine year old, or is withholding what the child wants the abusive action? Questions like these weren't even on the horizon a generation ago. Additionally, conversation is already becoming more normalized about polyamorous relationships.

---

71   Gen. 1–2.

72   Romans 3:23–24 and many other places.

73   For instance, males identifying as females and essentially eliminating female athletics, the rights for which have been fought hard over many decades and only recently achieved.

Protecting children in the middle of such shifting sands is going to be increasingly challenging.

Let's end with a few more quotes from Jackie Hill Perry.

> We are more than our sexuality.... [74] Marriage is not the pinnacle of the Christian faith.... [75] Singleness is not a curse.... [76] You are not your temptations.... [77] If He is the Creator, then we are the created. If He is Master, then we are servants. If He is love, then we are loved. If He is omnipotent, then we are not as powerful as we think. If He is omniscient, then there is nowhere to hide. If He cannot lie, then His promises are all true.[78]

---

74 Perry, *Gay Girl*, 178ff.

75 Ibid, 181ff.

76 Ibid, 184ff.

77 Ibid, 154.

78 Ibid, 160.

CHAPTER SEVEN

DONKEY FAVORITES

*Democratic Priorites that Jesus
Probably Likes*

IF you're skipping around instead of reading this in order, please make an exception and go back and read the first few pages of Chapter 6. In it you'll find much more information on how I'm approaching this material Biblically and culturally, and how I'm inviting you to do the same.

HERE'S MY INVITATION

Even if you're reading this chapter before the earlier material, commit that if you're reading this chapter, you'll read the previous one, too. And recognize that the predictable yet unhelpful reaction of cheering for one and booing for the other one is why I wrote the first half of the book!

Knee-jerk reactions are evidence of echo chambers—which are *not* our friends if we want peace to talk.

Caring for those experiencing poverty

The original title for this section was "caring for the poor." One of my blog readers, Rose Tederous, wrote, "'People experiencing poverty' is how I like to address and refer to someone who meets the poverty guideline. My reasons are: a) 'the poor' is not their identity, it's their current experience; b) experiences can change, and that's even more likely when we remove the stigma; and c) 'experiencing poverty' can stir the thought processes and close the gap between 'the rich' and 'the poor.'"[1] Brilliant! Only someone who's spent a lot of time with those experiencing poverty is likely to gain those insights. Imagine if we not only changed our language to "those experiencing poverty" but also to "those experiencing wealth." As surely as we're prone to think of poverty as an identity, we're even more likely to do so with wealth.

Jesus' cousin, John the Baptist, had been imprisoned for his preaching, probably more specifically for calling out the political leader Herod for his immoral behavior. John sent two of his followers to go ask Jesus if He was really the One they'd all been waiting for, the Messiah. Jesus replied, "Go back and report to John what you hear and see: The blind receive sight, the lame walk, those who have leprosy are cleansed, the deaf hear, the dead are raised, and the good news is proclaimed to the poor."[2]

Similarly, in what many commentators refer to as Jesus' inaugural address launching His public ministry, Jesus reads from Isaiah and says, "The Spirit of the Lord is on me, because He has anointed me to proclaim good news to the poor. He has sent me to proclaim freedom for the prisoners and recovery of sight for the blind, to set the oppressed free, to proclaim the year of the Lord's favor." With all eyes on Him as He takes His seat, Jesus announces, "Today this Scripture is fulfilled in

---

1   Rose Tederous, personal email correspondence, January 15, 2020.

2   Matt. 11:4–5.

your hearing."[3] The word "evangelical" literally means "bearer of good news."[4] How ironic that in our day "Evangelical" has become associated (rightly or wrongly) with a political position that sounds to many like good news to the rich, not the poor.[5]

This section will be more about perspectives than policy, because people far above my paygrade quote statistics and come to completely opposite conclusions on various policies relating to how best to care for those experiencing poverty. I'm a firm believer in the axiom, "where there's a will, there's a way," and it's the *will* that needs some attention. There's another axiom at play here: "perception is (some high percentage of) reality." If there's a perception problem, there's a problem, and there's no way on God's green earth that reducing poverty should be, or be seen as, a partisan issue. "Poverty is not a left-wing issue; it's a Christian issue, and it's time for us all to recognize that."[6]

There are literally *thousands* of verses in the Bible addressing the issue of poverty. It's one of the two most prominent themes in the Old Testament (the other being idolatry). One out of every 15 verses in the New Testament is about the poor or the subject of money. In Matthew, Mark, and Luke, that number bumps up to one in ten, and in Luke by itself it's one in seven.[7] When Mary was pregnant with Jesus, part of her exclamation while visiting her cousin Elizabeth includes these words, "He has brought down rulers from their thrones, but has lifted up the humble. He has filled the hungry with good things but has sent the rich away empty."[8] In Jesus' famous Sermon on the Mount, His opening statement is "Blessed are the poor (in spirit), for theirs is the kingdom of heaven."[9] In the early days of the Christian Church, "there

---

3   Luke 4:18–21, quoting Isaiah 61:1–2.

4   "Evangel" is the Greek word for "good news." The word used here in Matthew is literally "evangelized"; ironic since we tend to think of that word in spiritual terms, not material terms as it's used here.

5   Keep reading, elephants. I'll address trickle-down economics shortly.

6   Wallis, *God's Politics*, 226.

7   Ibid, 212.

8   Luke 1:52–53. This passage of Scripture is called the Magnificat.

9   Matthew 5:3 includes the phrase "poor in spirit;" Luke 6:20 just says "poor." Jesus probably said both.

was not a needy person among them" because the Christ-followers sold their property to help out anyone in need.[10] Jesus' half-brother James says, "Religion that God our Father accepts as pure and faultless is this: to look after orphans and widows in their distress and to keep oneself from being polluted by the world."[11] He goes on to directly call out any favoritism that might be expressed toward the rich.[12] And just in case we aren't convinced yet that alleviating poverty is a *major* Biblical theme, Jesus brings it home when He says that at the end of time, how we treated the hungry, thirsty, strangers, naked, sick, and imprisoned is how we treated Jesus Himself.[13] Mary Glover, a woman volunteering regularly in a food distribution line (and in need of a bag of groceries herself) understood Jesus well as she prayed every week, "Lord, we know that You'll be comin' through this line today, so Lord, help us to treat You well."[14]

It's impossible to read the Bible and not conclude that Jesus' heart beats for those experiencing poverty. Some branches of theology use the phrase "preferential option for the poor," with one stating, "The poor have the most urgent moral claim on the conscience of the nation."[15] Whether one subscribes to that language or not, it would be impossible to follow Jesus in a Biblically faithful manner and not want to care for those experiencing poverty in the most effective and compassionate ways possible. And it's certainly possible to care for those experiencing poverty without falling into the either/or trap and concluding that you have to attack those experiencing wealth in order to defend those experiencing poverty.

There's a scene toward the end of Jesus earthly life where a woman comes in and anoints Jesus with some very expensive perfume. Jesus'

---

10 Acts 2:44–45; 4:32–37.

11 James 1:27.

12 James 2:1–7.

13 Matt. 25:31–46.

14 Wallis, *God's Politics*, 217.

15 "Major Themes from Catholic Social Teaching," Office for Social Justice, Archdiocese of St. Paul and Minneapolis, accessed August 14, 2019, https://web.archive.org/web/20060216183419/http:/www.osjspm.org/cst/themes.htm.

disciples object, scolding her by pointing out how much money that perfume could have been sold for, "and the money given to the poor." Jesus, as He often had to do, corrects His *disciples*, and within His response makes the oft-quoted comment, "The poor you will always have with you."[16] Some have taken this as an escape route, assuming that since there will always be those among us experiencing poverty, we don't need to worry or do anything about it. Nothing would be more out of character for Jesus than such a sentiment. As Jim Wallis writes, "Jesus is saying, in effect, 'Look, you will always have the poor with you' *because* you are my disciples. You know who we spend our time with, who we share meals with, who listens to our message, who we focus our attention on."[17] Far from being a "get out of compassion free" card, Jesus is actually talking about our need to have *proximity* with those experiencing poverty at all times. He is also making a theological statement that if we don't want to suffer from compassion fatigue and burnout, we need to put Jesus first, drawing our strength and our compassion from the One whose well never runs dry. "The poor you will always have with you." Our question is, will we always be found *with* the poor?

THESE PROBLEMS ARE UNACCEPTABLE , MEANING THAT WE CANNOT JUST SIT BACK AND ACCEPT THEM.

So how bad is the poverty problem in America? Approximately 12% of the U.S., or 38 million people, live at or below the federal poverty threshold, which in 2018 for a family of four was $25,700. Even at the federal poverty threshold, basic necessities like food, clothing, shelter, education, and health care will be very difficult to achieve consistently. The rate for women (12.9%) is higher than for men (10.6%), and for single parent women (24.9%) it is nearly double that for single parent men (12.7%). Poverty discriminates by age, with 16.2% of all children living in poverty, meaning nearly one in six, which equates to about 12 million children. Poverty discriminates by

16   Matt. 26:6–13.

17   Wallis, *God's Politics*, 210.

ethnicity as well, with the poverty rate for Native Americans at 25.4%, Black 20.8%, Hispanic 17.6%, and White and Asian both at 10.1%.[18]

Before jumping to root cause or possible solution questions, which if you're anything like me you've already done, can we just pause for a moment to agree that the above paragraph points out numerous very serious problems? These problems are unacceptable, meaning that we cannot just sit back and accept them by misinterpreting Jesus' "the poor you will always have with you," or by prioritizing other issues to the exclusion of this one. Until the pandemic COVID-19 ravaged the global and national economies, poverty rates had dropped slightly in recent years for most subgroups.[19] Now, though, unemployment rates are skyrocketing as we try to protect as many citizens as possible from contracting the coronavirus, and those who were already experiencing poverty are by far the most vulnerable.

> The greatest moral question in American politics today is, "What is our prosperity for?" The Biblical prophets say that a society's integrity is judged, not by its wealth and power, but by how it treats its most vulnerable members. When our unprecedented economic growth exists alongside the embarrassing fact that one in six American children is still poor, and one in three children of color, the moral underpinnings of our prosperity are in great disarray.... We now have record prosperity and rising inequality [of wages] at the same time. The rising tide has lifted all the yachts, but not yet all the boats.[20]

I remember taking a class on economics in college and studying trickle-down economics—and that's about all I remember from that class—that

---

18   The statistics in this paragraph come from PovertyUSA.org, which draws from the U.S. Census Bureau. A quick Google search reveals multiple sources all with very similar information. ["The Population of Poverty USA," PovertyUSA.org, accessed August 20, 2019, http://povertyusa.org/facts.]

19   Jessica Semega, Melissa Kollar, John Creamer, and Abinash Mohanty, "Income and Poverty in the United States: 2018," United States Census Bureau, September 10, 2019, https://www.census.gov/library/publications/2019/demo/p60-266.html.

20   Wallis, *God's Politics*, 236–7.

the topic came up. The theory is that tax cuts to businesses and the wealthy stimulate the economy, eventually helping everyone. Well, the nature of theories is that they need to be tested, and good theories are those that will hold up under the testing. While there may be some evidence in support of trickle-down economics, such as how the improved economy in the last couple of years had reduced poverty rates until the pandemic took over, it's hardly the silver bullet that solves all the issues. In the 1950's the average CEO of an American company made 20 times the amount that the median worker's wages (median means the wage at which half the workers made more, half made less). By 2018 that ratio had risen to 361. The average worker's wages, adjusted for inflation, have been stagnant for the last 50 years, while the average CEO's wages have increased by 1000%.[21] The United States' CEO/Worker ratio is the highest in the world by a significant margin.[22] From a Biblical perspective, the issue isn't how much money a person makes as it is how much that person keeps. Yet the Bible also refers to the love of money as the root of all evil,[23] and the more you have, the bigger the temptation. Caring for those experiencing poverty needs to make our list of "important things to pay attention to" and "important priorities at the ballot box," and wage inequality is part of the backdrop.

My previous job included a concept of inviting people from all different domains and sectors (i.e. church, business, education, government, social services, etc.) to work together to address the city's systemic problems. The first systemic problem chosen was poverty reduction. I thoroughly agree with the premise that if one domain (say government, or education, or social services) could alleviate poverty all by itself, the problem would have been solved decades ago. The problem is our lack of collaboration, not only within sectors but even more so between

---

21   Diana Hembree, "CEO Pay Skyrockets to 361 Times That of the Average Worker," *Forbes*, May 22, 2018, https://www.forbes.com/sites/dianahembree/2018/05/22/ceo-pay-skyrockets-to-361-times-that-of-the-average-worker/#d960126776dd.

22   Erin Duffin, "Pay Gap Between CEOs and Average Workers, by Country 2018," Statista, March 20, 2020, https://www.statista.com/statistics/424159/pay-gap-between-ceos-and-average-workers-in-world-by-country/.

23   1 Tim. 6:10.

them.[24] This multi-domain multi-sector theory is one that actually has been tested, and the Center of Opportunity where my office is located is living proof. You can read more about it in the Appendix of this book.

The research in preparation for the poverty reduction taskforce from that previous job revealed a startling statistic. If three conditions are met (just three!), there is only a 2% likelihood of landing in poverty.[25] Those three conditions? 1) graduate from high school, 2) secure employment, and 3) wait until marriage to have a child. Donkeys and Elephants can work themselves into a tizzy over whether or not there should be a minimum wage and if so, how much, and what the tax rates should be for individuals, families, and corporations. Those are important questions, but smarter people than me haven't been able to lead the country to clear consensus on them yet. What I find so encouraging about the aforementioned research is how tangible and practical it is. There are all kinds of things we can do to make a difference in those areas. And there are policies that could be implemented that would make an immediate difference in reducing poverty.

> **"WE NEED A RENEWED COMMITMENT TO THE COMMON GOOD OVER THE BOTTOM LINE."**

That leads us directly to taking a closer look at the first item, education. Virtually everyone agrees that a quality education might be the single most important factor in a person's economic wellbeing. Here's where the cycle of poverty is the most vicious. The poorer a person/family is, the harder it is to get a decent education—including just graduating from high school, let alone anything beyond high school. Poorer neighborhoods have less resourced primary and secondary schools. Here in Arizona property taxes are a primary funding source for schools. The state has attempted to mitigate the obvious built-in disparity from a funding source based on property taxes by allotting a set amount per student

---

24   Go to 4Tucson.com for more information.

25   Ron Haskins, "Three Simple Rules Poor Teens Should Follow to Join the Middle Class," Brookings, March 13, 2013, http://www.brookings.edu/research/opinions/2013/03/13-join-middle-class-haskins.

regardless of district, with the state general fund making up the difference between what's needed and what's collected via property taxes. Yet the inequities are still built into the system because school districts can propose budget overrides for both operations and capital expenditures, as well as bond elections. Guess which districts have an easier time passing those overrides and bonds? The districts in more affluent neighborhoods. Furthermore, the system assumes an equal distribution of students, both in terms of percentages of special education students (for instance), as well as the neediness of the student population. Yet that isn't what happens at all, and the less resourced schools typically end up with the most higher need students. As Vail Unified School District Superintendent Cal Baker told me in a phone conversation, "We have to find a way to solve these inequities, if for no other reason than this: society cannot continue to economically carry a higher and higher percentage of the population."

For policy recommendations, how about this as a starting point? I see nothing partisan at all in a desire for steady employment at a livable family income, access to health care, a pathway to homeownership, and a chance to send your kids to good schools. Yet if you Google bipartisan efforts on reducing poverty, you won't find much. I agree with Jim Wallis when he writes that it will take liberals and conservatives working together to solve our issues and alleviate poverty.[26] We need a "renewed commitment to the common good over the bottom line and an ethic of both personal and social responsibility."[27]

Economic policies for a country and a Biblical worldview on money are not the same thing. Yet neither are they as disconnected as we tend to make them. One more quote from Wallis:

> Our anxious striving after affluence has also created a spiritual poverty. Nobody wants to say out loud that shopping doesn't satisfy the deepest longings of the human heart. We underestimate our spiritual impoverishment. The consumer economy is putting enormous

26 Wallis, *God's Politics*, 226.

27 Ibid, 238.

pressure on all of us, fueling a never-ending and relent-
less cycle of working and buying. Affluence often helps
to mask moral and spiritual poverty.[28]

And Biblically, we can clearly say that our spiritual health is directly
related to how we treat others, especially those in need.

How much income and asset redistribution should be voluntary by
individuals versus required by the government through taxes is an open
question, one that needs both Donkey and Elephant perspectives at the
table. Instead of one party monopolizing the conversation when it comes
to those experiencing poverty, we need a healthy "idea lab" where each
party's experiences bounce off one another until solutions are found and
good news is experienced by the poor.

Advocating pro-life (immigrants/refugees)

The irony of a phrase like "pro-life" is that each party has parts of
the picture, but neither party seems to do a very good job of seeing
how all the pieces are part of the same puzzle. "The tragedy is that in
America today, one can't vote for a consistent ethic of life."[29] This is
the Democratic chapter of the book, and one of the Donkey's pro-life
emphases has been concern for the lives of immigrants and refugees.

Let's play a quick light-hearted game of word association. Dear Mr.
Elephant, what word comes to mind when you hear the word "immigration"? Answer: border security. So let's address a couple items right up
front so that hopefully the rest of this section can be considered by the
Elephants in the house. I believe that nations have a right and responsibility to defend themselves against those who mean them harm. I do
not believe that a Christian worldview has to equate to open borders.[30]

---

28 Ibid, 237.

29 Ibid, 301.

30 The Bible is filled with stories of nations, and nowhere is it implied that they can't or shouldn't
    defend themselves. Furthermore, specific land (and hence, borders) is attributed to specific nations
    in the Bible.

The Old Testament spills a lot of ink talking about national borders. And I do believe that there are those who mean us harm, and so border security is a legitimate concern. Border security and immigration need to be a both/and in public policy, not an either/or.

Jesus was a refugee! Much like refugees all over the world today, Jesus and his parents Mary and Joseph were forced to flee from Israel when Jesus was somewhere between one and two years old, because Herod sought to kill him.[31] Refugees, in the technical sense of the word, are simply people seeking refuge in some other country because their homeland has become unsafe. Given their choice, they'd rather stay where they were, but that option has been removed from them. They are wholly dependent on some other nation's hospitality in order to survive.

As we saw in the last section, Jesus equates welcoming the stranger with welcoming Himself.[32] I did a little digging on the word Jesus used for "stranger," and foreign or alien is part of the connotation. The Greek word is *xenos*, from which our English word xenophobia comes, and which is defined as fear or hatred of strangers or foreigners. Thus, it doesn't simply (or only) mean someone we don't know, but implies someone from a foreign country. In a fascinating twist on language, the same word can be translated as "host, or one who extends hospitality."[33] I find it remarkable that the very word Jesus uses for stranger takes us directly to the need for hospitality. How we treat foreigners is how we treat Jesus—according to Jesus.

While national sovereignty is a position assumed and presumably validated by the Bible, that doesn't equate to a worldview in which a person from one country is worth more than a person from another country. When patriotism bleeds over into discrimination or prejudice, it needs to be called out for what it is. The Bible does that repeatedly.

---

31 Matt. 2:13–18.

32 Matt. 25:31–46.

33 *Xenos* is translated as host or hospitality in Romans 16:23, where Paul is passing along greeting from Gaius, the "xenon." [Walter Bauer and F. Wilbur Gingrich, *A Greek-English Lexicon of the New Testament and Other Early Christian Literature*, ed. William F. Arndt and Frederick W. Danker (Chicago, IL: The University Of Chicago Press, 1979), 548.]

Welcoming the stranger (or foreigner or alien) is a major theme in the Old Testament, primarily because the Jews themselves were foreigners or strangers in Egypt and again later during the Exile. There are four Hebrew words that variously get translated as stranger, foreigner, alien, or immigrant.[34] *Gehr*, the most common, refers to a permanent resident. The Hebrew word *Gehr* occurs 87 times and is always used positively. One example: "God defends the cause of the fatherless and the widow, and loves the foreigner residing among you, giving them food and clothing. And you are to love those who are foreigners, for you yourselves were foreigners in Egypt."[35] A related word *Toshab* refers to a more temporary foreigner, often a hired worker. *Nacher*, another Hebrew word translated "stranger," literally means "not recognized" and is almost always used negatively, often synonymous with "idolater." The fourth word, *Zar*, is similar to *Nacher* and can mean "unauthorized." All of us are strangers and aliens, in a sense—the land is God's and we are merely tenants passing through.[36] Taken as a whole, "foreigners" just like everyone else are made up of those with positive character and those with negative. God expects us to welcome those in need of hospitality, but it's appropriate to sift out those who might mean us harm. "God's people were to receive refugees and immigrants with generosity. But they were not commanded to adopt and anoint the practices of neighboring kingdoms as their own."[37]

America is a nation of immigrants. With the exception of Native Americans, all the rest of us (or our ancestors) immigrated to the country. The inscription below the Statue of Liberty states in part,

> Give me your tired, your poor,
> Your huddled masses yearning to breathe free,
> The wretched refuse of your teeming shore.

---

34 Thanks to Pastor Dan Johnson for his unpublished research on this topic, from which much of this paragraph is drawn.

35 Deut. 10:18–19.

36 1 Chron. 29:14, Heb. 11:13, 1 Pet. 2:11 and many others.

37 Greer, Horst & Heisey, *Rooting for Rivals*, 183.

> Send these, the homeless, tempest-tost to me,
> I lift my lamp beside the golden door![38]

These words have encapsulated the nation's attitude toward immigrants until recently, when the topic has become much more controversial. Part of the controversy comes from the fact that approximately 11 million people living in the United States either crossed the borders illegally, or came legally on a visa but stayed beyond the date authorized.[39] So the immigration question in our country consists of two distinct sets of people: how to address those who are already here without authorization, and how to address those who wish (or need) to come.

WHEN PATRIOTISM BLEEDS OVER INTO DISCRIMINATION OR PREJUDICE, IT NEEDS TO BE CALLED OUT FOR WHAT IT IS.

The Elephant news channel seems to find a way to report every instance of a heinous crime committed by someone here illegally, while the Donkey news channel seems to overlook those stories.[40] The fact that such stories exist is certainly cause for concern. But from a sheer numbers and percentage issue, I'm willing to bet legal residents of the country commit crimes at a higher rate than those here illegally or legally through a refugee resettlement program. Some of the negative news stories about crimes committed by people in our country without legal paperwork, and the ways some politicians have *used* those news stories, seem intent on fanning xenophobia into flame. Refugee isn't an identity, it's a condition, and one that ought to call forth empathy and compassion, not disdain and fear.

---

38   Emma Lazarus, "The New Colossus," *The NYC Insider Guide*, accessed October 4, 2019, https://www.nycinsiderguide.com/statue-of-liberty-inscription.

39   Elaine Kamarck and Christine Stenglein, "How Many Undocumented Immigrants Are in the United States and Who Are They?," Brookings, November 12, 2019, https://www.brookings.edu/policy2020/votervital/how-many-undocumented-immigrants-are-in-the-united-states-and-who-are-they/.

40   I know because I make it a habit at least daily to read both *Fox News* and *CNN* websites.

Perhaps the greatest travesty is that at a time when the number of refugees globally has never been greater, America is accepting the fewest in recent memory. The U.S. Refugee Admissions Program was established in 1980, when Congress passed the Refugee Act. President Trump's announcement cutting the limit to 30,000 in 2019 represents the lowest ceiling any president has imposed on the program since its creation.[41] At the same time, the United Nations estimates there are 25,000,000 refugees globally, with another 40 million displaced within their own countries.[42] The vetting process for legal refugees is incredibly extensive, with the average wait time being a minimum of 18 months and extending into decades. Only 1% of refugees are ever resettled, and those who are don't get to choose the country they are sent to. There has never been an act of terrorism that resulted in death committed on our nation's soil by someone who entered the country through the refugee admissions program. If a person wished to come to the U.S. to do the American people harm, it's inconceivable that he/she would choose the refugee resettlement program as the pathway to get here. Probably in part because we're accepting so few refugees legally, the number of asylum seekers is exploding, with an estimated 280,000 processed in 2019 by the United States alone. Someone seeking asylum declares that intention upon crossing over the desired host country's border. As a nation of immigrants, to accept the fewest number on record at a time when the need is the greatest it's ever been is unacceptable.

A close contestant for "greatest travesty" is how families are split apart when a parent is deported,[43] as well as how the private prisons benefit financially by criminalizing those whose crime was entering the U.S. illegally.[44] The vast majority of people who have come to our country without proper documentation did so with what most of us would

---

41 "U.S. Slashes Number of Refugees to 30,000," *BBC.com*, September 18, 2018, https://www.bbc.com/news/world-us-canada-45555357.

42 Ibid.

43 Melissa Cruz, "When Immigrant Parents Are Deported, the Entire Family Suffers, Survey Shows," *Immigration Impact*, November 14, 2018, https://immigrationimpact.com/2018/11/14/immigrant-parents-deported-family-suffers/#.XhkaGUdKi70.

44 Clyde Haberman, "For Private Prisons, Detaining Immigrants Is Big Business," *The New York Times*, October 1, 2018, https://www.nytimes.com/2018/10/01/us/prisons-immigration-detention.html.

consider the best of intentions: to better provide and care for their families. Even if their lives weren't at risk such that they were forcibly displaced, it's hard to fault someone for wanting food and education. Numerous documentaries have been produced on the risks of getting to the U.S.-Mexico border, let alone crossing it; conditions would have to be quite dire for most parents to take such risks.[45] Those here without legal documentation live in the shadows, constantly in fear of being deported. As such, they are easy targets for financial and physical abuse by unprincipled individuals looking to take advantage of someone. An employer, for example, could suddenly decide to withhold an undocumented migrant worker's wages for no apparent reason, and the pressure to not report harassment or other crimes in general is even more enormous for those living here with such little protection.

The United States can do better than this. We *must* do better than this. Where there's a will there's a way, and there needs to be a will for immigration reform. A bipartisan group of Christians known as the Evangelical Immigration Table has proposed a set of principles that seem like a great starting place to me. They are calling for immigration reform that:

- Respects the God-given dignity of every person.

- Protects the unity of the immediate family.

- Respects the rule of law.

- Guarantees secure national borders.

- Ensures fairness to taxpayers.

- Establishes a path toward legal status and/or citizenship for those who qualify and who wish to become permanent residents.[46]

---

45   As one such example, a group of us in Tucson went to see *"Who is Dayani Cristal?"* together.

46   http://evangelicalimmigrationtable.com/#PRINCIPLES.

Immigration reform is essential to address some of the systemic issues. But if you're looking for a place to personally be a blessing to immigrants and refugees who are already in our country, Tucson Refugee Ministry is a tremendous resource. There you'll find background material on the refugee vetting and resettlement process, as well as a series of steps we can take to make a difference in the lives of these vulnerable people who are already our neighbors.[47] All life matters to God—from womb to tomb—regardless of which side of the border that life is lived. Refugees and immigrants need advocates from both sides of the aisle.

Promoting racial equality

For several election cycles now, various demographics have been identified and studied to see which direction they would lean when casting their ballots. Sometimes it's as specific as the soccer Moms, other times it's as broad as female voters or college-educated. What needs little studying because it's entirely predictable is the role of race in elections. In the 2018 midterm elections, black voters voted Democratic by a margin of 90%. Seventy percent of Hispanic voters voted for Democratic candidates, as did 77% of Asian voters. White voters, the largest voting bloc, were the most closely contested, voting Republican by 54%.[48] When there's such a huge difference between one party and the other based on race, social justice as it relates to race matters is obviously and tragically a partisan issue.

What does Jesus have to say about racial issues? As discussed previously[49], Samaritans were the race that the Jewish majority culture was most likely to be prejudiced against, and so Jesus made a point of highlighting Samaritans positively in His stories, and going out of His way to treat them with respect and dignity. In His final commission, He commands His followers to take the good news to the entire world as

---

47 TucsonRefugeeMinistry.com.

48 Alec Tyson, "The 2018 Midterm Vote: Divisions by Race, Gender, Education," Pew Research Center, November 8, 2018, https://www.pewresearch.org/fact-tank/2018/11/08/the-2018-midterm-vote-divisions-by-race-gender-education/.

49 Pages 103–104.

opposed to keeping it only to themselves.[50] Many translations choose the word "nations" when describing Jesus' "Great Commission," but the Greek word translated "nation" is *ethnos*, and more literally means all people groups. Nothing in the gospel accounts of Jesus endorses racial inequality.

Some have argued that the Bible supports slavery, citing various passages where slavery is mentioned and nothing is said about abolishing the institution. The Bible is a library of 66 books, written by about 40 human authors over a span of 1500 years. Unlike some other religions, Christianity never claims that its Scriptures were penned without influence from human culture or human authors. Some of the Bible is simply descriptive, describing what's taking place, as opposed to prescriptive, prescribing what ought to be taking place. The difference between descriptive and prescriptive literature is essential to properly interpreting the Bible. Furthermore, when the Bible speaks with more than one voice on a topic, as it often does, the interpretive task is to determine which passage is more time-bound and which is more universal. The following statements sound universal to me: "God created man in His own image, in the image of God He created him; male and female He created them."[51] "So in Christ Jesus you are all children of God through faith…There is neither Jew nor Gentile, neither slave nor free, nor is there male and female, for you are all one in Christ Jesus."[52] "Here there is no Greek or Jew…barbarian, Scythian, slave or free, but Christ is all, and is in all."[53] Much of the section on caring for those experiencing poverty applies here, too, in the sense that the Bible consistently roots for the underdog, seeking justice for those who have been maligned.

How serious is our race problem in America? Some refer to racism as America's original sin, citing both our historical treatment of Native Americans as well as the fact that while the Declaration of Independence includes the statement, "All men are created equal," many of those very

---

50   Matt. 28:18–20.

51   Gen. 1:27.

52   Gal. 3:26–28.

53   Col. 3:11.

same authors owned slaves. "America's original sin has affected most everything about our nation's life ever since. Slavery and the subsequent discrimination against black people in America is of such a magnitude of injustice that one would think national repentance and reparations would be called for."[54] While a national apology doesn't change the past, from a Christian standpoint it's hard to imagine healing and forgiveness without some acknowledgment of the grievance. Reparations can be a thornier issue, but mostly because of the astronomical cost when the crime committed is on such a national scale. Reparations are everyday occurrences in lawsuits, so the objection to the topic is one of scale and proportion, not concept.

WHEN WE TALKED ABOUT RACISM WE WEREN'T EVEN TALKING ABOUT THE SAME THING.

Formal, official apologies for a variety of national atrocities have come in recent decades, along with reparations in some cases. In 1946 Congress created the Indian Claims Commission after Native Americans had enlisted in disproportionately high numbers to serve in the U.S. military during World War II. $1.3 billion in reparations was authorized, but a formal apology didn't happen until 2009. The Civil Liberties Act of 1988 included an apology and reparations for American citizens of Japanese descent who were detained during World War II. California Congressman Norman Mineta said, "The country made a mistake, and admitted it was wrong. It offered an apology and a redress payment. To me, the beauty and strength of this country is that it is able to admit wrong and issue redress."[55] The U.S. in 1993 apologized for its treatment of Native Hawaiians. The country officially apologized for slavery and segregation in 2009, but reparations have never been offered, although the topic has come up in Democratic primaries in the 2020 election.

---

54   Wallis, *God's Politics*, 308.

55   Erin Blakemore, "The Thorny History of Reparations in the United States," *History*, last modified August 29, 2019, https://www.history.com/news/reparations-slavery-native-americans-japanese-internment.

It's hard to decide which of our nation's racial injustices is the most heinous, but in the running is the Tuskegee Experiment begun in 1932, where 600 black men signed up for what they were told was free health care, when in fact they were unknowingly injected with syphilis and were monitored to see how the disease would eventually kill them, with autopsies as the only medical "intervention." The Experiment continued until 1972 when the story was first publicly reported and the outrage forced it to stop. In 1973 those who were still alive were paid $10 million each in an out of court settlement, and a public apology was finally issued in 1997. A similar apology was issued in 2010 for a parallel medical atrocity perpetrated by the U.S. government, this time in Guatemala. 700 prisoners, soldiers and mental patients were intentionally infected with syphilis between 1946 and 1948 without their knowledge or consent.[56]

Reactions to the above paragraphs probably vary widely. Some likely stopped reading, perhaps because it's too painful to consider. Some, especially in younger generations, view the country with shame instead of pride. Others hold to a Manifest Destiny position,[57] either consciously or subconsciously, and perhaps just filter out inconvenient realities from our nation's history. Extreme pride and extreme shame wouldn't be as prominent if the middle ground were occupied more frequently. It certainly ought to be an option to celebrate the country's positive attributes, of which there are many, while acknowledging its faults and correcting them where possible.

Even when apologies and reparations have taken place, the impact on those involved lasts for generations. The statistics shared in the section on caring for those experiencing poverty indicate a very strong racial correlation to the poverty rates. It's well documented that incarceration rates and severity of punishments are heavily influenced by the race of the (alleged) perpetrators. In 2017, Whites made up 64%

---

56   Elizabeth Nix, "Tuskegee Experiment: The Infamous Syphilis Study," *History*, last modified July 29, 2019, https://www.history.com/news/the-infamous-40-year-tuskegee-study.

57   The 19th-century doctrine or belief that the expansion of the U.S. throughout the American continents was both justified and inevitable. In a broader sense, the belief puts the country in a special or privileged position which makes it easier to avoid taking responsibility for sins.

of the U.S. population but only 30% of the prison population; Blacks were 12% of the general population and 33% of the prison population; Hispanics were 16% and 23% respectively. Fortunately, the gaps have shrunk some in the last ten years.[58] Median net worth of White families in 2016 was 4.6 times that of Black families for those in the lower income brackets, and 4.0 times that of Black families for those in middle income brackets. For White to Hispanic families, the ratios were 2.9 and 3.4 respectively.[59] Inequal access to quality education contributes to both the incarceration and net worth statistics.

THE TRAGEDY OF RACIAL SEPARATION ISN'T JUST THE INJUSTICES THAT REMAIN UNTOUCHED, BUT ALSO THE BLESSINGS THAT AREN'T EXPERIENCED.

Part of the challenge of talking about racial inequality and racism is that our worldviews vary dramatically by culture. White, European culture views life individualistically, while both Black and Hispanic cultures view life more collectively. I discovered in our monthly meetings of African American and Anglo pastors that when we talked about racism we weren't even talking about the same thing. My starting point was individual—does this individual person view other races as inferior to his/her own? But their starting point was collective—are there systems in place that favor one race over another? I remember a meeting where an African American pastor asked the question, "How many of you have given your son 'the talk'?" I thought at first he was referring to sex, but in fact he was referring to how to act if you're stopped by a police officer. Every African American in the group had had

58   John Gramlich, "The Gap Between the Number of Blacks and Whites in Prison Is Shrinking," Pew Research Center, April 30, 2019, https://www.pewresearch.org/fact-tank/2019/04/30/shrinking-gap-between-number-of-blacks-and-whites-in-prison/.

59   Rakesh Kochhar and Anthony Cilluffo, "How Wealth Inequality Has Changed in the U.S. Since the Great Recession, by Race, Ethnicity and Income," Pew Research Center, November 1, 2017, https://www.pewresearch.org/fact-tank/2017/11/01/how-wealth-inequality-has-changed-in-the-u-s-since-the-great-recession-by-race-ethnicity-and-income/.

that conversation with their sons, and it never once crossed my mind to talk to my sons about how to act if they were pulled over by the police. The reason for the difference, if you're like me a few years ago and have never considered the question, is that whether or not a person is given the benefit of the doubt has a huge correlation to their race. That isn't only true of the police; it's true of the general public walking down the street. Systemic issues go far beyond individuals who are racist. Anti-Semites and Klansmen, for example, exist and certainly are a problem, but they aren't the whole problem.

A friend of mine, Grady Scott, linked the following post on Facebook on August 21, 2019, from Shaka Senghor:

> Last Friday night I was standing outside of a barbershop in Cincinnati, OH, with a small group of mostly black men, when this officer walked over to a group of us. He looked around curiously and said "I don't see a car blocking an intersection" while shaking his head. I asked him what was he talking about. He said someone called and reported that we had a car blocking the intersection. He paused for a minute and shook his head again. In that moment we both nodded and acknowledged what had just happened. Someone basically saw our group and made a false report. I asked him how long he had been on the job and he said 10 months. He asked what we were doing at the barbershop and so I told him about the barbershop challenge Men of Courage and Ford Fund had sponsored. I asked if he wanted to come inside. He said he wanted to, but didn't want to spoil the fun with his presence. Again, we both nodded and acknowledged the reality of distrust between the community and police officers. I offered to take him inside so he could meet the owners and establish a relationship. I told him that someone has to take the first step to healing these relationships. He said he wanted to, but was unsure of what the reaction would be. I told him it would be cool and

that Jerome Bettis[60] and a host of other amazing people were inside. He lit up like a lightbulb and said "No way The Bus is in there," with a kid-like smile. I said hold on, I'll grab him and have him come out. Jerome Bettis came out and the officer stood there with his mouth agape before saying, "If my dad was still alive he would be so excited, because you were his favorite player." We all stopped and sat in the moment before they went on to take a selfie together. It was one of those moments that reminded me of our humanness, our frailties and our similarities. In that moment we were all just men navigating the world without the mask we are taught and trained to wear. I could have taken my offense to the call-out on the officer and accused him of being a racist cop. He could have believed the caller and acted based on stereotypes about black men in groups. But we chose to just see each other and talk like humans. It's ultimately a decision we can all make. When he lit up like a kid at seeing his dad's sports hero, I saw a little boy and the uniform no longer mattered. We can collectively choose to see beyond the uniforms we all wear. It's not easy and there is a lot of work to be done, but if we can at least start seeing each other, I believe things will get better. #writingmywrongs[61]

Race isn't our identity—our identity supersedes our race. But neither is race of no consequence. Our racial and cultural heritage are part of our gifting. Contrary to popular opinion, I don't believe the goal is to become "colorblind." The goal is to see the strengths that each color and culture bring to society as a whole, as well as to every workplace, congregation, and group of friends. The tragedy of racial separation, let alone racial inequality, isn't just the injustices that remain untouched,

---

60 Very famous NFL star, who played for the Rams and the Steelers, in case you didn't know. Nicknamed The Bus.

61 Shaka Senghor (@OfficialShakaSenghor), "Police officer with small group of mostly black men," Facebook photo, August 21, 2019, https://www.facebook.com/photo.php?fbid=2618045958248154.

but also the blessings that aren't experienced. I've been so blessed by the cross-cultural experiences of the last nine years that I can't wait to keep growing. Three of the books on my reading list are educational just from their titles, and all three were recommended by trusted sources who are moving toward greater racial interaction and equality.

- *Beyond Color Blind: Redeeming our Ethnic Journey,* by Sarah Shin

- *Multiethnic Conversations: An Eight-Week Journey Toward Unity in Your Church,* by Mark Deymaz and Oneya Fennel Okuwobi

- *Driven by Difference: How Great Companies Fuel Innovation Through Diversity,* by David Livermore

America still has a race problem, not only because of some horrific moments in history, and not simply because there are some individuals who view other ethnicities as inferior. Our race problem is systemic, as evidenced by inequal access to quality education, disparate incarceration rates and sentencing severity, and the assumptions made about complete strangers based mostly on race.

Racial equality must be a priority for all of us, not just half the country. We will likely end up with a variety of recommendations, some of which may remain partisan, but the conversation itself can't be the territory of only one party. When all of us decide that Rev. Dr. Martin Luther King Jr's "dream" is long overdue, progress will speed up significantly.

In the next chapter we'll begin to tackle some big picture yet practical solutions for the country, looking to see much more specifically how peace talks in the middle of a Donkey Elephant war.

PART III
NEW GROUND

CHAPTER EIGHT

GUIDANCE FOR
THE COUNTRY

*"I'm asking you to join me in rejecting the partisan loyalties
and rhetoric that divide and dehumanize us."*
—JUSTIN AMASH[1]

This should be obvious, but just in case, I believe everything in the last two chapters—all six topics—are important to Jesus. If they're important to Jesus, it's not only reasonable but it should be expected that they're important to His followers, too.

WHY I COVERED WHAT I DID
I picked three topics each that strike me as much more significant to one side of the political divide than the other (or where the other side might have an opposite point of view). When I hear Republicans get passionate, or when I look at Republican-favored news channels, I hear

---

1   Independent Michigan Rep. Justin Amash.

a lot about protecting religious liberty, advocating pro-life (meaning the unborn), and promoting marriage. When I hear Democrats get passionate, or when I look at Democrat-favored news channels, I hear a lot about caring for those experiencing poverty, advocating pro-life (meaning the immigrants and refugees), and promoting racial equality. When I read the Bible, I see all six.

It's a bit brash to say, "Here's what Jesus says" about contemporary issues, but I decided to jump in anyway. Most of the times when I've cringed at people playing the "Jesus" card it's been because they made Jesus sound like the talking points of their political party. There's a huge difference between asking Jesus to bless *my* plans or ideas and asking Jesus to help me align my plans and ideas with *His*. As an old quip says, "If Jesus is your co-pilot, switch seats." As we saw in Chapter 2, none of us walks through life bias-free. Jesus is bigger than the gap between the two political parties, and I've been abundantly blessed by expanding my circle of friends to include both Donkeys and Elephants.

PAINTING A BALANCED PICTURE OF JESUS, WHO IS CONCERNED ABOUT BOTH DONKEY AND ELEPHANT ISSUES, IS A HIGHER GOAL OF MINE THAN SAYING EVERYTHING THAT COULD BE SAID.

My hope remains that I am treating the Biblical material fairly, stating the issues clearly and accurately, and de-partisaning Jesus thoroughly. And I'm sure that as the dialogue continues, I'll be better-equipped the next time.

You might have a different list than what was offered in either Chapter 6 or Chapter 7. In fact, I'd bet on it. You might be Republican and think I should have talked about gun rights. You might be Democrat and think I should have talked about gun control. Both sides have worked plenty on their talking points, so if that's all you're looking for, you don't need this book to help you.

Both parties are passionate about taxes and tend to have strong opinions. One of the reasons the economy and social welfare is a debatable topic is that Christ-followers used to do much of the charitable work that is now the responsibility of the government. In years past, social welfare was the work of the Church, not the government. During some election cycles, it seems to me that the talking points are virtually identical: "Vote for our mammal and help the middle class." In some cases, the goals are the same but the strategies are different. Jesus calls us to follow in his footsteps, and if we do, that will mean good news for those experiencing poverty. Quoting Forrest Gump, "that's all I have to say about that." My hope is that this entire book becomes more of a "first word" than a "last word," anyway.

One final comment on the last two chapters: The topic I had the hardest time leaving out was the typically Democrat-favored issue of caring for the environment. The Bible instructs us to be good stewards of God's creation, and it's beyond unfortunate that one party seems to have a corner on that issue. It's also wrong that there's such a generational divide on the issue of the environment. My children worry if there will even be a world in which to raise their children. My only reason for leaving the topic out was my inability to find a concern of equal importance that would keep the numbers even in Chapter 6 and 7. Painting a balanced picture of Jesus, who is concerned about both Donkey and Elephant issues, is a higher goal of mine than saying everything that could be said.

Let's tie everything together and look at some specific solutions.

"If I cannot do great things, I can do small things in a great way."[2]

---

2   Often attributed to Rev. Dr. Martin Luther King Jr, particularly appropriate as I'm writing this on the day set aside to honor him. However, it appears that the statement was written earlier by Napoleon Hill, *The Law of Success in Sixteen Lessons*, 1928, p. 113.

Do you believe it? A majority of the country apparently doesn't.[3]

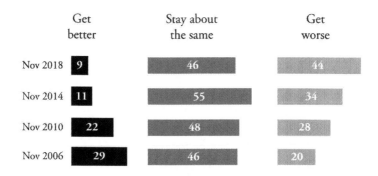

FIGURE 8.1 *More Americans expect partisan relations to get worse than did so after three prior midterms.* Percentage who say relations between Republicans and Democrats in Washington will_____ in the coming year. (Pew Research Center. 2018 and 2014 surveys conducted online on the American Trends Panel; 2010 and 2006 polls conducted via telephone. No answer not shown. Source: Survey of US adults conducted Nov. 7–13, 2018.)

The number expecting things to stay the same has . . . stayed the same. But every single election year since 2006 has made our Donkey Elephant war worse. Jonathan Haidt writes,

> There seems to be no alternative to a political process in which parties compete to win votes and money. That competition always involves trickery and demagoguery, as politicians play fast and loose with the truth, using their inner press secretaries to portray themselves in the best possible light and their opponents as fools who would lead the country to ruin. And yet, does it have to be *this* nasty? A lot of Americans have noticed things getting worse. The country now seems polarized and embattled to the point of dysfunction.[4]

---

3   Urban, Chapter 10, quoting Pew Research Center. 2018 and 2014 surveys conducted online on the American Trends Panel; 2010 and 2006 polls conducted via telephone.

4   Haidt, *Righteous Mind*, 319.

If not us, then who? If we don't change the trajectory, who's going to? If not now, when? How much worse does it have to get, when studies already say we're more divided than any time since the Civil War?

Let's do a quick review at how we got into this mess, so that we can discover some ways out of it.

Because of its meteoric growth, social media has changed the dynamics of communication. We can easily search out and surround ourselves with those who believe and talk the same way we do. And we can fire off snappy retorts to the other side with little caution and even less awareness of any damage. Making matters worse, foreign nations have decided that dividing the country and fanning the flames weakens us as a nation, so this isn't even just our own internal battle.

Political conversations light up the "fight or flight" part of the brain, turning would-be Scientists into Attorneys and Zealots who no longer seek the truth but rather merely seek confirmation of what they already believe.[5] Add in our Western culture's tendency to turn both/ands into either/ors, and it's readily apparent how easy it is for politics to turn into tribal warfare. Once we forget our primary and higher identity and instead settle for secondary identification with a political party, the Donkey Elephant war is on, possibly being waged in our own living rooms as it was in mine. How serious is the war? "This shift to a more righteous and tribal mentality was bad enough in the 1990's. America's hyperpartisanship is now a threat to the world."[6] That quote was from a few years ago; this one is from 2020:

> American politics is the biggest threat facing the world in 2020 and the looming presidential election will stress the country's institutions, influence economic and foreign policy and further divide an already polarized electorate, with potentially huge consequences for the climate,

---

5   In case you forgot this part, I'm referring to Tim Urban's brilliant analysis of the four rungs of a thinking ladder: Scientist, Sports Fan, Attorney, and Zealot. See page 43. for more explanation.

6   Haidt, *Righteous Mind*, 321.

business and investors. That's the view of experts at consultancies Eurasia Group and Control Risks.[7]

That was of course before the global pandemic of COVID-19 engulfed the planet. And we've yet to see if partisanship will be the cause of unnecessary suffering physically and financially due to the inability to address the pandemic together in a healthy bipartisan, "what's-good-for-everyone" approach.

Brief guidance at the ballot box

The ballot box might be the simplest place to start, so let's look at a few possibilities rapid fire before diving deeper.

- *Do we need more Christians in political office?* Maybe. Electing people who share your values is preferable to electing people who contradict your values. But since not all Christians have a Biblical worldview,[8] not all who claim the title Christian will share your values anyway, no matter what values they might be.

- *Do we need more Christians voting?* Probably. The fact that a majority of Christians opt out of the elections won't help Jesus' priorities become the country's priorities. If we sit it out, we have no right to complain.

- *Do we need more Christians voting for solutions instead of political parties?* Definitely. It's my opinion that the Donkey and Elephant brass think they own us, probably because they traditionally *have* owned us. Our identity has been too tied to a political party. Voting for solutions instead of merely red or blue straight down the line sounds good in principle, but is much harder to pull off in actuality. The whole battle isn't won or lost at the ballot box, however. We can *live* a both/and life even when it's

---

7   Charles Riley, "What Do Experts See as the Biggest Risk to the World in 2020? American Politics," *CNN*, January 15, 2020, https://www.cnn.com/2020/01/15/business/global-risks-2020-davos/index.html.

8   Discussed in Chapter 3.

hard to *vote* for one. For instance, Abby Johnson is most well known as a former director of a Planned Parenthood abortion clinic, who one day walked across the parking lot and joined the other side.[9] Her pro-life (unborn) advocacy would seem to plant her firmly with the Elephant tribe, yet on July 13, 2019, her Facebook page said this:

> I am headed to the Mexican border with some of my awesome friends to deliver #bottles2theborder! *And Then There Were None - Prolife Outreach*[10] and *New Wave Feminists*[11] have partnered together to help the immigrants at the border who desperately need us to help meet some of their basic needs.[12]

- *The Donkey and Elephant machines might be too big to stop. Do we need a third party that's Christian?* Probably not. The Church has been at its worst when it has power. Power and following Jesus are like oil and water. I'm sure you won't all agree with that, but I believe Church history is on my side in this one. I see no reason to try it again given how well it's worked (NOT) in the past. Let me say it again: historically, the Church has been at its worst when it has power, especially political power.[13]

- *Do we need more citizens to separate from their Donkey and Elephant parties and become independent?* Maybe. For me, becoming independent was an important outward manifestation of an inward truth, that I no longer gave primary allegiance to one side of the political war. It's helped me vote more for solutions than simply taking the easy way out and looking for my party affiliation. Interestingly enough, Tim Urban who I've read and

---

9   Abby Johnson, *Unplanned*, 2019. Her story is told both in a book as well as a movie by the same name.

10   https://www.facebook.com/ATTWNOutreach/.

11   https://www.facebook.com/NewWaveFeminists/.

12   Abby Johnson (@abbyjohnsonprolife), "On July 13, I am headed to the Mexican border," Facebook post, July 3, 2019, https://www.facebook.com/abbyjohnsonprolife/posts/2551258031550921/.

13   Two examples: Constantine arguably undid much of first century Christianity, and of course, the Crusades.

quoted liberally (pun intended) came to a similar conclusion from an opposite starting point.

> Whatever the cause of my attachment to the Democratic Party,[14] the Republicans of the 2000s...weren't helping the situation. As I tried to rid myself of the notion that the Democrats were "my people," the Republicans...would continually make it crystal clear that they were certainly not my people. Well good news! Over the past decade, the Left finally did it. They regressed so far that they became as "not my people" as the Republicans. They actually went insane enough to free me from my tribal handcuffs. I spent a lot of years saying I was "an Independent" while not truly believing it. Today, I can say it with a straight face. It's amazing how much clearer your vision gets when you really— actually—separate your identity from a tribe. I can see reality better now.[15]

- *Do we need more Christians in public service who are willing to step out of an old wineskin[16] (political party) and run (and vote) as Independents?* This one intrigues me. If Independents were free to support solutions instead of being bound to their parties, and if they had significant support from those who have an affinity for Jesus, including financial support, the Donkey Elephant war could be rendered irrelevant. Those are some gargantuan "ifs", but I'd sure love to give it a try.

---

14 At this point in his own political evolution, he claimed to be independent but kept defaulting to the party of his upbringing, Democrat.

15 Tim Urban, "Political Disney World," Chapter 9, The Story of Us, published December 15, 2019, https://waitbutwhy.com/2019/12/political-disney-world.html.

16 Reference to Luke 5:36–38 (and elsewhere), where Jesus talks about new wine needing to be poured into new wineskins, because the expansion would burst older more brittle wineskins. The parable commonly is taken to mean that there are times when we need not only new content but new methods.

That last idea, more candidates who understand their loyalty to something higher than their political party, has often been ridiculed as unrealistic given the incredible money generated by the Donkey Elephant machinery. It would be a massive uphill battle to finance an election outside the traditional Republican and Democratic alliances. And since the media has shifted from broadcasting to narrowcasting, it's harder still for Independents to get their name out in front of the public. Traditional media who are aligned right or left won't be friendly to Independents. For sure, if it was an easy thing to do, we'd see more candidates doing it. But perhaps there's hope! Maybe you saw this news story from Independence Day, 2019:

> July 4, 2019 Michigan Republican Justin Amash resigned his membership in the U.S. House Republican Party Conference. Excerpts from his accompanying letter: "The parties value winning for its own sake, and at whatever cost. Instead of acting as an independent branch of government and serving as a check on the executive branch, congressional leaders of both parties expect the House and Senate to act in obedience or opposition to the president and their colleagues on a partisan basis.... With little genuine debate on policy happening in Congress, party leaders distract and divide the public by exploiting wedge issues and waging pointless messaging wars. These strategies fuel mistrust and anger, leading millions of people to take to social media to express contempt for their political opponents, with the media magnifying the most extreme voices. This all serves to magnify the us-vs-them, party-first mindset of government officials.... Preserving liberty means telling the Republican Party and the Democratic Party that we'll no longer let them play their partisan game at our expense. Today, I am declaring my independence and leaving the Republican Party. No matter your circumstance, I'm asking you to join me in rejecting the

partisan loyalties and rhetoric that divide and dehumanize us.[17]

One person making such a move is unlikely to cause much more than a temporary ripple. Imagine if even five percent of Congress were to become Independent or Third Party?[18] The parties are so deadlocked that a five percent block of people whose priority was solutions untethered by party politics would change the landscape dramatically. Of course, now that Amash has decided to run for President as a Libertarian, it's impossible to predict as of this writing (early May, 2020) how big the ripple will get. We certainly have a new wrinkle to the Donkey Elephant war.

The opening quote about doing small things in a great way is debatably attributed to Rev. Dr. Martin Luther King Jr. Undeniably attributed to him is this: "In the end, we will remember not the words of our enemies but the silence of our friends."[19] I hope Rep. Amash's friends are not cowering in silence for fear of retribution from the lead Donkeys and Elephants. Similarly, Irish statesman and philosopher Edmond Burke is credited with saying,

"DARKNESS CAN'T DRIVE OUT DARKNESS; ONLY LIGHT CAN DO THAT."

"The only thing necessary for the triumph of evil is that good men should do nothing."[20] If we don't like the war we're in the middle of, let's change it. Those of us who are attracted to Jesus represent 70% of the country. It's time to stand up and be counted!

---

17   Justin Amash (@justinamash), "Today I sent the attached letter to Republican leaders," Twitter post, July 8, 2019, https://twitter.com/justinamash/status/1148339804272300032.

18   That would mean 5 U.S. Senators and 22 from the House of Representatives.

19   Martin Luther King, Jr., *The Trumpet of Conscience* (Boston, MA: Beacon Press, 1967), 96.

20   Though Burke, in the late 1700's, is often attributed with the quote, the earliest known citation in anything close to this form is from Rev. Charles Frederic Aked in 1920. [Last modified May 9, 2012, https://quoteinvestigator.com/2010/12/04/good-men-do/.]

Bad Strategy

The first step to being part of the solution is to stop being part of the problem. Last November (2019) my wife was driving around town and saw a pair of bumper stickers on the same car that grabbed her attention. The first said, "In God we trust." The second said, "Annoy a liberal: work, succeed, be happy." I imagine the car's owner is rather proud of his/her religiosity and cleverness. But that pair of messages is a classic example of being part of the problem. Presumably, someone who trusts in God would like to attract others to place their trust in God as well. That ain't gonna do it, either on the faith side or the politics side. In my daily time with God I was reading a sidebar about the family of Herods[21] in the Bible and came across this: "Religion was important only as an aspect of politics."[22] It's the identity issue all over again, and identity in Christ needs to be the big umbrella with politics the subset, informed by our identity in Christ. Herod seemed to reverse that. And this may be a jump, but I have to wonder if bumper sticker guy/gal isn't a current application of the Herod problem.

Consider what terrible strategy it is to demonize the opposition. We're certainly not going to win someone over who's currently on the other side, politically or spiritually. As Dr. King is particularly famous for saying, "Darkness can't drive out darkness; only light can do that. Hate can't drive out hate; only love can do that."[23] Love and respect will gain a far greater audience than ridicule. The voice of peace is preferable to the din of war.

What about those in the middle, the "independents" whether officially or just philosophically? I would wager that a majority of them landed there out of their disdain for partisanship, so additional partisanship sounds patently unwise. Biblically speaking, our "enemy" is never other

---

21 Herod the Great was on the throne when Jesus was born; son Herod Antipas was involved in Jesus' trial; grandson Herod Agrippa the First persecuted Jesus' followers after the resurrection and killed one of them, James; and Herod Agrippa the Second was one of the Apostle Paul's judges.

22 *Life Application Study Bible*, Herod Agrippa 1 sidebar.

23 Martin Luther King Jr., *Strength to Love* (Minneapolis, MN: Fortress Press, 1963), 168. Also found in a 1957 sermon of his.

people, but rather the spiritual forces that seek to divide and conquer.[24] And just in case there's someone we're thinking of who's so sold out to the dark side that we might at least consider their actions evil and therefore see them as an enemy, how did Jesus say we're supposed to treat our enemies? Love them and pray for them.[25] So it's not only bad political strategy, but unbiblical as well. Of course, part of the problem is that social media (and old school social media—bumper stickers) aren't usually aiming at people whose names we know, but rather the faceless straw man we paint as an idiot so we can eventually destroy him.

"PUT THE BEST POSSIBLE CONSTRUCTION ON YOUR NEIGHBOR'S WORDS OR ACTIONS."

The eighth commandment[26] is "You shall not bear false witness against your neighbor."[27] In politics it seems like bearing false witness against our neighbor is standard operating procedure. Martin Luther in his *Small Catechism* explains the eighth commandment as an instruction for us to put the best possible construction on our neighbor's words or actions.[28] When have the Donkeys and Elephants ever done that when talking about the other one? Answer: not in my lifetime. If we're going to wait for the political parties to heed the guidance of the eighth commandment, we're likely going to wait indefinitely. But we don't have to wait for someone else—we can decide both to *stop* painting the other side as negatively as possible and *start* looking for positive motives behind even the policies with which we have the most trouble. 2016 Presidential candidate John Kasich writes, "Societal change flows from the bottom up, and not from the top down, and it's

---

24   Eph. 6:12.

25   Matt. 5:43–47.

26   Seventh commandment depending on whether 1 & 2 are listed as one, or 9 & 10 are listed as one. Sorry for the confusion!

27   Ex. 20:16 (NRSV).

28   Martin Luther, *The Small Catechism* (The Book of Concord), accessed June 29, 2019, http://bookofconcord.org/smallcatechism.php#tencommandments.

almost always driven by the passion and purpose of selfless individuals who push for a way to make these changes happen."[29] He continues, "I'm troubled at how so many of us seem to hold fast to our narrow points of view, without making room in our thinking for different perspectives."[30] Regardless of your opinion of Kasich, I hope we can agree with his sentiments expressed here.

I wrote earlier how particularly passionate I am about protecting the life of the unborn. It was only in the writing of this book that I came to realize the degree to which I'd demonized the other side of the abortion issue. Do I really believe that all pro-choicers wake up in the morning hoping they can kill babies? No, of course not. I suspect the vast majority arrived at their position out of a loving concern for women with unexpected pregnancies. That's a praiseworthy desire, even if I strongly disagree with the conclusion that taking the life of the baby is the best or only way to care for the mother. Demonizing and dehumanizing the other perspective is both Biblically wrong and politically short-sighted.

My hope and prayer as you read through the positions in the last two chapters held by *the other side* is that you began to recognize the validity of the concerns, possibly for the first time. Let's put Luther's advice to the test with some of the specific policies addressed in Chapters 6 and 7.

- *Do most Republicans wake up hoping they can shove their beliefs down your throat?* Unlikely. They just want the freedom to express their faith in the "marketplace of ideas"[31] on level footing with everyone else. All people of faith would want that, I would presume. That's what's behind the call for religious liberty. And as a reminder, all people are people of faith in something. On the flip side, *are most Democrats all about censorship?* Unlikely.

---

29 John Kasich, *It's Up to Us: Ten Little Ways We Can Bring About Big Change* (Toronto, Ontario: Hanover Square Press, 2019), 18.

30 Ibid, 35.

31 Credit goes to Tim Urban for his brilliant use of this term in his "The Story of Us" series.

- *Do most Democrats hate America and hate Anglos?* Of course not. As every parent knows, pointing out things that are wrong is an act of love, not hate. *Do most Republicans hate all non-whites?* Again, ridiculous. Equal opportunity for all people regardless of skin color is a godly perspective. All life matters to God. Affirmative action can be debated—for instance, is there a point at which it's no longer necessary to truly create equal opportunity, and doing so instead becomes reverse discrimination? How would we know if we'd arrived at that point? But those arguing for or against are certainly not all racist individuals.

- *Do most Republicans hate immigrants and refugees?* Of course not. National security and caring for those around the world in dire situations is a both/and, not an either/or, and so the concern for safety and respect for a nation's laws is completely legitimate. It's simply bad strategy to play the "race card" indiscriminately, especially when racial intolerance is still a present reality that needs to be confronted head on. We damage our ability to fight the real problem when we label everything as racism.

- *Do most Democrats hate rich people?* Of course not. Some Democrats *are* experiencing wealth! They just want to be sure that when the tide rises, it brings all the ships with it, not just the yachts, as Jim Wallis said.[32] *Do most Republicans hate poor people?* Of course not. Some Republicans *are* experiencing poverty. When/if they're advocating tax breaks for the business owners and more well-off, it's most likely out of the belief that that's the best way to see the economic tide rise for everyone. Jesus calls all of us to care for those experiencing poverty. I believe we'd arrive at many more common-sense solutions if we saw those on the other side of the debate as our teammates instead of our opposition. For instance, there's broad consensus on both sides that a hand up is better than a handout, that helping someone achieve financial self-sufficiency is better than

---

32   Wallis, *God's Politics*, 236–7.

a lifetime (or more) of dependency. If we saw the other side as an ally whose life experience leads them to some perspectives we probably lack, we'd have a lot more success working together for solutions that benefit all. The Donkeys will likely bring a systemic approach, and the Elephants more of an individual approach, and guess what? The answer is a both/and.

- *Do most Republicans hate gays?* The ones I know don't. There's a logical fallacy at work that says that if you say something is wrong, you must hate the person who you see as doing the "wrong" thing. Do parents hate their own kids when they correct them? Of course not. Parents who do nothing to teach their children about morals would be widely and correctly viewed as negligent. Connect the dots here with me: 1) if there is a God, He's smarter than I am by definition; 2) the God Christians worship desires to communicate with people made in His image; 3) humbly desiring to stand under the written Word of God usually leads to a belief that God designed sexuality for lifelong marriage between a man and a woman; 4) Jesus showed what it looks like to uphold truth and at the same time treat people with grace. A critique that someone isn't treating others with grace is a fair critique; what isn't fair is to call a proclamation of truth that you happen to disagree with "hate speech." And flipping it around, the motivation for the vast majority of those advocating LGBTQ+ rights isn't to abolish marriage between a man and woman, but a civil rights concern for people who've been oppressed. This could be a book all of its own, and I recognize the risk I'm taking in raising it at all when the focus of the book doesn't allow me to fully explore the topic. My point in this context is merely that demonizing the other perspective is not only unbiblical, but unwise and thoroughly unhelpful.

Quoting again from one of my new friends[33] from the other side of the tracks, Tim Urban says, "There's a term we need to start using:

---

33   We've never met or conversed. I just find his analyses incredibly insightful, even though he uses language for shock value at times, that I think unnecessarily alienates people he could otherwise attract.

political bigotry." He goes on to note that we typically haven't viewed political intolerance as negatively as, say, racial intolerance, probably because we see politics as a field of ideas rather than a group of people. But isn't that the very definition of dehumanizing—forgetting that there are actual people being referenced who hold the political views we're mocking? It's a short step from mocking ideas to mocking the people who hold them, as 2019 rhetoric has shown us all too frequently. A study was done showing scientifically that political intolerance is worse than any other kind in terms of its severity, and equally pronounced on both the right and the left.[34]

Urban shares personally why he's particularly concerned about our level of political bigotry.

Here are four reasons this scares me:

1. We're losing our ability to gain knowledge.

2. We're losing our ability to think together.

3. We're losing our ability to cooperate. A polarized country that isn't capable of building broad coalitions can't take forward steps—it can only self-inflict.

4. We're doing that thing that people do before really, really awful things happen. Disgust should scare you as much as it scares me. If our species were a person, it would have a mix of beautiful and unadmirable qualities—but its darkest quality would be the ability to dehumanize.[35]

---

34   Christine Reyna, "The Ideological-Conflict Hypothesis," *Current Directions in Psychological Science* 23, no. 1 (February 2014), 27–34, https://www.researchgate.net/publication/256050159_ The_Ideological-Conflict_Hypothesis.

35   Urban, Chapter 10.

Another new friend, Jonathan Haidt, concludes something similar. "We all get sucked into tribal moral communities. . . . We think the other side is blind to truth, reason, science, and common sense, but in fact everyone goes blind when talking about their sacred objects."[36] We end up in "ideological teams that fight each other as though the fate of the world depended on our side winning each battle. It blinds us to the fact that each team is composed of good people who have something important to say."[37]

Guidance for the long haul

I hinted toward the beginning of the book that I found myself surprisingly encouraged in reading Tim Urban and Jonathan Haidt, despite the fact that I can't really imagine people whose backgrounds, interests, areas of expertise, and perspectives differ more from mine. Haidt concludes his book with a couple of comments I found noteworthy:

> If you can have at least one friendly interaction with a member of the "other" group, you'll find it far easier to listen to what they're saying, and maybe even see a controversial issue in a new light.[38] . . . We all have the capacity to transcend self-interest and become simply a part of a whole. It's not just a capacity; it's the portal to many of life's most cherished experiences.[39]

I know exactly what he's talking about and experience it regularly.

Urban references a fascinating report called "The Hidden Tribes of America"[40]—a year-long study that collected the views of over 8000 Americans—which found that two-thirds of Americans fall into what they call the "Exhausted Majority." This large block of people is fed up

---

36   Haidt, *Righteous Mind*, 364.

37   Ibid, 366.

38   Ibid, 364.

39   Ibid, 370.

40   http://hiddentribes.us.

with the polarization plaguing American government and society. They feel forgotten, overlooked, and without voice. They're politically flexible, willing to endorse different policies according to the precise situation rather than sticking ideologically to a single set of beliefs. And they believe we can find common ground.[41]

The reason I find those comments so encouraging is that I strongly believe the world I'm most familiar with, the Church, is best equipped to carry out such suggestions. I'm so convinced of this that I've devoted an entire additional chapter (Chapter 9) to fleshing that idea out. But I want to end this chapter with some suggestions that could apply to anyone regardless of their connection to Christian communities (church congregations) or not.

Remember that at the apex of His life, Jesus looked out at the future and could have prayed anything He wanted. He prayed His followers would love one another. As long as there are followers of His who are both Elephants and Donkeys, as there certainly are, we can become an answer to Jesus' prayer and forge a hopeful path forward for the country simultaneously. Let's break that big idea into parts:

1. MAKE FRIENDS

Writer Gene Knudsen Hoffman says, "An enemy is one whose story we have not heard."[42] It's hard to dehumanize people you know personally. Anglican Priest Tish Harrison Warren writes, "Communities can have opposing ideologies, yet not silence one another, but instead learn to live as neighbors and, more radically, as friends."[43] I may have unintentionally minimized the opposing ideologies by emphasizing Donkey and Elephant priorities that Jesus' followers can all celebrate. We'll come back to this point in the section below on anger, but it's possible to befriend people without accepting their views—perhaps even

---

41   Urban, Chapter 10.

42   Gene Knudsen Hoffman, "An Enemy Is One Whose Story We Have Not Heard," *Fellowship* (May/June 1997), https://newconversations.net/communication-skills-library-of-articles-and-teaching-materials/gene-knudsen-hoffman-articles/an-enemy-is-one-whose-story-we-have-not-heard/.

43   Greer, Horst & Heisey, *Rooting for Rivals*, 172.

strongly opposing their views. Jesus left heaven in order to befriend people who put Him on a cross. Nothing we're being invited to do will match that.

This isn't just theory; it's happened at pivotal points in our nation's history. Abraham Lincoln famously asked, "Do I not destroy my enemies when I make them my friends?"[44] Lincoln opted for a rare political strategy: grace. He appointed all three of his Republican primary opponents to his cabinet. He also appointed several Democrats to his cabinet. He was the first to apologize when conflicts arose. He famously wrote his most honest frustrations in "hot letters" to leaders with whom he was in conflict that were "never sent, never signed."[45] The partisanship Lincoln experienced was arguably worse than anything in our day, yet Lincoln's approach changed the direction of our nation.

> **AS LONG AS THERE ARE FOLLOWERS OF JESUS WHO ARE BOTH ELEPHANTS AND DONKEYS, WE CAN BECOME AN ANSWER TO JESUS' PRAYER.**

Fast forward to the 60's and we find Rev. Dr. Martin Luther King Jr echoing Lincoln's own words. He wrote in a sermon, "Love is the only force capable of transforming an enemy into a friend."[46] King's nonviolent love for his enemies once again changed the trajectory of the nation. He wrote, spoke, and lived his adage about light driving out darkness and love driving out hate. We can follow in Lincoln's and King's footsteps today, knowing that more than likely we won't have to pay the ultimate price to do so, as both of them did.

While we may be as divided now as 50 (Rev. King) and 150 (President Lincoln) years ago, we can also find modern day examples of the same

---

44   Ibid, 180.

45   Ibid, 181.

46   Ibid, 179.

behavior. Evan Low is a California Democratic Assembly member of the LGBT caucus, and Barry Corey is the president of Biola University.[47] They've become friends and stated, "You don't need to see eye to eye to work shoulder to shoulder."[48] The fantastic book *Rooting for Rivals* includes a chapter on "Vengeance vs Grace" that includes multiple examples of pro-life (unborn) organizations befriending workers at abortion clinics. "These sorts of friendships can feel impossible for people of deep conviction. Yet they are not only possible but essential if we are to bridge the growing divides in our world."[49] I found myself challenged in that chapter, having to reexamine some of my own faulty assumptions where I had meshed ideologies I reject with the people who hold them.

With our culture fixated on all things sexual, issues surrounding sexuality are particularly divisive. But we need similar examples in other partisan arenas as well, and fortunately we have them. *CNN* has a series called, "Fractured States of America," and the following story by Julia Song caught my attention regarding the immigration issue because it shows how relationships can lead to stronger consensus:

> Still, despite our differences, I felt she and I shared a common set of values—compassion, patriotism and a belief that our shared country could be a better version of itself. We may disagree on how to accomplish this— through a border wall or increased refugee intake, for example—and we may even disagree on the priorities of the federal government, but we agreed that illegal immigration is a challenge, and comprehensive immigration reform is vital to solving that problem. To know a Democrat also cares about the issue of immigration but may have a different approach to reforming the system, helps me make peace with our policy differences. Instead of being a faceless liberal, Rremida is now a fellow American with a unique set of experiences that color the

---

47   Biola is a well-known evangelical Christian university in Southern California.

48   Greer, Horst & Heisey, *Rooting for Rivals*, 185.

49   Ibid, 185.

way she sees the world—and the role she thinks America should play in it. And our ability to meet in the same living room, to get out of our red vs. blue silos, gives me a tremendous amount of hope. Among the biggest takeaways, I learned that much of the groundwork for bridging political divides starts in homes across America. It starts at the community level, where Americans who are already united by ties to a specific place can come together and hash out their differences.[50]

Interested but unsure how to start? I recently learned of a program springing up in cities all over the country called Make America Dinner Again.[51] The program is a nationwide effort to pair Democrats and Republicans over a meal together, out of the belief that we can learn greatly from one another if only we're in the right setting and frame of mind. The website contains incredibly practical suggestions for how to make this happen. I noticed that my own city of Tucson isn't on the map yet, and recently had someone suggest that my ministry, J17 Ministries, needs to consider being a local organizer. Check that one off; whether as the organizer or just as a participant, unless someone beats us to the punch, we will be happy to take the lead in this practical way. We need to reverse the very strategy that tribalized Washington, DC by actively preventing cross-party friendships and dinner engagements. Another group we're familiar with, Preemptive Love, has some great tips for a similar type of get-together, what they call Love Anyway Gatherings.[52]

The "polite dinnertime conversation rule" needs to change. Avoiding political topics is better than breaking out the knives and forks and carving one another up, but better still is to learn how to have mutually respectful political conversation among those with whom we already have a strong bond of trust, like family and friends. Julia (above) is correct

---

50   Julia Song, "Conservative: She Was Not a Faceless Liberal," *CNN*, December 4, 2019, https://www.cnn.com/2019/12/04/opinions/living-room-conversation-republican-perspective-song/index.html.

51   http://www.makeamericadinneragain.com/.

52   https://preemptivelove.org/feast-faq/.

and spot on: "much of the groundwork for bridging political divides starts in homes across America."

Bible Translator Todd Peterson[53] believes that three principles and Christ-like attributes—generosity, humility, and integrity—lead to friendship and ultimately guide greater partnership. When both (or all) parties honor these principles above their own agenda, the relationship thrives.[54] In my citywide work for Christian unity, I've become thoroughly convinced that unity goes as far as humility takes it, and no further. So let's turn next to the necessary ingredient of humility.

2. HUMBLE YOURSELF

Politics isn't known for bringing out our humble sides, whether among the politicians or among the armchair quarterbacks posting on Facebook. Urban writes, "While humility is a permeable filter that absorbs life experience and converts it into knowledge and wisdom, arrogance is a rubber shield that life experience simply bounces off of."[55] Humility will be aided simply by recognizing that the other party is made up of people, some of whom we probably already know and love.

UNITY GOES AS FAR AS HUMILITY TAKES IT AND NO FURTHER.

Once again, we can look to Jesus for direction. Listen to what He says: "Let me teach you, because I am humble and gentle at heart."[56] The person with the least reason or need to be humble, Jesus, chose the humblest of paths at every step of the journey. Nobody else has ever been in full control of the circumstances of his birth or death, but Jesus was. He chose a poor unmarried young girl as His mother, smelly disrespected shepherds as His entourage, and a cattle trough as His birthplace. Though He was entitled to all the riches of the world He helped create, His only possession when

---

53   Peterson was chairman emeritus and interim CEO of Seed Company, a Wycliffe Bible Translators affiliate.

54   Greer, Horst & Heisey, *Rooting for Rivals*, 172.

55   Urban, Chapter 7.

56   Matt. 11:29 (NLT).

He died was the robe that used to be on His back, and soldiers gambled for that while He hung on a cross and died. If Jesus chose humility, how utterly ridiculous for us to choose anything different.

Humility assumes that I don't already have all the answers, and that my opponents aren't evil, foolish, or stupid. Humility asks more questions than it spouts out answers. Humility seeks to understand even more than it seeks to be understood. Humility tears down the walls that arrogance builds. "To listen well and seek to learn from those with whom we disagree helps us to see our own blind spots and reflects the character of Jesus."[57]

We can cut ourselves some slack simply by recognizing that many factors have conspired against us when it comes to doing politics well. Technology, psychology and media are all major forces at play. Being WEIRD,[58] as most of us are by global standards, means that we're going to default to an either/or paradigm, making big picture consensus that much more difficult. We're all prone to over-identifying with secondary things—and when we recognize we've done that and then put what we've idolized back in its proper place, we often simply replace that idol with another one. None of these are Republican or Democratic problems, they're human problems. That fact alone can help us grow in humility.

No one by him or herself is an expert at how to run a country. Life experience and culture play huge roles in which side of the political aisle we tend to align ourselves. All life experience matters! All cultures have strengths! To think that we can solve the enormously complicated issues besetting the nation and the world by cutting out anyone who's unlike us is simply foolish. Humility goes looking for the gems in the other mammal's platforms and perspectives. A humble approach to politics can be like a treasure hunt. Doesn't that sound a lot more enjoyable than a war?

Does all of this invitation to friendship and humility mean that we shouldn't be passionate about our convictions? Not at all . . .

---

57   Greer, Horst & Heisey, *Rooting for Rivals*, 187.

58   Western, educated, industrialized, rich, and democratic.

3. ACCEPT ANGER, BUT EXERCISE SELF-CONTROL

I get angry when I think about babies being tortured and killed due to abortion. And it angers me that our immigration policy separates families and forces children to become even more vulnerable than they already were. The invitations in this chapter are not instructing us to hold fewer convictions, or to hold them less passionately.

There's a principle in the New Testament that many Christians aren't aware of, let alone the culture as a whole. It says, "Be angry and do not sin; do not let the sun go down on your anger."[59] Rarely has any significant cultural change happened without someone getting angry first about an injustice. Do you think Lincoln was angered by slavery, and King by discrimination? I'd bank on it. Yet as we've already seen with both of them, they were able to separate their anger from their actions. Tim Keller explains,

> Anger is always an outgrowth of love. Anger is that which rouses you and rallies all of our faculties to defend that which you ultimately love. You get angry to the degree you love something. If our loves are rightly ordered, there are times when we should and will be angry.[60]

Even when I'm angry over positions that I believe are hurting people, I can still humble myself and recognize that very possibly there are godly motives that are part of the picture for the person holding positions untenable to me. "Gracious leaders still display righteous anger. They are confident in their beliefs and unafraid of befriending those who do not share them. And they model humility, acknowledging their own stereotypes and faults first, before pointing them out in others."[61]

Self-control means resisting the urge to "share" the latest political dig on Facebook, let alone write it myself. It means refusing to laugh

---

59   Eph. 4:26 (ESV).

60   Tim Keller, "Wrath; The Case of Esau," *Gospel in Life*, April 2, 1995, sermon audio, https://gospel-inlife.com/downloads/wrath-the-case-of-esau-6377/.

61   Greer, Horst & Heisey, *Rooting for Rivals*, 185.

at snappy quips that dehumanize half the country, even if the clever comment happens to align with a view I already hold. Self-control makes us more human as we treat others with greater humanity. Just because there's less friction in faceless communication doesn't mean we need to engage in the ugly side of it. Also in the New Testament is a section that lists nine different aspects as fruit of the Holy Spirit.[62] The last one on the list is self-control. The list is often erroneously referred to as the fruits (plural) of the Holy Spirit in English, but in the Bible it's singular. The work of the Holy Spirit in our lives includes producing more self-control, along with all the other eight qualities.

My son Mike and I have disagreed on a number of topics politically and spiritually. In fact, when he first pitched the idea of helping me write parts of this book—yes, it was his idea!—the conversation went something like this:

"Isn't one of your main points, Dad, that people can disagree and yet still hold respectful and mutually edifying conversations?"

"Yes, son, it is. Let's talk!"

Since then we've been able to work together on this book, discussing fairly heavy political and spiritual topics with grace and respect. We are each aware that the other desires the best outcomes, and we're both passionate to help each side of the political aisle understand the other side better, creating greater unity.

In one of those subsequent conversations, Mike introduced me to a new word, sonder. Sonder is "the profound feeling of realizing that everyone, including strangers passed in the street, has a life as complex as one's own, which they are constantly living despite one's personal lack of awareness of it."[63] It's truly a unique, humbling emotion that can strike you with awe like few other experiences can. Take a moment

---

62   "The Spirit produces the fruit of love, joy, peace, patience, kindness, goodness, faithfulness, gentleness, self-control…" Gal. 5:22–23 (NCV).

63   "Sonder," Wiktionary, last modified January 16, 2020, https://en.wiktionary.org/wiki/sonder.

to truly understand that every other person walking this Earth has felt just as much heartache, love, fear, and desire as you. The barista, the cashier, those joggers, everyone on that bus, your teachers, your children's friends, your extended family, and every single person commenting on Facebook. They wrestle with decisions, sometimes act out emotionally, are just as unfathomably complex as you, and they each have dozens of other miraculously intricate people whom they love or who care for them. We would all do well to embrace this feeling of sonder more as we interact with the people around us. All our interactions with others are sacred, because we all bear the image of God.[64]

4. BUILD A BIGGER TRIBE

Donkey tribes and Elephant tribes aren't big enough. We need to start seeing our tribe as the human race. From a Biblical perspective, we'd say that the tribe we're working for is the Kingdom of God, something that transcends all the smaller tribes.

Urban and Haidt summarize the need to build a bigger tribe exceptionally well. While "progressivism" and "conservatism" don't exactly translate to Democrat and Republican, there's a strong correlation. And "high-rung" is a reference to Urban's "thinking ladder," where he advocates that we function more like Scientists or maybe Sports Fans than like Attorneys or Zealots.

> If a nation is a boat, high-rung Progressivism tries to make improvements to flaws in the boat and build newer, better features, while high-rung Conservatism tries to protect the existing boat against damage and deterioration. Given that any nation, like any boat, has some things working well and others working poorly—along with the capacity to be both improved and damaged over time—Progressivism and Conservatism, the way we're currently defining them, are simply the two sides of the "Let's make this the best boat we can" coin. Two halves of a single

---

64   Both this and the prior paragraph were coauthored by Mike and Dave Drum.

noble quest for a more perfect nation.... Evolution [in a societal sense] is driven by progressive ideas and policed by conservative sensibilities. In any of these situations, people with a progressive mindset feel like they're dragging more conservative people upward to a better place, while people on the conservative side feel that the progressive effort is dragging things downward to a worse place. Progressivism and Conservatism each worry about one half of every issue, and together, they make sure we're paying enough attention to everything that matters.[65]

Haidt lands on very similar conclusions, using the term "liberalism" where Urban uses "progressivism".

"A PARTY OF ORDER OR STABILITY, AND A PARTY OF PROGRESS OR REFORM, ARE BOTH NECESSARY ELEMENTS OF A HEALTHY STATE OF POLITICAL LIFE."

Liberalism—which has done so much to bring about freedom and equal opportunity—is not sufficient as a governing philosophy. It tends to overreach, change too many things too quickly, and reduce the stock of moral capital inadvertently. Conversely, while conservatives do a better job of preserving moral capital, they often fail to notice certain classes of victims, fail to limit the predations of certain powerful interests, and fail to see the need to change or update institutions as times change. John Stuart Mill said that liberals and conservatives are like this: "A party of order or stability, and a party of progress or reform, are both necessary elements of a healthy state of political life."[66]

---

65   Urban, Chapter 9.

66   Haidt, *Righteous Mind*, 343.

For the health of our country, we simply must find ways to turn more of our political "either/ors" into "both/ands". And the starting place is how we view the people who make up the parties.

A few more recommendations

Let's end this chapter with a couple more very practical takeaways. Since we don't typically get to vote for platforms, and rather must vote for candidates, consider making it your number one criterion that you'll vote for individuals who treat the other candidates and parties at least respectfully. I contend that our country needs unifiers possibly more than anything else. When one of those isn't available, I've started writing in candidates unless I can clearly identify a "lesser of two evils" candidate. If we continue to function like warring tribes, the prospects are bleak indeed. And if we keep on doing what we've always done, well, that's the very definition of insanity.

I don't know what kind of traction it's getting, but I was intrigued to learn of a new Emancipation Party, led by John Rankin, with the Golden Rule[67] as one of the three founding assumptions of the party: "The Golden Rule in political context is when all other partisan ideas are first given an honest listen."[68]

Civil Politics is a non-profit whose mission is "to educate groups and individuals who are trying to bridge moral divisions by connecting them with scientific research." They define civility this way: "the ability to disagree productively with others, respecting their sincerity and decency. By civility we do NOT mean agreement. We think citizens are well served when political parties represent different viewpoints and then compete vigorously to recruit voters to their side."[69]

I mentioned earlier in a footnote that I've made it a habit for the last few years to visit both *Fox News'* and *CNN's* websites at least daily.

---

67   Do unto others as you'd like them to do to you. Matt. 7:12.

68   https://www.teii.org/first-the-gospel-then-politics/emancipationparty/.

69   http://www.civilpolitics.org/.

By listening to what both sides are saying, it's easier to sift out the bias and not get infected by the animosity. Allsides.com is worth checking out—they rate media bias and even tell you how they do it! Another option would be to attempt to find a more unbiased news source. *Newsy* is my wife's and my current favorite in that regard.[70]

A chapter like this feels like it needs to end with some music! Ryanhood, an acoustic group that also calls Tucson home, recently released a song called "The Fight." Here are the lyrics to the bridge:

> Take the comments section
> From the last election
> Take the things we write
> And take our misdirection
> Take the fear that makes us
> Wanna drive them out
> And makes us act the same
> As what we're mad about
>
> Take the inquisition
> Think of prohibition
> Think of "Shock and Awe"
> Against Sharia law
> Take crusades and hate
> And mobs and frenzies
> Crews and cliques
> The crucifixion
> Ethnic cleansing
>
> And it isn't only all about the pain and hurt
> But also that it never really seems to work
> Because the heavier the hand that holds and squeezes
> The more you break the thing into a million pieces
> And every little spore is gonna grow again

---

70   https://www.newsy.com/.

You can call that hell or you can call that sin
But the only revolution is the one within
Until we throw ourself into the light
We will never win the fight

Take me
Take me
Take me
Take me[71]

Donkey Christians and Elephant Christians need to lead the way in civil, positive, honoring, solution-based conversation. Jesus said that we're salt and light—not that we should be, but that we are. We will either flavor the world with maturity or immaturity. There are many others calling for the same thing, so we need to link arms with anyone, regardless of their faith background, in promoting common kindness and the common good.

The next chapter will delve more deeply into some invitations specifically for the Church.

---

71 Reprinted, with permission, from Cameron Hood, "The Fight," Ryanhood. The song hasn't been released yet, but you can find the band at ryanhood.com.

CHAPTER NINE

GUIDANCE FOR
THE CHURCH

"Lead us not into temptation,
but deliver us from the evil one."
—Matthew 6:13[1]

Chapter 9 is *supplemental* to Chapter 8. If you consider yourself part of the Church, everything in Chapter 8 applies to you, too. You might also consider reviewing the recommendations in Chapter 5, because while Jesus' John 17 prayer has points of application for everyone, it specifically concerns His followers. But there's more that needs to be said, since many of Jesus' instructions were specifically for His followers, not the watching world. So let's jump right in.

Remember Pastor David Platt? Way back in Chapter 1 I told the story of how Platt unexpectedly had been asked by President Trump to

---

pray for him during a service in June of 2019, setting off a firestorm of controversy within his own congregation. As a result, he said, "I was labeled a far right-wing conservative and a far left-wing liberal in the same week." I listened to his sermon the following Sunday and am going to start this chapter by quoting from his message,[2] since it's a message to a local congregation. "This last week didn't create problems," Platt said, "it uncovered them. The Church is not healthy." Platt isn't only referring to his own congregation. Capital C Church refers to the whole Christian Church—in this case, the Church in America.

> The Bible doesn't say "don't have conviction or feel strongly about things". Romans 14:5–6 is counter-intuitive, because it says to have "deep conviction". Doesn't that make unity even harder? Not if we follow the rest of the guidance from the Word....

Platt used Romans 14 as the basis of his message, because the Church in Rome was struggling with different divisive issues, and the principles apply powerfully in our own day and situation.

> WHEN OTHERS IN THE CHURCH HAVE DIFFER-ENT CONVICTIONS ON ISSUES THAT ARE NOT CLEARLY AND ESSENTIALLY ADDRESSED IN GOD'S WORD, LOVE THEM [Caps were used in Platt's published sermon notes]. Listen to and respect others. James 1:19 says, "be quick to listen, slow to speak," (and we could add, "be slow to tweet, be slow to post"). The culture entices us to share our thoughts behind a screen instead of face to face.... Find someone who believes different than you do, and just listen. If you can't find someone different than you, broaden your rela-tionships.... Refuse to disparage or quarrel with others. (Romans 14:1) We live in a culture of contempt....

---

2   David Platt, "On Unity in the Church," *Radical*, June 9, 2019, sermon video, 1:05:03, https://radical.net/sermon/on-unity-in-the-church/.

We can decide that we simply are not going to disparage or quarrel with others. And that is indeed half the battle. Whether in my own family, with other leaders in the Church, or wherever I go, I can decide that if I disagree, I don't have to voice my opposition.[3] I'll share my opinion when asked, but otherwise follow the advice of Proverbs and keep quiet.[4] But that truly is only half the battle.

> Even if we aren't sharing our thoughts, we can be feeding our pride about how right we are and how wrong others are. Pray for a deep spirit of humility and a commitment to never disparage brothers or sisters in Christ....

We talked about humility in the last chapter. There are things we can do to humble ourselves, but ultimately God will have to work on our hearts for humility to come from within. Humility is the other half of the battle. Platt continued, "Build your relationship with others on what is clear and essential in God's Word." Granted, we don't all agree on that, even within the Church. But among humble Christ-followers willing to dialogue, there's remarkable agreement on what's essential and what's peripheral. This quote isn't from Platt, but applies: In essentials, unity. In non-essentials, liberty. In all things, charity.[5]

> Is the core problem not disunity but idolatry? Have we at any point let our politics and our opinions become idols in the Church today? Do we love our politics or our opinions as much as or more than we love Jesus and what He has clearly and essentially said in His Word?...

This is the problem of identity theft that we discussed in Chapter 4. The answer to Platt's rhetorical questions is a resounding yes, but keep in mind, Platt was preaching this to people he personally knows and loves

---

3   Eccles. 5:2, "Do not be quick with your mouth, do not be hasty in your heart to utter anything before God. God is in heaven and you are on earth, so let your words be few."

4   Prov. 17:28, "Even fools are thought wise if they keep silent, and discerning if they hold their tongues."

5   The quote is often attributed to St. Augustine, but actually dates much later to Rupertus Meldenius in 1627.

and with whom he has direct personal contact. All of that is much riskier than writing it in a book.

Finally, "Look for opportunities to please others in the Church who have different convictions than you," Platt said, referencing Romans 15:1–2. Even and especially with those where our deeply-held convictions are polar opposites, taking a position of service and generosity is following in Jesus' footsteps, who did exactly that with each and every one of us.

In case something happens and you never get to read anything else in this chapter, I wanted you to hear highlights from Platt's sermon right up front.

Trumped

Has the Kingdom of God been trumped by politics?

President Trump doesn't get credit for the mess we're in—he's not that powerful! As mentioned previously, there is a Divider-in-Chief, and it's always a spiritual force, not a person.[6] I would point out how proud I am of myself for having made it this far in the book without saying anything about our current Commander-In-Chief's contributions to the mess . . . except that I just wrote about humility and that wouldn't be very humble. And with the one teeny tiny exception of the very public spat between Trump and Pelosi at the 2020 State of the Union that made its way into the first chapter. Anyway . . . the problems started before #45 took office, and they'll continue after he's left office, whether that's 2021 or sometime later.

A book like this wouldn't be complete without some discussion of the President, even though few topics are more divisive than President Trump. A July 5, 2019 article with the title, "The Deepening Crisis in

---

6   Eph. 6:11–12, "Put on the full armor of God, so that you can take your stand against the devil's schemes. For our struggle is not against flesh and blood, but against the rulers, against the authorities, against the powers of this dark world and against the spiritual forces of evil in the heavenly realms."

Evangelical Christianity"[7] recently caught my attention. *The Atlantic* has a bias, as all publications do—remember the discussion in Chapter 2? So the first thing I did was as much research as I could on the author, Peter Wehner, who's not only a contributing editor at *The Atlantic* but a senior fellow at The Ethics and Public Policy Center, which describes itself as "dedicated to applying the Judeo-Christian moral tradition to critical issues of public policy." My conclusion is that the two biases come as close to cancelling one another out as we can reasonably hope for. These quotes from the article can help give us some insight into how a block of voters is thinking.

> Last week,[8] Ralph Reed, the Faith and Freedom Coalition's founder and chairman, told the group, "There has never been anyone who has defended us and who has fought for us, who we have loved more than Donald J. Trump. No one!" ... The data seem to bear this out. Approval for President Trump among white evangelical Protestants is 25 points higher than the national average.[9] ... For "evangelicals," Trump is a man who will not only push their agenda on issues such as the courts and abortion; he will be ruthless against those they view as threats to all they know and love. For a growing number of evangelicals, Trump's dehumanizing tactics and cruelty aren't a bug; they are a feature. Trump "owns the libs," and they love it. He'll bring a Glock to a cultural knife fight, and they relish that. ... Jerry Falwell Jr., the president of Liberty University, one of the largest Christian universities in the world, put it this way: "Conservatives & Christians need to stop electing

---

7   Peter Wehner, "The Deepening Crisis in Evangelical Christianity: Support for Trump Comes at a High Cost for Christian Witness," *The Atlantic*, July 5, 2019, https://www.theatlantic.com/ideas/archive/2019/07/evangelical-christians-face-deepening-crisis/593353/.

8   Meaning June of 2019.

9   Philip Schwadel and Gregory A. Smith, "Evangelical Approval of Trump Remains High, but Other Religious Groups Are Less Supportive," Pew Research Center, March 18, 2019, https://www.pewresearch.org/fact-tank/2019/03/18/evangelical-approval-of-trump-remains-high-but-other-religious-groups-are-less-supportive/.

'nice guys.' They might make great Christian leaders but the United States needs street fighters like @realDonaldTrump at every level of government b/c the liberal fascists Dems are playing for keeps & many Repub leaders are a bunch of wimps!"[10]

Give me a moment while I wipe the tears from my eyes...and in case you're wondering, they aren't tears of joy. Even though "evangelical" is such a good and meaningful word, I almost can't use it anymore due to its political connotations. It's positively frightening to me that so few Christian leaders seem able or willing to separate out policies they support from methods and tactics that they can't possibly support—at least not in the name of Christ. One who did do so, however, was Michael Brown in an excellent article called, "Christian First, Patriot Second."[11]

"This article is not about President Trump," Brown wrote. "It is about us. About our behavior as followers of Jesus. About our words. About our attitudes. About our priorities." Brown continued:

> [The Apostle] Paul wrote, "Walk in wisdom toward outsiders, making the best use of the time. Let your speech always be gracious, seasoned with salt, so that you may know how you ought to answer each person" (Colossians 4:5–6, ESV). Sorry, but I didn't get the memo where God rescinded these verses. I didn't get the memo where He changed the fruit of the Spirit into the works of the flesh (see Galatians 5:17–24)....What has become of godly speech? Of civility? Of graciousness? Of respect? When did God send out the memo that it was now fine for His children to savage one another, to act

---

10   Brett Samuels, "Jerry Falwell Jr.: Conservatives and Christians Need to Stop Electing 'Nice Guys,'" *The Hill*, September 30, 2018, https://thehill.com/blogs/blog-briefing-room/409151-jerry-falwell-jr-conservatives-and-christians-need-to-stop-electing.

11   Michael Brown, "Christian First, Patriot Second," *The Christian Post*, July 31, 2019, https://www.christianpost.com/voice/christian-first-patriot-second.html.

like animals, to be cruel and cutting and nasty? . . . And the sword cuts both ways. I have seen Christians who are Trump critics bash other Christians who voted for him. "You can't be a Christian if you voted for Donald Trump! You are an ignorant fool bringing mockery to Christ's name." And I have seen Christian Trump supporters brand anyone who would dare criticize a single thing he says or does as un-American and un-Christian. . . . Have we lost our corporate minds? Have we lost our individual souls? . . .

Just like Platt told his congregation, the division in the body of Christ over politics isn't *caused* by President Trump as much as it is *revealed* by his tenure in office. I completely understand being passionate about policies that affect the lives of others, and I share that passion. And while I resigned my membership in the Republican party and became Independent, I respect those who remain Republican, pointing out some of the positives that have come during these last few years. What I fail to understand is how Christian

> **DIVISION IN THE BODY OF CHRIST OVER POLITICS ISN'T *CAUSED* BY PRESIDENT TRUMP AS MUCH AS IT IS *REVEALED* BY HIS TENURE IN OFFICE.**

leaders give him a pass on his morals, his behavior, and the regular toxic words coming from his mouth. Even if character ranks far below "job performance" for some, I still struggle to understand how Christians justify the character on display from the White House.

My conclusion is that there's an identity theft issue—party loyalty has trumped primary loyalty, partly over a failure to view the world through a both/and rather than an either/or lens. The official Elephant talking points have become such a thick lens that nothing else gets through, and the end justifies all means. If you've read this far and find that offensive, I would love to learn what I'm missing. We don't have to deny positives in order to address negatives. It's a both/and, not an either/or.

Jesus said, "What good is it for someone to gain the whole world, and yet lose or forfeit their very self?"[12] I think the same could be said nationally for followers of Christ. What good is it if we get Biblical policies passed for the nation while the Kingdom of God gets tarnished over the methods used to achieve those political victories? Jesus was so clear that His Kingdom is not of this world.[13] If loyalty to the Kingdom of God and loyalty to a political party are sparring with one another, there's no question which needs to come out on top for those who claim the name of Jesus as their identity. The ends cannot be used to justify any and all means, no matter how godly those ends might be. In fact, the godlier the ends are, the more incongruent it is to use ungodly means to achieve them. Besides calling it idolatry, which David Platt did, I think we need to call it a massive lack of trust, confusing our power and our ways with God's. Don't you think God would rather have us trust Him to accomplish His purposes in His own ways and timing, than implement a coup and place ourselves on the throne?

The Lord's prayers

Enough on that topic! I wrote several pages in the last chapter about how if we want to be part of the solution, we first have to stop being part of the problem. My premise is that one of Jesus' prayers, the one recorded in John 17, points us in the best direction for the country to have a prayer of ending its ever-more-damaging Donkey Elephant war.

What if even at this point, eight plus chapters in, you're not convinced that the war should end? Or at least not end with a cease-fire? What if a) you might see the best solution as the other side surrendering after getting sufficiently trounced in the court of public opinion? Or b) perhaps you see value in relatively even numbers on both sides assuring

12   Luke 9:25.

13   John 18:36.

that Washington *doesn't* get much done—an over-active Washington might be a bigger concern than a stalemated one.

Both a) and b) above have enough merit to need some additional conversation. Hopefully I've made it clear thus far that I'm not simply advocating compromising on everything, toning down our convictions, and/or pretending that there aren't any differences of real consequence. While I don't think the answer is one party pummeling the other into submission, the positions I advocated in Chapters 6 and 7 are worth fighting for. All of them. And that's just a start. The point is that no one party holds a monopoly on Jesus' values. So one party eliminating the other isn't the solution.

And I agree very much with the idea that robust discussion from different perspectives is healthy. Jesus' prayer in John 17 wasn't that we all be *alike*, it's that we all be *aligned*. Politically speaking, that means aligned toward the goal of a healthier country for everyone. A 50/50 split if there are only two parties in the running clearly has some merit, as only three times in the last 50 years has the country opted to keep the same party in control of the White House and both houses of Congress.[14] Voters clearly appreciate the founders' concern for balance of power, distributing it roughly equally between political parties for most of the country's history. I'm not troubled by a Donkey Elephant *contest*; it's when the contest becomes a *war*, with casualties, that we ought to be concerned.

Jesus was praying specifically for His followers, not for political parties, and His prayer was not that we come to agreement on philosophies, political or otherwise, but that we love one another. Love implies listening, respect, humility, service, and so forth. Since Jesus has followers in both parties—in large numbers—our current political climate is unacceptable.

---

14   Jimmy Carter had four years of Democratic control of both houses of Congress between 1977–1980, and George W Bush had six years of Republican control of both houses of Congress between 2001–2007.

Early on in Jesus' most famous sermon, the "Sermon on the Mount,"[15] he says of His followers that they're the salt of the earth and the light of the world.[16] In other words, the Church flavors and influences and guides the world. He doesn't say we *ought* to be these two things, He says we *are*. I believe disunity in the Church has contributed to disunity in the world. When we should have been *flavoring* the world to respond more like Christ, we've been *favoring* the world in its unChristlike ways. I'm thoroughly convinced that disunity and immaturity are circular, meaning that both lead to more of the other.[17] Therefore, I believe the immaturity of the culture is partly the responsibility of the Church.

Two other prayers of Jesus provide further illumination. The one we're most familiar with is the one we've dubbed The Lord's Prayer, even though it's the prayer that He taught, not one that the Bible ever records Him directly praying. The prayer goes like this (though this probably isn't the version you learned, if you learned one):

> "Our Father in heaven,
> hallowed be your name,
> your kingdom come,
> your will be done,
>   on earth as it is in heaven.
> Give us today our daily bread.
> And forgive us our debts,
>   as we also have forgiven our debtors.
> And lead us not into temptation,
>   but deliver us from the evil one."[18]

Let's apply each part to our current situation. The first request is that God's name be kept holy. I would argue that that's exactly the opposite of what happens when party loyalty and Kingdom-of-God loyalty get

---

15 Matt. 5–7.

16 Matt. 5:13–16.

17 Ephesians 4 makes this point clearly. Chapter 2 of my last book, *If It Was Easy, Jesus Wouldn't Have Prayed For It* lays out the argument.

18 Matt. 6:9–13.

mixed up. "Your kingdom come, your will be done, on earth as it is in heaven" is why I decided to write this book. Jesus never separates "spiritual" things from "earthy" things, as if He's concerned about the former and unconcerned about the latter. Jesus became human—clearly He's interested in what goes on down here. Let's take one of the most spiritual things you can imagine—Jesus, the Son of God, praying—and apply it to one of the least spiritual things you can imagine—partisan politics.

"Give us today our daily bread" again shows Jesus' concern for the most practical needs of life (and also speaks to His concern for those who lack the daily needs of life). "Forgive us our debts as we forgive our debtors" could make for some exciting policy discussion, don't you think? We typically take that request spiritually, especially if the translation we're used to uses the word "trespasses" instead of "debts." The prayer certainly includes a spiritual application, but Jesus in His ministry used examples of both spiritual debt caused by sin as well as monetary debt.[19] It's a both/and, not an either/or.

DISUNITY AND IMMATURITY ARE CIRCULAR. BOTH LEAD TO MORE OF THE OTHER.

"Lead us not into temptation, but deliver us from the evil one." YES! That's exactly how we need to be praying every time we turn on the TV, comment on Facebook, or engage in conversation at work during a break. We need to recognize partisanship as temptation, and pray for deliverance.

Another relevant prayer Jesus prayed happened later the same evening as His John 17 prayer—probably within the next hour or two. He was in the Garden of Gethsemane, agonizing over the suffering He was about to endure momentarily, and He prayed, "Father, if you are willing, take this cup from me; yet not my will, but yours be done."[20] The act of surrendering our own will is one of the hardest things we ever have to do, but we're invited to do that all the time. Jesus compared it

19   Matt. 9:2 and Luke 7:40–50 as two examples.

20   Luke 22:42.

to taking up our own cross,[21] because it's a form of death to ourselves and demands that things go a certain way. In the Garden, an angel came and strengthened Him, not to spare Him the hardship, but rather to give Him the strength to endure. In fact, it was *after* the angel appeared that His prayer became so anguished that He literally sweat blood.[22] Divine intervention often isn't to relieve us of hard and painful situations, but to give us the strength to endure them. It will not be an easy task to break through years of encrusted partisanship and forge a new path of conversation, but the Lord is not only *calling* us forward, He's *equipping* us to carry out the call.

So what, specifically, is Jesus' call to His Church in times of war, the Donkey Elephant kind? I submit four parts to that call.

1. CALL TO UNITY/HARMONY

I wrote in a previous book that in terms of imagery, harmony is actually a better translation than unity, because harmony implies different voices and different instruments but the same sheet of music. Jesus calls His Church to harmony, to harmonious relationships with people who are different from ourselves (which would be... everyone).

For followers of Christ, "Winning is when we are united, not when one has won and the other has lost."[23] The truth of that statement has impact at multiple levels. I'm completely convinced that one of the reasons that the number of Christians in America is decreasing (by percentage of population) while it's increasing dramatically in other parts of the world[24] is because in the U.S., congregations on many corners duke it out for market share just like the fast-food chains McDonalds and Burger King. And I'm certain that the number of church attendees is decreasing faster than the number of Christ-followers. If the Church

---

21   Luke 9:23.

22   Luke 22:43–44.

23   Ajith Fernando, "The Way of Unifying Passion," July 24, 2017, video teaching, 55:48, https://www.youtube.com/watch?v=mgOn8rgBZlY.

24   Aaron Earls, "7 Surprising Trends in Global Christianity in 2019," Facts & Trends, June 11, 2019, https://factsandtrends.net/2019/06/11/7-surprising-trends-in-global-christianity-in-2019.

merely offers "more of the same," no wonder consumers turn elsewhere. There is competition, that's for sure, but it's not with the congregation down the street. Kids' soccer and the NFL are far more likely to explain the number of empty seats than the nearby congregation. As I shared back in Chapter 5 with the story of the bank teller, a unified Church is enormously attractive to the world. That's probably why Jesus prayed what He did! Through harmony God will release His eternal blessing, the promise of life forever![25] Harmony within the Church will release His healing and unifying power in the world. Can I get an Amen?!

In the New Testament the big theological and political struggle that threatened to split the Church in half was whether or not Gentiles had to become Jews before they could become Christian. The new Christian Church wasn't a generation old yet, and it was a very real possibility that it wouldn't survive the conflict intact. The skirmish became severe enough that congregations wrote back to the leadership in Jerusalem and asked them to weigh in. Acts 15 tells the story along with the resulting letter sent out to Gentile congregations. "The point of the letter was to obligate Gentiles believers to maintaining unity in the Church. Corporate unity would require personal sacrifice."[26] "They decided unity in the Church was more important than the law of Moses. This was an extraordinary day in the history of the Church. It was precisely what Jesus prayed for just before He was arrested."[27]

By contrast, the Center for the Study of Global Christianity counts 45,000 denominations around the world, with an average of 2.4 new denominations forming every day![28] Even accounting for the fact that many of these are simply national subgroups, like "The Lutheran Church in America" or "The Lutheran Church in Canada," and not necessarily completely different denominations, that still seems a wee bit excessive. There aren't 2.4 new countries springing up every day. The Church is

---

25   See Psalm 133, the Old Testament's version of John 17.

26   Andy Stanley, *Irresistible: Reclaiming the New That Jesus Unleashed for the World* (Grand Rapids: Zondervan, 2018), 128. Capital C for Church is my addition.

27   Ibid, 130.

28   Greer, Horst & Heisey, *Rooting for Rivals*, 31.

likened to a Body, so having lots of parts isn't necessarily a problem. The problem is only when the parts are in competition with one another or think that they're the head instead of submitting to the head. (I didn't know it was possible for a body part to refuse to do what the head told it to until someone tried to teach me how to downhill ski at about age 40. The knees were the guilty party.) I fear that "my way or the highway" is what's ultimately behind many of those 2.4 new denominations forming daily.

This call for harmony is so totally possible! In my hometown of Tucson, AZ, we've been working quite diligently at harmony in the Church since our first three-day pastor prayer summit in 2009. I'm sure there was work done prior to that as well, and that first summit was the fruit of others' labors. As God worked it out, an amazingly representative group of 20 pastors climbed the mountain north of town[29] to spend several days getting to know both God and one another better through prayer . . . and that event shifted the spiritual atmosphere of our city. Tucson's first successful structural attempt at uniting the body, 4Tucson, was birthed six months later.[30] In the 1990's and early 2000's I rarely recall hearing someone say, "How can we do this together?" Now it's the norm. I met with a group of about 40 pastors yesterday over breakfast, another 30 over lunch, and there was nearly a multicultural gathering to see a movie in the evening, though the movie event has been postponed until later. Denominational and ethnic walls are *SO* much shorter than they used to be. We haven't grown *past* our differences, we've grown to *appreciate* our differences.

> **IF WE'RE GOING TO HEED THE CALL TO HARMONY EFFECTIVELY, WE'RE GOING TO HAVE TO ADDRESS AND RECONCILE PAST HURTS.**

---

29   Okay, we drove.

30   I say successful and structural because 11 years later it's still doing good work in our city, with a continually growing understanding of the role God has called it to play.

Disunity in the Church leaves the world without an example or source for better behavior. In Tucson, a bigger issue than animosity had been our isolation. We didn't have a lot of racial tension in our city, but we certainly had plenty of isolation. Everybody loses when we act like amputated body parts. Rev. Dr. Martin Luther King Jr. is famously and repeatedly quoted for saying, "11:00 Sunday morning is the most segregated hour in America." I am happy to report that that is no longer the case in my hometown, and not just because most church services are done by 11. Our Pastor Partnership continues to grow, resulting in many cross-congregational efforts that spill beyond "churchy" activities. In August of 2019, the Partnership's leader was wondering if we'd run our course and should stop meeting. Every single group member said, "Absolutely not. This barrier-breaking unity is not only the country's best hope, it might be its only hope." And so in 2020, we're stronger than ever. Just in time, too, as the COVID-19 pandemic is going to require unity and collaboration like never before.

People are people wherever we go, and the Church is certainly no exception. Anyone who tells you that Church people are better than others needs to repent. There are few things more wounding and heart-breaking than a church fight, and I've seen plenty of them. Some of the new congregations in your community are very probably what we call "splants"—a hybrid between an intentional new church plant or outgrowth and a church split that was the result of an unresolved disagreement. What's amazing about God is that He still uses broken people to accomplish His purposes. We minister out of our brokenness if we're authentic leaders. I've often commented that one of the strongest proofs for God to be found anywhere is the fact that after 2000 years, the Church is not only still around, but still growing. You certainly can't explain that by the Church's stellar, visionary, and flawless human leadership!

If we're going to heed the call to harmony effectively, we're going to have to address and reconcile past hurts. Whenever I meet people who are on a mission against Christianity, more often than not there's a very painful story in their past. The reconciliation work we're called to do needs to encompass both those who are no longer part of the Church, as well as those who are warring body parts. Musekura, the Rwandan pastor and friend who I introduced in the first chapter, bases his entire ministry around reconciliation,[31] in his case between warring Hutu and Tutsi tribes in East African countries. If it can work there, certainly us Donkeys and Elephants in America ought to be able to pull it off.

The Bible says judgment starts with the house of God.[32] When it's a brother or sister who's demonizing the other animal, we need to rachet up the courage, speak the truth in love, and call for laying down our verbal machetes and ending the tribal genocide. Will some be offended? Probably, no matter how perfectly Christlike you are in your confrontation. But you can dramatically lower the likelihood of offense if you go into the conversation prayerful and humble, admitting some of the times you've blown it yourself. That's a far cry from a quick email blast or Facebook share. But if we keep doing what we've always done . . . we'll leave an even bigger mess for our kids to clean up.

I mentioned in the last chapter that I was excited when I read Haidt's and Urban's conclusions, and that's because it felt like they'd just handed the baton to the Church. The very thing that is needed—cross-political friendships—is the very thing the Church is uniquely equipped to do. One, all but the most strident and politically active congregations have Donkeys and Elephants fellowshipping together in them already—probably without even knowing it. And whether we do or not, if we take Jesus' John 17 prayer seriously, then we know we're family with the brothers from another mother across the street, too. J17 Ministries has developed a number of programs in Tucson that bring people together from all different congregations,[33] resulting in plenty of opportunity for some Donkey

---

31 2 Cor. 5:17–19, "Therefore, if anyone is in Christ, the new creation has come: The old has gone, the new is here! All this is from God, who reconciled us to himself through Christ and gave us the ministry of reconciliation: that God was reconciling the world to himself in Christ, not counting people's sins against them. And he has committed to us the message of reconciliation."

32 1 Pet. 4:17.

33 One national one is Tres Dias—see if there's a chapter in your area at http://www.tresdias.org/locations. Another national one is the Global Leadership Summit, and you can find one near you at https://globalleadership.org/global-leadership-summit/. See the Appendix for more information on J17 Ministries, or www.J17Ministries.org.

Elephant love. What I'm calling for isn't something new, but a return to how it was at the beginning. Andy Stanley describes life in Jesus' day wonderfully: "People who were nothing like Jesus liked Jesus. And Jesus liked people who were nothing like him. As followers of Jesus, we should be known as people who like people who are nothing like us."[34]

2. CALL TO SERVE

If the Church wants to shift from being part of the problem to part of the solution, the first step is a call to harmony. The second step is a call to serve. Many congregations exist to serve themselves, and lest you think I'm taking unfair shots at the Church, let me tell you a little story.

I had been the lead pastor of a congregation for 15 years when I realized how inward-focused we'd become. And part of the reason is that we lacked clarity on our primary purpose for being a church in the first place. I had nobody to blame but myself after 15 years! The good news is that this is a fixable problem. We entered a season of serious reflection and change, and came out with great clarity that the primary purpose of the Church is to go.[35] It's not merely to welcome those who happen to find us, though I'm in favor of hospitality. It's to go where people are and love them right there.

Why? Because followers of Jesus are called to follow Jesus! And there's never been a more outward focused person than Jesus Himself. He left the safe and perfect confines of heaven to enter our messy world, knowing full well the cost. The evening He prayed the John 17 prayer for harmony, he began by doing the dirty service work that nobody else wanted to do, washing feet. He served the betrayer and the first pope equally.[36] His example is clear; the only question is if we'll pay attention and do likewise as His followers.

---

34   Stanley, *Irresistible*, 21.

35   I tell the full story in Chapter 6 of *If It Was Easy, Jesus Wouldn't Have Prayed For It*, and have had the privilege of helping a number of congregations regain an outward focus, so contact me!

36   John 13. Jesus washed the feet of Judas the betrayer and Peter, referred to by the Catholic Church as the first Pope. Peter also would betray Jesus later that evening, but unlike Judas, he repented and received Jesus' forgiveness. Jesus not only washed both of their feet, He also served both of them the Last Supper (Luke 22:7–23).

The Church in the first century gained a reputation for following well. "See how they love one another" was the world's observation of the Church, but that's because they loved not only their own, but society's rejects. When disease would ravage an area, it was the Christians who stepped in to care for the dying at risk of their own life. It was the Christians who cared for the widows and orphans—ironically what the Bible defines as true religion.[37] In later centuries it was usually the Christians who would step in and start schools and hospitals. The global pandemic is providing another opportunity for the Church to shine like it did in its early days.

How unbelievably tragic that the primary reputation of the Church in America today is the group that judges the rest of the culture. "Judgmental" and "hypocritical" are the words most likely to be associated with "Christian" by today's culture.[38] It's certainly true that there are many aspects of the culture today that don't line up well with Biblical values. But that was equally true in Jesus' day—possibly even more than today. The Bible is very clear that judging the world is not our job.[39] But this misunderstanding, too, has been there from the beginning. Two of Jesus' followers, James and John, saw a village that had rejected Jesus, and asked Jesus if He wanted them to call down fire from heaven to destroy the infidels, who, of course, happened to be Samaritans.[40] You may have heard that there's no such thing as a dumb question, but I don't know... Don't you think if Jesus thought that would be advisable, He could have handled it directly without James' and John's assistance? The only thing James and John had right in this scenario was that they took their dumb question to Jesus. The irony is that the one time fire from heaven *was* called down and destroyed the offenders was in the story of Elijah and the prophets of Baal, and afterward, Elijah felt even more alone and fearful, not less. Even when it worked, it didn't work.

---

37   James 1:27.

38   Kinnaman, *UnChristian*.

39   Matt. 7:1–2, John 16:7–11.

40   Luke 9:51–56.

The best way to preach an unconditional gospel is unconditionally. That's how Jesus serves us—without condition. His sacrifice on the cross—the ultimate act of service—carries with it no guarantee that those being served will even accept the gift. Yet He gives the Gift freely, with no strings attached. If we want to be part of the solution in our culture, leading the way through the Donkey Elephant war, it will start with service.

This, too, is imminently possible! Over the last decade we've emphasized churches adopting a neighborhood public school, not to point out what's wrong, but merely to ask where they might need help. The creativity has been endless, with churches supplying copy paper, hand sanitizer and facial tissues; remodeling teachers' lounges, washing windows, and replacing broken-down flooring; providing meals and gifts to faculty, staff, and needy students and their families; grandparents reading to kids who are behind grade level in reading; tutoring and mentoring; serving refugee and homeless children; sitting on site councils and parent teacher associations; cheering for a high school football team whose kids had nobody in the stands cheering for them; and on and on. We have a list of 101 ways and more that a local church can serve a local school. Over 80% of the public schools in our city have been adopted by at least one local church, with the presenting question always being from the church to the school, "What do you need and how can we help?" It's slowly starting to change the reputation of the Church in our town.

IF WE WANT TO BE PART OF THE SOLUTION IN OUR CULTURE, IT WILL START WITH SERVICE.

Here's another example. I received a call one day about five years ago from the program director for the county Department of Child Safety (DCS), or Child Protective Services (CPS) as it's sometimes called, that went like this, "We've heard how your churches have adopted schools. Would you consider adopting us, too?" Fast forward to today, and there's a church/DCS partnership called Care Portal that has served literally thousands of children in the foster care system in a few years.[41]

There have been a few churches in Tucson experimenting with a "Service Worship" Sunday where instead of the congregation gathering to worship, they gather to serve. One congregation has been doing that every fifth Sunday of the month. A new church is forming this year called "To Go Church" where they'll spend three Sundays of the month out in the community and only one "in." Several churches—at last count at least fifteen—have committed to a Sunday this Fall where we'll all do this together.

Because those kinds of relationships were already in place, it only took a week or two to mobilize the Church to serve the city once the stay-at-home edict came from the Mayor and Governor in response to the COVID-19 pandemic. We're currently mobilized to serve elderly and other high-risk people who shouldn't leave their homes to go shopping. And government leaders are actively seeking out the Church as a valued partner in serving the community. Churches are also collaboratively connected to all the hospitals in town, providing child care and care packages for front-line medical workers. And together we're exploring creative ways to bless graduates who are missing out on key celebrations.

I published numerous portions of this book in a weekly blog over many months, seeking feedback in order to improve the final product. I mentioned in the section "caring for those experiencing poverty" about one reader whose reply has forever changed my perspectives, since "poor" and "rich" aren't our identity, they're just our temporary experience. She also wrote this:

> Recently I took a lady experiencing poverty to a church
> food pantry. I became overwhelmed walking into a small
> space with so many children and adults waiting for their

---

41   Care Portal is a national program of the Global Orphan Project. Check it out at https://careportal.org/.

turn. The physical space had no pictures, the area was dull, and people looked like "We are poor, so we deserve it." None of them said that, I just think that's what they would say if asked. Although the food given was amazing and plentiful, I wondered what was given to the spirit and soul of those waiting. The pantry may not be able to help the long wait, but the congregation can help shape what experience people have while they are waiting. The pantry may not have a bigger space, but they can make a beautiful place out of the space they have. And, the congregation may not have enough staff to engage those waiting, but they could provide something to read for adults, games for kids and music to soothe the soul. The question is, "How are we really being the hands and feet of Jesus...in the real world?"[42]

3. CALL TO AUTHENTICITY

"Faith minus vulnerability equals politics, or worse, extremism."[43] Wow. What a powerful statement from Brené Brown, not only about communities of faith, but about politics and extremism as well. The difference can be as simple as humility, transparency, and vulnerability, major themes in Brown's book.

"All the answers are here" is as ugly in the Church as it is in politics. Allow me to repeat something from the last chapter. Unity goes as far as humility takes it, and no further. How refreshing to hear from a pastor or a politician, "I don't have all the answers, so let's find them together." I don't know if a politician could get elected on a platform of unity and humility, but if not, what a sad statement about the electorate. Can you imagine a politician in a debate who genuinely shared what he/she had to offer, but in a gracious manner that sought to build others up instead of tear them down?

---

42   Thanks to Rose, "Correspondence," for these great suggestions!

43   Brené Brown, *Daring Greatly: How the Courage to Be Vulnerable Transforms the Way We Live, Love, Parent, and Lead* (New York: Penguin Random House, 2012), 177.

One of the most quoted verses in the Old Testament is this: "If my people, who are called by my name, will humble themselves and pray and seek my face and turn from their wicked ways, then I will hear from heaven, and I will forgive their sin and will heal their land."[44] This is a call to the Church, not the entire country, and it starts with humbling ourselves. Could it be that our political partisanship is one of the areas of repentance for which God is eagerly waiting? And that if we did do what the verse says we're supposed to do, God would also not only forgive our sin but heal our land? God knows our land needs healing in dramatic ways.

I refuse to accept that politics the way it's done now is how it will always have to be. I want to see more candidates lead with godly character along with godly solutions. Talk about being salt and light! The difference would be impossible to miss! I may be naïve, but I believe enough of us in this nation are sick and tired of business as usual that we'd rally behind unifiers.

I REFUSE TO ACCEPT THAT POLITICS THE WAY IT'S DONE NOW IS HOW IT WILL ALWAYS HAVE TO BE.

I'm a big sports fan, especially basketball, and the defining characteristic of a strong point guard is one who makes the rest of his or her teammates better. Me-first point guards may score lots of points, but their teams don't win championships. Why can't we function like a team as a nation? Why do we have to accept that zingers are the only way to get attention?

Humility is often misunderstood as "I'm a poor loser with nothing to offer." Nothing could be further from the truth! Biblical humility looks like confidence, not poor self-esteem. People groveling and downplaying their own gifts and strengths are still focused on themselves. The key insight and core foundation of humility is: It's not about me!

---

44   2 Chron. 7:14.

"Humility isn't thinking less of yourself, it's thinking of yourself less."[45] In the past I've attributed that quote to C.S. Lewis, not Rick Warren, but since both wrote so well about humility, neither will likely care! What Lewis said is equally powerful: "A really humble man will not be thinking about humility; he won't be thinking about himself at all."[46] Humility focuses on others, confidently bringing to the table the gifts and experience God has given us, while also identifying and seeking out the gifts and experience others have that we lack.

Unless the Church leads out in this, I see no possibility of change happening. The very beginning of a person's relationship with Jesus is an act of humility—recognizing that I don't have what it takes to save me from myself. Even though we've done so poorly at it so often, Christ-followers *ought* to get humility. If we can keep reminding ourselves and others of the centrality of Jesus in all we do and say and are, we can recognize our brokenness and lead with authenticity.

It's been said that true intimacy is "into-me-see," an invitation to see the real me, warts and all. If we can't be loved for who we really are, it's hard to be loved at all. Love of a caricature isn't very fulfilling. So much of politics in our internet and visual age is about image management. I don't think we can roll back the clock on the role of media in our political elections, but surely we can find a way to celebrate authenticity in the public square.

The Old Testament short story called Ruth is a case study in authenticity. Naomi was Ruth's mother-in-law, and life had delivered Naomi one hard blow after another. Naomi's relationship with God was painfully real and transparent, so much so that Ruth left her own family, culture, and religion to join and follow Naomi and her God. Ruth apparently was more interested in a living God you could argue with and complain to than the idols with which she was familiar. And because of Ruth and Naomi's vulnerability with each other, their harmony transcended massive cultural, generational, and political differences. The

45 Rick Warren, "Day 19," *The Purpose Driven Life* (Grand Rapids, MI: Zondervan, 2002), 148.

46 C.S. Lewis, *Mere Christianity* (New York: HarperCollins Publishers, 1996), 121–8.

story is incredibly poignant and powerful, and even helps explain some of Jesus' ancestry, so check it out!

The word hypocrite is rooted in the Greek word *hypokrites*, which means "stage actor, pretender, dissembler."[47] Greek stage actors literally wore masks, and we've been following in their footsteps figuratively ever since. That's why true authenticity is so refreshing! True Christian community is where everyone from the leaders to the first-time guests recognize that it's an unconditional, undeserved Love that binds us together, and that the masks have to go. All of us have blind spots, and if we're healthy, we're willing to have them exposed.

TRUE CHRISTIAN COMMUNITY IS WHERE EVERYONE FROM THE LEADERS TO THE FIRST-TIME GUESTS RECOGNIZE THAT IT'S AN UNCONDITIONAL, UNDESERVED LOVE THAT BINDS US TOGETHER.

This is what we need to bring to the table as we seek to build relationships with the other mammal. We can do this! I'm watching it happen every month in some of the groups in which I participate. It's so lifegiving to show up without having to pretend that we have all the answers. In fact, the expectation is the opposite— we know we have a lot to learn, and we're eager to get started. If the Church experiences her own Reformation from the inside out, we have something to offer the country when it comes to authentic cross-party relationships that bring out the best in all of us.

Proud people desire to be a success. Broken people are motivated to be faithful and to make others a success. That is so radical that it might not be possible in today's political climate, but wow, would I ever love to see such an attitude attempted. Like John the Baptist, may I become

47   "Hypocrite," Vocabulary.com, accessed February 1, 2020, https://www.vocabulary.com/dictionary/hypocrite.

less and You more.[48] How entirely different than the Donkey Elephant war and its culture of self-promotion and other-deprecation.

4. CALL TO LOVE

Andy Stanley delivered an all-time classic sermon called, "The Separation of Church and Hate"[49] back in 2010. Here are a few highlights:

> I grew up in a denomination that was against everything. Neither Jesus nor Paul position themselves against everything in culture or even against the Roman empire. In fact, the only thing those two guys were consistently against were the people on the religious side of the aisle that were against everything. . . . Making you feel guilty for what I think you're doing wrong is different than instructing you in what to do right. . . . It's easy to make a point. It is very, very, very difficult to make a difference. . . . Jesus and Paul constantly leaned relationally in the direction of those they disagreed with the most. And because their approach was so different, they were always butting heads with the people—listen—they agreed with the most. . . . The Church loses its influence in culture to the degree it tries to police the behavior of people who aren't even a part of the Church. The Church has its greatest influence when it polices its own behavior. . . . Jesus said, 'I've not come to abolish the law or the prophets, I've come to fulfill them.'[50] This isn't either/or, this is both/and.[51] . . . Paul said, 'Let your conversation be always full of grace, seasoned with salt.'[52] Do you know what 'full' means in Greek? It means 'full,' like there's hardly any room for anything else, full. Do you know what we've done for the past

---

48   John 3:30.

49   Stanley, "Church and Hate."

50   Matt. 5:17.

51   Yes, Andy really worded it that way.

52   Col. 4:6.

fifty years in conservative evangelical Christianity? We've had our conversation full of salt, then sprinkle a little grace.... We cannot be content to sit back and make points. We've got to be about our Father's business to make a difference.

We looked at the topic of religious liberty back in Chapter 6. The need for the topic tells us quite a bit about the present makeup of the country. Instead of lamenting what was, what if God is calling us to function like we would if we were sent as missionaries to a foreign country hostile or at least ambivalent to the Gospel? Mark Labberton, president of Fuller Theological Seminary, the largest multi-denominational seminary in the world, has suggested a shift in the way American Christians conceive of their calling. Rather than seeing ourselves as living in a Promised Land and "demanding it back," perhaps we need to live a "faithful, exilic life." Labberton speaks about what it means to live as people in exile, trying to find the capacity to love in unexpected ways; to see the enemy, the foreigner, the stranger, and the alien, and to go toward rather than away from them. He asks what a life of faithfulness looks like while one lives in a world of fear.[53]

Jenn Johnson sings a song "For the One" that has captured both my wife's and my hearts. Here are some of the lyrics:

> Let me be filled
>   with kindness and compassion for the one....
>   for humanity....
> Help me to love with open arms like You do
> A love that erases all the lines and sees the truth
> So that when they look in my eyes, they would see You
> Even in just a smile, they would feel the Father's love."[54]

---

53   Wehner, "Deepening Crisis."

54   Brian Johnson and Jenn Johnson, "For the One (Lyric Video)," Bethel Music, January 27, 2017, music video, 4:06, https://www.youtube.com/watch?v=e_bj6mjUj7k.

Abu Saada, who is introduced in the first chapter, is the PLO hitman turned Christian who's working for reconciliation between Jews and Arabs—in Jesus! His ministry is launching in the United States under the title, Lead with Love. That's exactly right. Don't you think we'll get so much further leading with love than leading with political zingers?

> Love looks like listening.
> Love looks like listening more and talking less.
> Love looks like taking the initiative.
> Love looks like courage in the face of fear.
> Love looks like identifying walls
>   and tearing them down.
> Love looks like seeing the other person
>   in the best possible light.
> Love is patient and kind.
> Love sounds like asking questions
>   instead of giving answers.
> Love sounds like, "Help me understand."
> Love sounds like putting the other person first.
> Love sounds like, "You have a point there."
> Love doesn't envy or boast.
> Love isn't proud.
> Love isn't rude.
> Love isn't self-seeking.
> Love keeps no record of wrongs.
> Love doesn't delight in evil but rejoices with the truth.
> Love jumps in where angels fear to tread,
>   believing that even politics is a good place for love.
> Love always protects.
> Love always trusts.
> Love always hopes.
> Love always perseveres.
> Love never fails.[55]

---

55   Several items in this list can be found in 1 Corinthians 13:4–8. You might recognize some of them from the last wedding you attended.

Let's look like love to the world around us. Let's make sure that peace talks louder than conflict, louder than agitation, louder than cutthroat competition. Jesus said, "I have told you these things, so that in me you may have peace. In this world you will have trouble. But take heart! I have overcome the world."[56]

We could end right there except for two little words in Jesus' statement: "in Me." Please prayerfully turn to the epilogue so that "in Me" becomes good news for you.

---

56   John 16:33.

EPILOGUE

*"Come to me, all you who are weary and
burdened, and I will give you rest."*
—Matthew 11:28[1]

J esus can be more than a good example.

Make no mistake, He's an excellent example. He models humility, He reaches out to the disenfranchised, He listens well, He breaks down walls of division, and on and on. His love doesn't keep record of wrongs, praise the Lord.

He isn't the only great example of becoming part of the solution instead of part of the problem. President Abraham Lincoln and Rev. Dr. Martin Luther King Jr. were two examples we looked at earlier of

---

1   Jesus, Matthew 11:28.

bridgebuilding while still standing firm on one's convictions. Célestin Musekura and Tass Abu Saada were two contemporary examples we saw at work in other cultural settings. And along the way there have been multiple stories told of this work being done today, in our country, like Abby Johnson and Julia Song.

Examples can inspire us, but they can't take us all the way home in and of themselves. We need more than a good example. Here's another way to say it: we need more than a map—we need a driver, someone who can take us where we want to go. Making friends from across the aisle, humbling ourselves, exercising self-control—even if we *want* to do those things, wouldn't it be great if we actually had the power and capacity to pull it off, consistently? And when our "lower minds"[2] take over and we disappoint ourselves and others, wouldn't it be awesome to have a 100% reliable way of starting fresh without having to carry around bags of guilt that just get in the way?

If you're already adding your Amen because you've already experienced Jesus as the source and voice of peace from within you, then ask Him to bring someone else to mind right now as you read this. Maybe this invitation is for a friend or family member of yours.

I shared back in Chapter 4 the story of how our multi-racial Pastor Partners got started and the question I was asked that would normally have led to a defensive response. I honestly don't believe it was simply my stellar self-control kicking in; I think it was a much higher power operating through me, in spite of me. Later, in Chapter 5, I described the GPS pattern for prayer out of Jesus' own John 17 prayer. When conversation starts to get tense around the dinner table, God goes to work from the inside, reminding me to pray like Jesus prayed, and I'm telling you, that makes all the difference in the world.

And all the times I blow it, and disappoint myself, my wife, or somebody else? Wow, am I ever thankful that Jesus is more than just a great

---

2   Urban's language for the worst versions of ourselves.

example for how to live. He literally steps in, takes my hand, leads me back to the cross where He reminds me of all He did to set me free from guilt and shame, and gives me the power to reengage in the battle in healthy ways. There's no possible way I could self-generate that kind of capacity for a fresh start.

Jesus is the Prince of Peace, and His Peace can cover our fears, whether the fears are related to health, finances, political conversations, or just the unknown. Jesus brings us to a place of peace, so we can be peacemakers in the world around us.

The icon

There's a difference between knowing *about* Jesus and *knowing* Jesus. It's the difference between reading a book about my wife and learning through that book what a great musician she is, what a wonderful teacher and mother she is, how stunningly beautiful she is, and several other facts . . . versus meeting her in person, dating her, asking her to marry me, and living our lives together.

Most people in our country know some things about Jesus—although not all people do. I remember several years ago when our church was conducting a day camp for kids, and our teenage daughter Amy brought along a friend of hers from school to help out. Amy's friend had been listening to the stories for a few days, and then said to me, "Wait . . . Jesus is a *person*? I thought that was just a swear word." So not *everybody* in our country knows about Jesus, even if most do.

If as you've been reading this book you've sensed a hunger to know more about Jesus—or better yet, to know Him personally and have Him know you personally—do you know why that is? My guess is that Jesus' own prayer is being answered. Jesus didn't just pray for unity as the end goal. While I believe He's praying for each of us to be the voice of peace that talks louder than the Donkey Elephant war, I also believe His sights are set even higher. He prayed that you and everyone else watching would come to know Him and How much God loves you. Unity is the means to the end, according to Jesus Himself.

If a hunger is indeed stirring in you, there are several great places you can turn. Not knowing your background, I'd rather assume too little than too much, so forgive me if you're already past these beginning suggestions. The original source document for Jesus is the Bible, a library of 66 books divided into two parts. You'll want to start with the New Testament and pick out one of the first four books. Many people find John[3] a great place to start, because John has some tremendous personal stories in it but also clearly points out that Jesus was more than just a good man or a good example. But if you particularly want to see how He fulfills Old Testament prophecy, or if you want to especially focus on Jesus the teacher, Matthew[4] is a great choice. If you are just looking for the basic story with very little embellishment, Mark[5] is your man. Alternatively, Luke[6] emphasizes Jesus' compassion for the marginalized; plus Luke was a doctor and historian, so those interests come through in His biography of Jesus. If you don't have a Bible and want one, download one of the Bible apps on your phone, or just Google "free Bible" or visit a nearby church—they'll probably be glad to give you one.

JESUS IS THE ICON OF THE INVISIBLE GOD. CLICK ON JESUS, AND YOU GET TAKEN DIRECTLY TO GOD!

But reading the Bible is only one way to experience Jesus. One of the most powerful currently-unfolding depictions of Jesus I've seen is the first multi-season made-for-television series called *The Chosen*.[7] Download The Chosen App for free and enjoy! Following Jesus is a team sport, not

---

3   The fourth book in the New Testament.

4   The first book in the New Testament.

5   The second book in the New Testament.

6   The third book in the New Testament.

7   https://studios.vidangel.com/the-chosen.

something private—it's kind of hard to follow Jesus religiously *on your own* when He constantly taught us to love *one another*. So if you want a community of people to explore this stuff with, I have a recommendation for you: The Alpha Course. There's a very good possibility, no matter where you live in the world, that there's an Alpha Course somewhere near you.[8] You can find out by going to the link in the footnote. Alpha is the first letter of the Greek alphabet, and The Alpha Course is a safe place to ask hard questions and start at the beginning. No prior knowledge is assumed or required.

I've shared extensively in this book what Jesus passionately prayed before heading to the cross, and what a difference that prayer can make in our current political climate. I've also shared some about his character and his values, particularly as we looked at some of the favorite platforms of each party. Now I'm going to take one more passage from the Bible and unpack a little bit of it, because it has one of the best modern titles for Jesus embedded right upfront, and it's such good news! This ultimately is my reason for hope in the midst of the Donkey Elephant war being waged around us.

> Jesus is the image of the invisible God, the firstborn over all creation.[9]

The word "image" in the original Greek is also an English word: icon. Jesus is the icon of the invisible God. While it's possible you might think of ornate religious paintings with the word icon, the way we use the word in modern technology is the definition I'm thinking of: "a graphic symbol on a computer display screen that represents an app, an object (such as a file), or a function (such as the command to save)."[10]

Jesus is the icon of the invisible God. Click on Jesus, and you get taken directly to God! Like icons on our computers or phones, Jesus makes it easier to access God. Try comprehending all that God is and

---

8   https://www.alpha.org/try-alpha/.

9   Col. 1:15.

10   "Icon," *Merriam-Webster*, accessed April 1, 2010, https://www.merriam-webster.com/dictionary/icon.

you can spin yourself in circles; Jesus is a lot easier to understand, and much more relatable. God gave up everything in order to make it possible for us to relate to Him personally, and Jesus is how that happened. If we want to know God, look to Jesus.

But there are so many religions—how can I be so exclusive in saying Jesus is the way to know God?

First, I'm not the one saying it; I'm just quoting what He said. Just consider this possibility for a moment . . . God is Spirit, and yet wants a relationship with the pinnacle of His creation, human beings. What better way to make that possible than to become human Himself? That is the central claim of Christianity—that Jesus is God in the flesh, that He came at a specific point in time and a specific place on the globe, that He lived, died, and rose again. All of that can be evaluated like you would evaluate any other historical claim. Jesus isn't just a great example: He claimed to be far more than that. He's either crazy or telling the truth: you decide. But it's worth an investigation, don't you think? Anyway, this is the kind of stuff the Alpha Course wrestles with, so if each question starts spawning several more, seriously consider checking it out.

> For in Him all things were created: things in heaven and on earth, visible and invisible, whether thrones or powers or rulers or authorities; all things have been created through Him and for Him.[11]

That's a mouthful. To say much about that verse here would be beyond the scope of this book. Suffice it to say that good people don't allow such claims to be made about themselves, let alone make such claims on their own.[12] Jesus either is the real deal, or an egomaniac of such magnitude that no politician could ever hold a candle to Him.

---

11   Col. 1:16.

12   If you've never noticed Jesus saying such things about Himself, just read the Gospel of John. You won't have to get very far. The people listening understood how radical His claims were, and either accepted them as true, or sought to put Him to death for blasphemy. See John 5:18, for example.

The other piece of great news in this verse is that every single person is an image-bearer of the Almighty God. Genesis 1:26–31 says that all of us were created in God's image. That's not only true of Democrats and Republicans, but of Christians, atheists, Muslims, LGBTQ+, and any other label you can come up with. All people are created in the image of God and therefore have infinite value.

> He is before all things, and in Him all things hold together.[13]

I love this verse for very personal reasons. Quick story: I had been a pastor for maybe ten years or so, and I was learning that leading a church has some things in common with politics! People are people wherever they go, and trying to keep a church unified can be exhausting. My mistake was in thinking that was *my* job, when ultimately, it's *His* job. I certainly had a role to play: I could be part of the solution or part of the problem. That's one of the main points of this book! But during a particularly challenging season, I happened to be preaching on this passage from Colossians. I got to this verse and literally fell apart in the pulpit. That isn't normal behavior for me, but the emotions just caught up with and overwhelmed me. I thought, and said, "It isn't my job to hold everything together. That's His job." I still have goosebumps thinking about the magnitude of that realization.

ALL WE HAVE TO DO IS ACT LIKE WHO WE ALREADY ARE. LET HIM WORRY ABOUT ALL THE DETAILS.

This truth applies politically, also. It's His job to hold relationships together between Donkey Christians and Elephant Christians. It's His job to empower us to listen well, give us the desire and will to humble ourselves, and ultimately to enable us to reach across the aisle. We can of course treat people respectfully whether they're Christian or not, and in fact we have all the more reason to be gracious in our conversation with those

---

13   Col. 1:17.

who *aren't* following Jesus. It's just that there's a spiritual unity *that's already true* when we're talking about Christians from the other party. All we have to do is act like who we already are. Let Him worry about all the details. Just do our little part, our small thing done in a great way.

> He is the head of the body, the church; He is the begin-
> ning and the firstborn from among the dead,[14] so that
> in everything He might have the supremacy. *[15]*

This by itself, apart from anything we know about Jesus, could sound like very bad news. Someone wanting or claiming supremacy over everything sounds really scary. But the way Jesus exercised His authority was by serving.[16] The One we've been talking about throughout this entire book has the power to make a difference in the world, and He exercises that power in acts of service, both directly (Him serving us) and indirectly (Him serving others through us).

And specifically, this tells us that Jesus is the head of the Church. Pastors and bishops aren't ultimately in charge—Jesus is. All Jesus-followers, no matter our roles, experience, degrees, faithfulness, or unfaithfulness... all who follow Jesus are just parts, body parts with Jesus as our head. Under the direction of Jesus, coordinated by Him and working together, parts can do some pretty amazing things.

> For God was pleased to have all His fullness dwell in
> Him, and through Him to reconcile to Himself all things,
> whether things on earth or things in heaven, by making
> peace through His blood, shed on the cross.[17]

This isn't just any old good news, this is THE good news. This is literally the gospel, the good news. Jesus, the Prince of Peace from His birth onward, has made peace through His blood shed on the cross.

---

14 A reference to Jesus rising from the dead.

15 Col. 1:18.

16 Reread John 13:1–3 as one powerful example.

17 Col. 1:19–20.

We don't have to live in hostility toward God, we don't have to live in hostility toward one another, and we don't have to live in hostility toward ourselves. No matter what! It says "all things", so that means no exceptions!

To reconcile means to restore friendly relationships. God can reconcile us to one another! The war is not destined to carry on unabated. Jesus can put an end to our internal war with our conscience, our shame, our failures, and our disappointments. And He can put an end to the external wars we've been waging in our families, our workplaces, and our country.

Such. Good. News.

> Once you were alienated from God and were enemies in your minds because of your evil behavior. But now He has reconciled you by Christ's physical body through death to present you holy in His sight, without blemish and free from accusation.[18]

All of us have things we aren't proud of. Imagine if there were a computer screen above our heads constantly displaying our thoughts. That would be terrible! By playing the comparison game, we can convince ourselves that "evil behavior" isn't a label we need to apply to ourselves. Of course, we usually pick Hitler as the person we're comparing ourselves to . . . but this verse makes no reference to comparisons. It simply says what's true. If we had to do away with all image management, and others could see every thought crossing our minds, without the benefit of a comparison to someone worse, well, "evil" as a description wouldn't be so hard to swallow.

But the amazing good news is that God doesn't look at us in our raw unedited version. He looks at us through His Son Jesus, which is why the verse says that we are now holy in His sight. God looks at *Jesus* when He evaluates *us*. And because we've been given a fresh start and

---

18   Col. 1:21–22.

a clean record, we can give that same gift to others, not holding their past sins against them.

Jesus is the icon of the invisible God in all His holiness. How astounding is that.

Overcoming objections

In just a few minutes (pages), I'm going to invite you to cross a line of faith if you haven't already done so. If you already have, don't stop reading but continue on and pray for someone God brings to mind. I'd love nothing more than to bring everyone along when we get there, so let's briefly address a few of the most common possible reservations.

- *If I become a Jesus-follower instead of just a Jesus-fan, does that mean I have to be become anti-homosexual, anti-women, and anti-environment?* If you haven't already, read through one of the gospels—any of them, you pick. Does Jesus seem anti-homosexual, anti-women, or anti-environment to you? Me neither. In fact, like Andy Stanley pointed out, the only thing He was consistently "anti-" about was anti-religious leaders who were the ones who were anti-everything.[19] The most famous Bible verse in the world starts, "For God so loved the world..."[20] Another verse says, "If God is for us, who can be against us?"[21] Following Jesus doesn't make you anti-people. If anything, it gives you a love for people that previously you didn't want to be around. That was my wife's immediate testimony when at age 16 she became a follower of Jesus.

  As for the environment, taking care of it was the main job Adam was given at the start of creation. God is pro-environment, so we can (and need to) be too.

---

19   Stanley, "Church and Hate."

20   John 3:16.

21   Rom. 8:31.

This question is really a subset of the next one...

• *Jesus I like, it's His followers I can't stand.* I'm so sorry. Really and truly, if we were in the same room having a conversation, that's the main thing I'd want to convey to you. I'm so sorry for rotten things that have happened to you by people who should have known better.

C.S. Lewis, arguably the most influential Christian writer of the 20th century, said that you can't compare Christians to non-Christians, because none of us really know the details of other people's lives. (That's the word "sonder" my son introduced me to. It applies here.) Lewis said the comparison that needs to be made is with a person before and after his/her relationship with Christ has begun. What difference does Christ make in a person's life as compared to life without Him?

As I mentioned before, the strongest proof of God's existence to me is the fact that the Church is still going and growing 2000 years after its inception, because you certainly can't explain that on the basis of its great human leadership. If I do a lousy job representing the One I claim to follow, that's a reflection on me, not Him. But regardless—I'm sorry. Whatever it was, and however badly it still hurts, it shouldn't have happened.

For exactly this reason, you may have noticed that more often than not I'll use the phrase "Jesus-followers" or something similar rather than Christian, because Christians have so poorly reflected Christ, and Christianity has so often acted more like a religion than a relationship. Which leads to the next objection...

• *What about the Crusades? Hasn't religion caused more problems than it's solved?* There are some ugly chapters in religious history, without a doubt. This may come as a surprise to you, but not once did Jesus indicate a desire to start a new religion. With

Jesus it's all about relationship. Religion is humanity's attempt to reach or relate to God. The Jesus story is all about the opposite—God's attempt to reach us.

Religion usually brings with it a bunch of rules, which has always amused me. We have a hard-enough time following the directions Jesus specifically laid out—why on earth would we have a desire to add additional rules to the ones we aren't following already?

I am not the least bit compelled to attempt to defend religion. Whether religion has caused more problems than it's solved is probably a matter of perspective, but I'm not in the religion business. At its best and truest version of itself, Christianity is simply a group of people who've been rescued by Jesus, striving to help one ano-ther follow Him as we serve the world.

CHRISTIANITY IS SIMPLY A GROUP OF PEOPLE WHO'VE BEEN RESCUED BY JESUS, STRIVING TO HELP ONE ANOTHER FOLLOW HIM AS WE SERVE THE WORLD.

- *What about all that horrific stuff in the Bible that nobody follows anyway, and that I wouldn't want to follow either?* I briefly mentioned in the section on racial equality in Chapter 7 the difference between Biblical literature that is descriptive and that which is prescriptive. Quite a bit of the Old Testament in particular is simply describing what happened—it's not even claiming to say what *ought* to have happened in that moment, let alone in future millennia. That simple distinction between descriptive (what is) and prescriptive (what ought to be) doesn't solve all the issues, but it can help with a bunch of them.

I trust the Bible because I trust Jesus, not the other way around. Because I've met and experienced Jesus, and know that I can trust Him with my life, I can also trust Him with His perspectives. He revered the Scriptures (which would have mostly been the Old Testament), and the New Testament was assembled on the basis of which writings most-helpfully point to Jesus. God wants a relationship with us, and ultimately, the Bible is God's love letter to us. Some of it doesn't read that way, for sure, but keep the big picture in mind.

Martin Luther said, "If you come across a passage of Scripture you can't understand, go back to one that you *can* understand." That's good advice. There are plenty of questions I have about various verses and stories in the Bible. Someday it will all be clear. In the meantime, I want to stick close to Jesus.

Crossing the line
Our unity with one another doesn't start with one another.

Jesus' prayer not only emphasizes our unity with one another—it emphasizes our unity with Christ. "May they be *in us* so that the world will believe that You sent Me."[22] Jesus invites us to unite with Him. When *that* happens, we'll have all the power we need to set about the task of uniting with others . . . because it won't be *our* power, but *His*.

A ceasefire in the Donkey Elephant war seems unattainable by human means. And a ceasefire doesn't come close to what I'm pleading for: actual friendships and collaboration, with new solutions emerging that are stronger than what either side brings to the table on their own. I don't intend this to be flippant in any way—that will take an act of God.

Fortunately, that's possible! Fans of Jesus can become followers of His, such that He Himself is the One at work in our world, through

---

22 John 17:21 (NLT), italics mine.

us. That's what it will take, and that's what Jesus prayed would happen. We don't have to wonder if God's in favor of such work—Jesus prayed for it directly. And as we saw in Chapter 5 while studying Jesus' prayer, the solution doesn't paper over the very real and substantive differences, where one position is qualitatively closer to God's intent than the other. If mutually respectful, Christ-honoring, benefit-of-the-doubt conversation takes place by people whose identity is on a higher plane than political parties, God's truth will rise to the top and most will be able to acknowledge it.

So, are you ready?

There is no one set formula for crossing the line of faith. If you feel like you know enough of Jesus that you want to not only live for Him, but to have Him living in and through you, then you're ready. None of us know everything about Jesus—don't wait for that! Anyone who claims to know it all proves in that very same instant that he/she is wrong. A hunger for more is quite sufficient.

Find a quiet place—in your house or car or wherever you're reading this, but also in your spirit. Psalm 46:10 is most often translated, *"Be still, and know that I am God..."*[23] The word for "be still" is a Hebrew word that can also mean cease or abate,[24] and given the context, it can appropriately be translated, *"Stop your fighting, and know that I am God..."*[25] Wherever there's fighting (with family, friends, or fellow citizens), and whatever the cause (politics, past or present sin, demanding our own way), or even if the fighting is within yourself (resisting God's call, clinging to guilt and shame, or simply struggling to relinquish control)... *Stop your fighting, and know that I am God.* And isn't it fascinating that John 17 could be the connection between those two phrases—as we stop our fighting, as we show love for one another, God's identity is revealed, not only for others, but maybe even for ourselves.

---

23 Ps 46:10 (NIV) and many other translations.

24 "7503. *Raphah*," *Strong's Exhaustive Concordance*, accessed April 1, 2020, https://biblehub.com/hebrew/7503.htm.

25 Ps. 46:10 (CSB) and some others.

The full verse can be translated, *"Stop your fighting, and know that I am God, exalted among the nations, exalted on the earth."* As Jesus is exalted, we are drawn not only to Him but to one another as well.

Nicky Gumbel in the Alpha Course outlines the process of crossing the line of faith in three short words or phrases: *sorry, thank you,* and *please.* I've found that to be a very simple and helpful way of praying with others who are wanting what Jesus Christ alone offers. The ultimate solution for you, in my opinion, is entering into a relationship with the One whose love for you is constant, unchanging, and undying. Find a quiet place in your day and in your surroundings, *be still and know that I am God,* and simply talk to Jesus...

SORRY

Lord Jesus, I'm sorry for things I've said and done that I shouldn't have, as well as for things I should have said or done but didn't...

THANK YOU

Thank You for leaving heaven to come to earth, and willingly taking the worst that humanity could dish out to You. Thank You for not only giving Your life for the world, but giving Your life for me...

PLEASE

Please forgive me for my shortcomings and failures. Please come into my life and live through me from this day forward...

Some people feel the presence of God immediately when they pray a prayer like the above. Others don't feel any different at all at first. Our faith doesn't rest in our feelings, because our feelings vary with the wind and with last night's dinner. Jesus promised that if we open the door to our hearts and invite Him in, He'll come in.[26] Not even death itself could stop Jesus from keeping His promises, so you can bank on it. You invited Him in... He's in!! He knows you fully, better than you know yourself, and He loves you completely, more completely

---

26   Rev. 3:20, "Here I am! I stand at the door and knock. If anyone hears my voice and opens the door, I will come in and eat with that person, and they with me."

than anyone else ever will. Let me repeat that: Jesus knows you fully and loves you completely!

Your next step is to go find a community to love and learn from and share the gifts God's given you. Don't be discouraged if it takes you a few tries. Following Jesus is a team sport, and it helps to find a team with whom you're comfortable. A team that prays for one another and encourages one another in this peacemaking journey is absolutely vital. Don't try to go it alone!

You aren't alone! I believe there are millions of others just waiting for someone to forge a path of peace through the Donkey Elephant war. Some of them are waiting for you!

You aren't alone! Jesus is with you, inside you, giving you strength and courage and direction. If you're praying what Jesus prayed, you can have high confidence He'll answer that prayer. Just ask Him, and He'll show you where to start. He's even hungrier than we are to bring an end to the wars we've been waging in our families, our workplaces, and our country.

You aren't alone! You are the bearer of Good News.

About J17 Ministries

J17 MINISTRIES was founded October 20, 2018, and its mission is to Unite the Body of Christ FOR a broken world. J17 Ministries takes its title from Jesus' prayer in John chapter 17 for the unity of His followers. John 17 is Jesus' strategy for fulfilling the Great Commission.

Founder David Drum worked as the Church Domain Director of 4Tucson from the summer of October 2011 through the fall of 2018, after having served as the pastor of a Tucson church for 21 years. J17 Ministries advances the work Dave began at 4Tucson with greater focus, intentionality, and sphere of influence, while continuing to partner with 4Tucson in various avenues.

J17 Ministries is based in Tucson, AZ, and working anywhere God opens up doors. Programs have been developed for pastors, leaders, and the entire body of Christ. Programs include prayer summits, discipleship retreats, topical symposiums, and cross-cultural relationship training. Resources include books and videos developed by founder David Drum.

J17 Ministries has its office at the amazing collaborative H.S. Lopez Family Foundation Center of Opportunity. The Center of Opportunity is a one-stop shop for the homeless, directed by the Gospel Rescue Mission. The ribbon cutting ceremony was a visible manifestation of the kinds of partnerships described in this book, as Elephants and Donkeys had a fiesta together celebrating what can happen through collaboration. Government agencies and 30 non-profits make it possible for a person to come off the street and receive emergency shelter, meals, and clothing.

Dental and medical assistance are available on site. Legal services can help track down identification cards—an absolute essential for any other services. Whatever might have been contributing to homelessness—substance abuse, refugee status, prison reentry, and more—there's a ministry on site to help tailor services to the person experiencing extreme poverty. Job training is available at the site, and the hotel tower is being converted into low income housing. Our part as a non-profit is contributing to the atmosphere of unity and collaboration.

For more information about J17 Ministries, contact:
inquires@j17ministries.org

Acknowledgments

No project worth pursuing is ever accomplished in isolation. But this book required even more team members than my previous two.

Thank you to my loving and lovely wife Valerie. She cheered me on when I was discouraged, and eagerly desired to partner with me in the project. She was one of my valued proofreaders and was willing to ask the hard questions that make the finished project so much more . . . finished. I love you with all my heart.

Thank you to my whole team of readers and editors: Valerie Drum, Tasha Campbell, John Cepin, Tessa Dysart, Craig Meyer, Cameron Hood, and Mike Drum. Each of them read through the manuscript and caught not only typos and other fine details, but spoke into the overall flow of the book. A special thank you goes to Tasha Campbell, who also took on the unenviable task of following up on all my footnotes, making sure that we had the appropriate copyright permissions.

Thank you to my son Mike Drum. He contributed way more than a valuable chapter. He also was one of the people who read through the entire manuscript and provided insightful feedback and direction. We'd never tried collaborating before on anything of this magnitude, and the experience was awesome!! I'm so proud of you!

Thank you to a small group of investors who caught the vision early and helped offset some of the development costs: John & Patty Cepin,

Jim Cords, Peter Santaniello, Dave & Judy Strong, an anonymous donor, and Ashley Hughes, who helped with some of the fundraising.

Thank you to my teammates, fellow staff members Tasha Campbell and Karen Henley. Both picked up extra responsibilities to free me up for writing and editing, especially during crunch time.

Thank you to my son Daniel Drum for his social media help. Most of what I know on the social media front I've learned from my kids.

Thank you to my typesetter, graphic designer, and friend Cameron Hood. Aren't his chapter drawings outstanding? Aren't you glad I talked him into doing them?!

Thank you to our Pastor Partners group of the last eight years. The patience, grace, laughter, and hunger for learning that have marked this group have created a rich atmosphere for growth, and this project would have never even been conceptualized without the experience of this group of dear friends.

Thank you to many other authors and speakers around the country who are working in the same field. Some are Christ-followers, others are not, but I've been introduced to some amazing people while researching this book, and I'm forever grateful.

And finally, thanks to our Lord and Savior Jesus Christ, who is rich in mercy, slow to anger, and infinitely patient with us.

Also available by David Drum

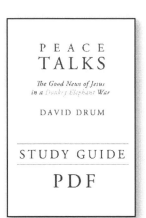

Study Guide for
Peace Talks: The Good News of Jesus in a Donkey Elephant War

FREE downloadable PDF available at: *www.J17Ministries.org/resources*.

SUGGESTED USES:

- As a personal resource to process the material from the main book.

- As a path toward greater understanding within your family or extended family. Discuss with your teenage or adult children; or ask the uncle whose political comments always make Thanksgiving uncomfortable if he'd be willing to read and work through the book with you.

- As a church small group. Grow in appreciation for how each of you can be part of the solution instead of part of the problem. This can be especially effective if both political parties are represented in the group.

- As a multicultural small group between churches. Grab a friend from your church, link up with a friend from another church who has a different cultural (and probably political) background, and invite that friend to bring along a friend. Form a foursome and work through the material together.

Jesus' Surprising Strategy: A Mandate and a Means for City Transformation

Paperback available from Amazon and *www.J17Ministries.org/resources*.
Kindle version also available.

Drum's first book introduces John 17 and studies its description of unity in detail. Another chapter outlines the Biblical basis for the City Church, forever changing how you read the New Testament. The middle section of the book looks at five different levels of unity, places where unity tends to break down, and how to break through them. The final section looks at the strategy behind 4Tucson, a ministry working toward Biblical city transformation.

Also available in Spanish as *La Sorprendente Estrategia de Jesús*.

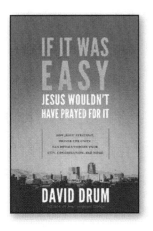

If It Was Easy, Jesus Wouldn't Have Prayed For It: How Jesus' Strategic Prayer for Unity can Revolutionize your City, Congregation, and Home

Paperback available from Amazon and *www.J17Ministries.org/resources.* Kindle version also available.

Drum's second book shows how John 17 creates the unity it describes. *If It Was Easy* addresses multiple challenges to seeing Jesus' prayer answered: the relationship between unity and maturity, cross-cultural differences, lessons from marriage, Western individualistic worldview, and more. Visible unity tells powerful stories of Jesus' prayer being answered. *If It Was Easy* ends with seven bridge building tools all of us can put into practice.

Made in the USA
Monee, IL
02 September 2020